Evolutionary Archaeology

Contributors

ALYSIA L. ABBOTT, Department of Anthropology, University of New Mexico, Albuquerque

ROBERT C. DUNNELL, Department of Anthropology, University of Washington, Seattle

MICHAEL W. GRAVES, Department of Anthropology, University of Hawaii, Honolulu

THOMAS D. HOLLAND, U.S. Army, Central Identification Laboratory, Hawaii, Hickman Air Force Base

GEORGE T. JONES, Department of Anthropology, Hamilton College, Clinton, New York

THEGN N. LADEFOGED, Department of Anthropology, University of Auckland, New Zealand.

ROBERT D. LEONARD, Department of Anthropology, University of New Mexico, Albuquerque

TIMOTHY D. MAXWELL, Office of Archaeological Studies, Museum of New Mexico, Santa Fe

HECTOR NEFF, Research Reactor Facility, University of Missouri, Columbia

MICHAEL J. O'BRIEN, Department of Anthropology, University of Missouri, Columbia

ANN F. RAMENOFSKY, Department of Anthropology, University of New Mexico, Albuquerque

PATRICE A. TELTSER, Department of Anthropology, University of Arizona, Tucson

Evolutionary Archaeology
◆◆ Methodological Issues

edited by
Patrice A. Teltser

THE UNIVERSITY OF ARIZONA PRESS
Tucson & London

The University of Arizona Press
Copyright © 1995
Arizona Board of Regents
All Rights Reserved
∞ This book is printed on acid-free, archival-quality paper.
Manufactured in the United States of America.
00 99 98 97 96 95   6 5 4 3 2 1
Library of Congress Cataloging-in-Publication Data
Evolutionary archaeology : methodological issues / edited by Patrice
    A. Teltser.
        p.   cm.
    Includes bibliographical references and index.
    ISBN 0-8165-1461-5 (cl : acid-free). — ISBN 0-8165-1509-3 (pb :
acid-free)
    1. Archaeology—Methodology.   2. Evolution.   I. Teltser, Patrice
A., 1954– .
    CC75.7.E96   1995   94-30423
    930.1—dc20   CIP
British Library Cataloguing-in-Publication Data
A catalogue record for this book is available from the British Library.

◆◆ Contents

Evolutionary Archaeology

I

The Methodological Challenge of Evolutionary Theory in Archaeology

Patrice A. Teltser

◆◆ For more than fifteen years a variety of archaeologists have advocated the application of Darwinian evolutionary theory to explain variation in the archaeological record. Programmatic statements, critiques of traditional anthropological evolutionary models, and considerations of the implications of evolutionary theory have become an increasingly prominent part of the archaeological literature (e.g., Braun 1991; Dunnell 1980, 1982, 1989; Leonard and Jones 1987; Marks and Staski 1988; Neff 1992, 1993; O'Brien and Holland 1990, 1992; Rindos 1984, 1989). This literature has taken a decidedly theoretical direction in recognition that applying evolutionary theory to the archaeological record cannot be accomplished by analogy or simple theory borrowing, but really involves an *expansion* of evolutionary theory as we currently understand it. In short, expanding evolutionary theory to explain variation in the archaeological record requires building new archaeological theory and method.

Even though critiques of traditional evolutionary models from an evolutionary perspective have proven insightful (e.g., Dunnell 1988; Leonard and Jones 1987; Rindos 1986, 1989), and the logic extending evolutionary theory to behavior and the archaeological record is relatively straightforward (as will be discussed below), evolutionary theory has yet to be applied in a cogent way to a significant portion of the archaeological record. It is equally plain that discussions of theoretical concepts have been far less clear about how those concepts translate methodologically and analytically (see Neff 1993 for an exception). This situation is only partly the consequence of a poorly developed theoretical base. Equally important, but given far less attention, are the *methodological* implications and requirements of evolutionary theory. Taken together, these implications constitute a considerable challenge to evolutionary archaeologists.

In this volume, twelve researchers attempt to provide more concrete methodological expression for expanding evolutionary theory to archaeology. This involves methodological expression for why and how evolutionary explanations differ from more traditional anthropological evolutionary models, why and how different units of measurement must be created, and how these implications carry enormous, but fairly specific, data requirements.

The General Problem

For many archaeologists, explaining variation in the archaeological record in terms of evolutionary processes is an important and legitimate disciplinary goal. While the day-to-day business of our work may not always entail direct engagement with theoretical issues, most archaeologists would hope that their more proximal analytic tasks are directed toward, and in some way contribute to, this ultimate goal. And yet, how we view evolutionary processes on a general level has implications for the way in which more specific analytic tasks are conceived and carried out (cf. Bettinger 1991; Hill 1972). These views, whether implicitly or explicitly recognized, specify the terms in which we conceive of a problem, the causal mechanisms we invoke to explain a particular phenomenon, the observations we consider relevant to solve a problem, the language we choose to make those observations, the way we sample the archaeological record, and the way we might organize our observations and analyze a particular body of data.

These are methodological concerns, the domain of general theory that specifies the measurement of theoretically relevant variables (or dimensions) and the explanation of a particular class of phenomena in terms of theoretically relevant processes. As a subset of theory, method should not be confused with the more common connotation of "procedure" even though it may have procedural implications.

In general, two major sources of variation can be recognized in the archaeological record: that which is the result of human behavioral variation and that which is the result of postdepositional processes. Determining the difference between these two sources of variation is essential to any archaeological theory, evolutionary or otherwise. Understanding and accounting for sources of variation introduced by postdepositional processes is usually placed within the general topic of formation process theory (Schiffer 1988). Understanding sources of behavioral variation is a matter of general or explanatory theory. While there is considerable interaction between these two bodies of theory, the analytic distinction is useful in that the sources and methods associated with them have been quite different. For example, most work carried out to understand sources of variation in the formation of the archaeological record has been conducted within the framework of "behavioral archaeology" (e.g., Reid et al. 1975; Schiffer 1972, 1976, 1987), a research program directed toward studying and explaining the relationships between human behavior and material culture in all times and places. On the other hand, general or explanatory theory stipulates the explanatory basis of those relationships, and research is directed toward determining the empirical and dynamic sufficiency of those theoretically determined relationships.

When the content of explanatory theory and the role of research are stipulated in this way, the subject matter of archaeological explanation is the archaeological record rather than human behavior or motives. This does not necessarily deny a role for human behavior but places it in an explanatory role rather than the role of subject matter. When methodological issues are the focus of concern, criticisms of behavioral reconstruction associated with the evolutionary literature in archaeology (see especially Dunnell 1978, 1982, 1989) are valid to the extent that they take issue with the methodological role which behavioral reconstructions have come to play in many archaeological studies, rather than a denial of the importance of behavioral inferences per se (see Neiman 1990 for a similar argument). Because the archaeological record does not provide any direct observational access to human behavior, the methods used in an evolutionary archaeology will look very different than, for example, an evolutionary ethnography. The chapters in this book address the methodological challenges of expanding such an explanatory framework to include explanation of variation in the archaeological record.

The general difficulties encountered when expanding evolutionary theory to behavior and the archaeological record are primarily twofold. On the one hand, evolutionary theory was formalized in the context of biology, and written and understood almost entirely in biological terms (e.g., genes, organisms, species). Even though biologists have long accepted behavior as an important part of the phenotype, classic evolutionary theory does not include the necessary terms to address behavioral phenomena, much less the products of that behavior as manifest in the archaeological record. On the other hand, anthropologists and archaeologists have been reluctant to embrace an evolutionary framework, and, consequently, the terms in which they conceive their problems and organize their observations are largely incompatible with such a framework. This is most clearly illustrated when one considers the role of theory in specifying how research questions are asked and what kind of observations are required to address them.

To the extent that theory determines the relevance of one question or observation over another, it follows that the terms in which we ask many of the "big questions" of archaeology (sensu Binford 1983) are paradigmatically determined. Consequently, the way in which we have addressed long-standing issues of archaeological interest, such as the origins of agriculture or the evolution of complex societies, requires a reorientation.

Reorientation of specific archaeological questions is no simple exercise. For example, Rindos (1980, 1984) has only begun to redefine and redirect inquiry into the origins of agriculture in evolutionary terms. This kind of effort is evident in much of the existing literature on evolutionary theory (e.g., Braun 1991; Leonard 1989; Neff 1992, 1993; Neiman 1990, 1995; Rindos 1985, 1986; also Ramenofsky, chapter 7, and Graves and Ladefoged, chapter 8), but Rindos's model for the origins of agriculture remains the most well-developed example. Rindos's success is marked by the ability of evolutionary theory to generate a model for the origins of agriculture that does not ultimately depend on population pressure or climate change, treat agriculture as an "invention" attributed to the omniscience of early farmers, or relegate it to the status of "trait" that can diffuse in much the same way as a ceramic design. Rather, agriculture is defined in terms of specific classes of highly variable behaviors or activities (e.g., planting, protecting, and harvesting) that arise in the context of a specific kind of relationship between plants and people (domestication). The differential persistence of agricultural activities, or the relative frequency with which these activities are performed, determines the degree to which a population at a given point in time and space (e.g., any given "system") is dependent upon them. Defining agriculture in terms of specific classes of *activities* is a significant departure from defining it as a kind of *system* that must be distinguished from other kinds of systems (e.g., incipient agriculture or horticulture).

Criticisms of Rindos's evolutionary model for the origins of agriculture are equally enlightening here. These criticisms usually point to the failure of this model to incorporate the intentions of human actors as causal (e.g., Flannery 1986). While an evolutionary approach would make a distinction between processes that account for the source of behavioral variants (e.g., innovation) and the processes that account for the differential persistence of those variants, the real point of conflict is that an evolutionary model does not incorporate the same terms that traditional formulations of the question require. The difference is paradigmatic. The terms in which evolutionary approaches frame long-standing anthropological problems are likely to differ.

Methodological Implications of Evolutionary Theory

Evolutionary theory is a framework for understanding the differential persistence of variation (Dunnell 1980:38; Lewontin 1970). It applies to biological populations whose members have the capacity to reproduce and transmit information to succeeding generations. Most of evolutionary theory derives from the notion that if there is inherited variation within a population, evolution will occur. If some of that variation contributes to an individual's ability to survive and reproduce, evolution by natural selection will occur (Lewontin 1970:1; Mayr 1988:117; see also Neff 1993). Extending evolutionary theory to what is loosely regarded as the "cultural" domain is based on the premise that behavior is an important component of the phenotype. Because natural selection acts on the phenotype, behavior—as well as morphology—is subject to evolutionary forces (Dunnell 1989:44–45; Leonard and Jones 1987:213). At the same time it is also recognized that most human behavior is the product of learning. Consequently, applying evolutionary theory to people requires an expansion of classic neo-Darwinian theory to allow for nongenetic mechanisms of transmission and its consequences. Further extending these notions to the archaeological record requires that some classes of artifacts be conceived as part of the behavioral segment of the human phenotype (Dunnell 1989:44).

Evolutionary theory provides a general model in which change is defined in terms of the differential persistence of alternative traits through time. Here, the notion of trait is expanded to include behavioral aspects of the phenotype (regardless of scale) transmitted through learning processes; and differential persistence does not imply the action of any particular causal mechanism. This basic model carries specific methodological implications.

First, the notion of differential persistence implies the transmission of information. That is, evolutionary change occurs within historically related populations wherein information is transmitted and evolutionary explanations are relevant to features that are transmitted through an inheritance system. Consequently, some means to measure the transmission of information is required for evolutionary studies (Teltser, chapter 4, and Neff, chapter 5).

Recognizing learning processes (cultural transmission) as a system of inheritance is one of the primary ways that studies of cultural evolution require an expansion of classic evolutionary theory. The consequences of nongenetic transmission are still poorly understood and theoretically contentious, opening the door to entirely new kinds of research into learning processes in general. For example, information transmission through learning is not confined to parent-offspring relationships or traditional biological generations. This has implications for the rate of change (Rindos 1985) as well as the scale at which some evolutionary processes could potentially occur (Dunnell, chapter 3). Furthermore, nongenetic transmission of information does not necessarily imply reproduction. Consequently, some authors have argued that these complexities of cultural transmission could establish conditions under which additional mechanisms are operative to sort variation during transmission (e.g., biased transmission, see Boyd and Richerson 1985). Since the consequences and the conditions under which such mechanisms operate are so poorly understood, other authors have taken a more pragmatic and parsimonious position by using the notion of replicative success

(Leonard and Jones 1987:214). This concept applies only to the differential persistence of the traits themselves, making no assumption regarding the biological fitness or reproductive success of their bearers. While this concept is not without theoretical and empirical problems, it does provide a useful temporary solution in some cases. Preliminary consideration of nongenetic mechanisms of transmission has raised a number of important, and as yet unresolved, questions. No doubt additional questions will be raised in the future. Most of these questions are ultimately empirical issues. Regardless of how they are resolved, an evolutionary archaeology requires a set of well-developed methods to measure and track the transmission of information.

Second, the notion of differential persistence of alternative features suggests that change is quantitative, not qualitative (Dunnell 1980:38). Actually, this is only a methodological expression of the distinction between population thinking and typological thinking (Mayr 1959; Hull 1967; Sober 1980). When change is conceived in terms of frequency changes of *analytically* discrete features, the scale of analysis shifts from systemic entities, such as phases or cultures, to the individuals that comprise those entities. Appreciating the appropriate scale at which evolutionary processes occur and the characteristics of the empirical entities on which they operate (Dunnell, chapter 3) has important consequences for the appropriate scale of analysis. Indeed, the difference between defining agriculture in terms of certain classes of analytically discrete behaviors or activities rather than a kind of system illustrates just such a shift in analytic scale. Furthermore, the quantitative nature of change has obvious implications and requirements for how we sample the archaeological record.

Third, the notion of differential persistence says nothing about the source of variation, only about the sorting or patterning of variation through time. In a Darwinian framework, evolution is conceived as a two-step process in which the introduction of new variation is independent of (i.e., governed by different mechanisms than) the processes that pattern that variation through time. The concept of undirected variation is a somewhat contentious issue for anthropologists on a theoretical level because it does not specify human intention as causal to the direction of evolutionary change. This topic, including the role of human intention, has been considered in some detail (Dunnell 1980:60–63, 1989:38–39; Rindos 1989). The Darwinian position taken in regard to undirected variation differs from the Lamarckian position in which the introduction of variation is controlled by selective forces. As Dunnell points out, the Lamarckian position is not used in contemporary evolution because no mechanisms have been identified whereby selective conditions generate variation. "The key point is, however, that Lamarckian evolution is not inherently unscientific; it is rejected because current understanding of mechanisms renders it *unparsimonious* in relation to the Darwinian model. *The choice between the two is empirically founded.* Should a general mechanism for generating directed variation be documented, Lamarckian evolution would become just as valuable to science as Darwinism has proved to be" (Dunnell 1989:39, emphasis added).

Traditionally, emphasis has been placed on the role of natural selection as the primary mechanism responsible for sorting variation through time. This emphasis is particularly evident in the archaeological literature (e.g., Dunnell 1980, 1989; Leonard and Jones 1987; O'Brien and Holland 1990, 1992; see Jones et al., chapter 2, and O'Brien and Holland, chapter 9) where reference to an evolutionary program is sometimes referred to as a "selectionist" framework. Despite this bias, evolutionary theory also incorporates other mechanisms such as immigration, drift (Teltser, chapter 4), linkage of neutral traits with those that are under selection (Ramenofsky, chapter 7), in addition to the role of historical contingency (Gould 1989; Neff 1992). Such mechanisms are taking on an increasingly more prominent role in evolutionary studies to account for the differential persistence of variation. The expectations generated by such mechanisms require methodological consideration in much the same way that natural selection has been considered.

The differential persistence of variation can be explained in one of two general ways. Features that directly affect an individual's potential to survive and reproduce can be attributed to natural selection or deterministic processes, while those features that are neutral with respect to selection can be attributed to transmission processes alone. These definitions of function and style (Dunnell 1978) imply different kinds of distributions in time and space. Generally, those features that are under selection will exhibit nonrandom distributions in relation to environmental constraints, while those that are neutral with respect to selection will display random distributions. Even though different kinds of distributions can suggest the nature of different kinds of causal mechanisms operative, additional information regarding mechanisms of interaction is required. For example, nonrandom distributions of traits can result from their linkage to other traits under selection. Here, evaluating differences in potential fitness of alternative features through comparative or engineering analyses has been suggested (e.g., Maxwell, chapter 6; Neff 1992, 1993; O'Brien and Holland 1992) to further assess the nature of causal mechanisms. This not only emphasizes the complimentary relationship between functional/mechanistic and evolutionary explanations, but also emphasizes the notion that different features affect fitness only in relation to the environment in which they occur. To establish the nature of the causal mechanism responsible for the patterning of variation (whether it be spatial or temporal), and ultimately the extent to which natural selection or other mechanisms are operative, requires both mechanistic and distributional kinds of information and description. This ultimately depends on understanding the historic context in which specific changes occurred.

In summary, evolutionary theory generates a series of expectations in which change is treated as the differential persistence of alternative features through time. This model gives methodological expression to many of the basic theoretical aspects of evolutionary theory. These methodological issues specify that evolutionary change occurs within empirically and historically related populations requiring methods to measure information transmission; that change is measured in terms of changes in the frequency of analytically discrete features or variants; and finally, that understanding the mechanisms responsible for evolutionary change is context specific, requiring both distributional and mechanistic kinds of information and descriptions. Unfortunately, evolutionary theory, as currently formalized, provides no further guidance regarding the specific terms and methods by which this framework can be extended to explain variation in the archaeological record. The solutions to these problems must be anthropological in nature. Biological solutions (to the extent that we are biological creatures) will be necessary but not sufficient because evolutionary theory has yet to integrate behavior and nongenetically transmitted information into its program either formally or analytically.

The authors of this book attempt to meet the methodological challenge of finding solutions to these problems. The first three chapters do so from a theoretical perspective; the following four chapters do so in the context of specific topics. Jones, Leonard, and Abbott (chapter 2) begin with a discussion of how the structure of evolutionary explanations differs from the structure of other explanatory frameworks. While this discussion covers some familiar territory (e.g., Dunnell 1980, 1982; O'Brien and Holland 1990, 1992), the authors specify the methodological implications and advantages of evolutionary explanations. In chapter 3, Dunnell extends the discussion to the definition and identification of units of evolution. Using the biological concept of "species" as an example, he points out that while it is a problematic concept for biologists, there is far more agreement about the characteristics of units that evolve and units that are selected. At issue is determining precisely what empirical entities meet those criteria. By focusing on the scale at which evolutionary processes occur, and drawing from these theoretically specified characteristics (and taking into account the nature of archaeological data), it is possible to identify units of selection and evolution in archaeological analysis. In chapter 4 the issue of unit formation is extended to the measurement of information transmission through the method of frequency seriation. By separating frequency seriation as a method from the overall explanatory framework of culture history, the questions of how and why this method is consistent with an evolutionary archaeology can be specified. This historical treatment emphasizes how evolutionary theory can potentially subsume, on an explanatory level, the more cogent historical methods (and results) generated by previous archaeological work.

In the following four chapters, the methodological implications of evolutionary theory are examined in the context of specific research topics. Neff (chapter 5) uses compositional analysis of ceramics to identify historically related pottery traditions and to assess the nature of selective agents in the evolution of serving vessels during the Classic and Post Classic periods in Guatemala. In chapter 6, Maxwell uses engineering analysis and the comparative method to formulate and assess hypotheses about the nature of selective agents operating on rock-mulch fields among late prehistoric agricultural populations in the lower Rio Chama of New Mexico. These methods have long since been important to historical or archaeological research and, in this chapter, Maxwell specifies the articulation of these methods in an evolutionary framework. Ramenofsky (chapter 7) evaluates frameworks for the explanation of artifact change during the post European contact period. In redefining this topic in evolutionary terms, she presents this phenomenon as one with the potential to examine the role of sorting at different scales of inclusiveness. Graves and Ladefoged (chapter 8) take on the task of redefining a topic of long-standing concern into evolutionary terms. These authors examine the timing and distribution of ritual architectural features in Polynesia. Their analysis emphasizes some of the complementary aspects of ecological and evolutionary frameworks by specifying precisely which aspects of the same phenomenon each framework is capable of addressing. The final chapter provides a concluding overview for this volume. Here, O'Brien and Holland make a rather critical assessment of evolutionary theory as a paradigm, and specify those aspects of evolutionary archaeology over which there is emerging disagreement.

Acknowledgments

I am grateful to all the contributing authors in this volume for their efforts and their enthusiasm and encouragement toward completing this project. I am also grateful to Robert Dunnell, Michael Schiffer, and two anonymous reviewers for commenting on previous versions of this introduction, and to Michael Schiffer and William Walker for providing a sounding board for my ideas.

References

Bettinger, R. L.
1991   *Hunter-Gatherers: Archaeological and Evolutionary Theory.* Plenum Press, New York.

Binford, L. R.
1983   *In Pursuit of the Past.* Thames and Hudson, New York.

Boyd, R., and P. J. Richerson
1985   *Culture and the Evolutionary Process*. University of Chicago Press, Chicago.

Braun, D. P.
1991   Selection and Evolution in Nonhierarchical Organization. In *The Evolution of Political Systems*, edited by S. Upham, pp. 62–86. Cambridge University Press, Cambridge, England.

Dunnell, R. C.
1978   Style and Function: A Fundamental Dichotomy. *American Antiquity* 43:192–203.
1980   Evolutionary Theory and Archaeology. In *Advances in Archaeological Method and Theory,* vol. 3, edited by M. B. Schiffer, pp. 35–99. Academic Press, New York.
1982   Science, Social Science, and Common Sense: The Agonizing Dilemma of Modern Archaeology. *Journal of Anthropological Research* 38:1–25.

Dunnell, Robert C.
1988   The Concept of Progress in Cultural Evolution. In *Evolutionary Progress,* edited by M. H. Nitecki, pp. 169–194. University of Chicago Press, Chicago.
1989   Aspects of the Application of Evolutionary Theory in Archaeology. In *Archaeological Thought in America,* edited by C. C. Lamberg-Karlovsky, pp. 35–49. Cambridge University Press, Cambridge, England.

Flannery, K. V.
1986   The Research Problem. In *Guila Naquitz: Archaic Foraging and Early Agriculture in Oaxaca,* edited by Kent V. Flannery, pp. 3–18. Academic Press, New York.

Gould, S. J.
1989   *Wonderful Life: The Burgess Shale and the Nature of History*. W. W. Norton and Company, New York.

Hill, J. N.
1972   The Methodological Debate in Archaeology. In *Models in Archaeology*, edited by D. L. Clarke, pp. 61–107. Methuen, London.

Hull, D. L.
1967   The Metaphysics of Evolution. *British Journal for the History of Science* 3:309–337.

Leonard, R. D.
1989   Resource Specialization, Population Growth, and Agricultural Production in the American Southwest. *American Antiquity* 54:491–503.

Leonard, R. D., and G. T. Jones
1987   Elements of an Inclusive Evolutionary Model for Archaeology. *Journal of Anthropological Archaeology* 6:199–219.

Lewontin, R. C.
1970   The Units of Selection. *Annual Review of Ecology and Systematics* 1:1–18.

Marks, J., and E. Staski
1988   Individuals and the Evolution of Biological and Cultural Systems. *Human Evolution* 3:147–161.

Mayr, E.
1959   Typological versus Population Thinking. In *Evolution and Anthropology: A Centen-*

nial Appraisal, edited by B. Meggers, pp. 409–412. Washington Anthropological Society, Washington, D.C.

1988 *Toward a New Philosophy of Biology.* Belknap Press, Cambridge, Massachusetts.

Neff, H.

1992 Ceramics and Evolution. In *Archaeological Method and Theory,* vol. 4, edited by M. B. Schiffer, pp. 141–194. University of Arizona Press, Tucson.

1993 Theory, Sampling, and Analytical Techniques in the Archaeological Study of Prehistoric Ceramics. *American Antiquity* 58:23–44.

Neiman, F. D.

1990 *An Evolutionary Approach to Archaeological Inference: Aspects of Architectural Variation in the 17th-Century Chesapeake.* Ph.D. Dissertation, Department of Anthropology, Yale University, New Haven.

1995 Stylistic Variation in Evolutionary Perspective: Implications for Middle Woodland Ceramic Diversity. *American Antiquity* in press.

O'Brien, M. J., and T. D. Holland

1990 Variation, Selection, and the Archaeological Record. In *Archaeological Method and Theory,* vol. 2, edited by M. B. Schiffer, pp. 31–79. University of Arizona Press, Tucson.

1992 The Role of Adaptation in Archaeological Explanation. *American Antiquity* 57: 36–59.

Reid, J. J., M. B. Schiffer, and W. L. Rathje

1975 Behavioral Archaeology: Four Strategies. *American Anthropologist* 77:864–869.

Rindos, D.

1980 Symbiosis, Instability, and the Origin and Spread of Agriculture: A New Model. *Current Anthropology* 21:751–772.

1984 *The Origins of Agriculture: An Evolutionary Perspective.* Academic Press, New York.

1985 Darwinian Selection, Symbolic Variation, and the Evolution of Culture. *Current Anthropology* 26:65-88.

1986 The Evolution of the Capacity for Culture: Sociobiology, Structuralism, and Cultural Selection. *Current Anthropology* 27:315-332.

1989 Undirected Variation and the Darwinian Explanation of Cultural Change. In *Archaeological Method and Theory,* vol. 1, edited by M. B. Schiffer, pp. 1–45. University of Arizona Press, Tucson.

Schiffer, M. B.

1972 Archaeological and Systemic Context. *American Antiquity* 37:156–165.

1976 *Behavioral Archaeology.* Academic Press, New York.

1987 *Formation Processes of the Archaeological Record.* University of New Mexico Press, Albuquerque.

1988 The Structure of Archaeological Theory. *American Antiquity* 53:461–485.

Sober, E.

1980 Evolution, Population Thinking, and Essentialism. *Philosophy of Science* 47:350–383.

2

The Structure of Selectionist Explanations in Archaeology

George T. Jones, Robert D. Leonard, and Alysia L. Abbott

◆◆ All archaeologists agree that human societies evolve; that is to say, their content and organization change over time. What they do not agree about, however, is that societal evolution proceeds according to processes akin to those governing biological evolution, namely natural selection. Neither have they reached a consensus about whether cultural and biological evolution can be, in principle, wedded under a single inclusive evolutionary structure. Owing to the history of thought in anthropology more generally, ideas about evolution and evolutionary explanations have been tied to the assertion that humans are fundamentally unique (see Binford 1992 for a recent argument to this affect). As the argument goes, because of the uniqueness of humans, particularly in our species' apparent capacity to guide its own evolution, biological evolution is at best an analogous process. This paradigmatic bias, remarked upon at one time or another by many of the authors in this book, has limited any attempt to build a unified evolutionary theory.

As a number of the authors in this book have argued before, however, it should be possible to build an inclusive evolutionary theory (Leonard and Jones 1987). This conclusion follows from the simple theoretical premise that natural selection will operate, inevitably, in any mutable system meeting three conditions. First, the system must contain individuals that vary in form. (Both the individual and formal variation are matters of theoretical and methodological specification.) Second, mechanisms must exist for the "faithful" transmission and preservation of variation between generations. (The concept of generation is also a matter of theoretical specification.) Third, conditions or selection criteria that differentially favor particular variants must be present (Campbell 1965; Dunnell 1980; Mayr 1991). This last point is operative in the concept of fitness.

Cultural systems meet those criteria. They encompass behavioral variation, described by Schiffer and Skibo (1987), for example, as the different capacities of individuals or groups often reflected in technology, and heritability as defined by Boyd and Richerson (1985) as "modes of cultural transmission." When these qualities are combined with selective criteria that affect the viability of variants relative to one another, we reach the inference that selection must operate in cultural systems. Thus, it is axiomatic that the differential persistence of cultural traits—behaviors, artifacts, or technologies—is significantly influenced by natural selection. Recognizing that an instance of cultural change is the consequence of selection, however, is not the same as explaining that event. For this reason natural selection is often criticized as tautological and not explanatory in the usual sense of specifying cause and effect. To address what is an adequate explanation minimally requires a more complete understanding of the historical context in which the event took place.

The purpose of our chapter is to examine the structure of selectionist explanation in archaeology in order to see what sorts of inferences about the archaeological record are necessary to this perspective. In turn, these classes of inferences justify the particular methodologies developed elsewhere in this book. We have divided our study into three parts. First, we begin with a brief consideration of explanation. Next, selectionism is contrasted with the dominant processual model in archaeology to identify modes of explanation distinct to each. Finally, we examine the products of selectionism. They consist of two kinds of explanation. The first is an accurate rendering of the patterns of differential persistence of material and inferred behavioral traits through time—an evolutionary description. The second explanation links the description with selection factors to build an argument as to why such patterns exist.

A Note About Explanation

So that it is clear what kinds of explanations selectionism offers, we need to examine briefly the general issue of explanation in archaeology. Formal and substantive aspects of explanation have received a considerable amount of attention over the past thirty years (e.g., Kelley and Hanen 1988; Renfrew et al. 1982; Salmon 1982; Watson et al. 1971). Even so, explanation is discussed with some consternation today. In some quarters, it is treated skeptically; indeed, it may be ridiculed as the goal of a suspect intellectual exercise. Where explanation has remained a respected goal among avowed processualists, it often seems unattainable in practice.

The processualist critique of the 1960s and 1970s brought explanation front and center (e.g., Watson et. al. 1971). In seeking different explanations than those supplied by culture history, archaeologists have looked to make improvements by working out the most appropriate logical form of explanation. The deductive-nomological model (Hempel 1966) was an early rallying point. Subsequently, the D-N model has been strongly criticized generally for inaccurately portraying scientific practice, and specifically for misrepresenting how scientific explanations are developed.

Is it possible, indeed appropriate, for a historical and observational science like archaeology to posit invariant or universal laws of behavior from which "good" explanations necessarily follow deductively? We have learned that it is not. Still, lacking a unified body of explanatory principles and a clear means to evaluate hypothetical explanations formally is not an ideal situation. How is the adequacy of explanation to be evaluated?

According to Hanen and Kelley (1989), archaeological explanations in practice assume a somewhat weaker form of deductive reasoning. The logic of the reasoning is to work from a hypothesis to implications about the empirical world. If observations made of empirical phenomena conform to those implications, the hypothesis is supported. The problem with such reasoning lies in the fact that, although the observations may be sufficient to support the hypothesis, they may not be a necessary consequence of only the causal process or processes specified in the hypothesis. In short, other explanations may also account for the same observations. Hanen and Kelley remark that "this pattern of reasoning is deductively invalid and yet it seems to play an essential role in hypothesis confirmation" (1989:16). While such arguments clearly are flawed, Hanen and Kelley observe that purported explanations seem to recover their usefulness when alternative hypotheses for the observations can be evaluated and are found wanting (method of multiple working hypotheses).

This form of explanation is especially well suited to cases that can reference lawlike propositions which either are widely accepted in the discipline or have bases in physical laws. The form may be a suitable mode of explanation for more complex phenomena and processes as well, such as those involved in cultural evolution.

In a substantive vein, what do we seek to explain? Renfrew (1982) suggests several fields. The first is a specific event. While Renfrew has in mind complex events like the Classic Maya collapse, we can imagine seeking explanations for events from a continuum of complexity. Whether simple or complex, events share the fact that they are unique occurrences. Renfrew's second field is "classes" of events. Here, Renfrew refers to events that are historically distinct and because of similar form and content are believed to have common processual qualities, and thus would permit a common explanation for all cases. The origins of food production are an example. A third field relates to processes. For example, an explanation might be sought for the persistence of equilibrating processes as they relate to population size. Lastly, Renfrew points out that we attempt to build explanations for empirical patterns either directly from the archaeological record or derived from it. These patterns may be synchronic, as in the case of a settlement pattern, or diachronic, as in the reorganization of settlement over time.

When we closely examine Renfrew's distinctions (the "whats" of explanation), it seems clear that these are not so much exclusive phenomenal fields as they are different phases in archaeological inference. Empirical patterns arise from the formal and spatial qualities of artifacts (Spaulding 1960). Events and processes are more involved inferences derived from the empirical record. When we attempt to explain events and processes, arguments are constructed to link events, variables and relations among variables, and processes that provide coherent statements as to why events transpired as they did. To construct such arguments, however, means working through an empirical record comprised of artifacts, which Binford has described as static, rather than dynamic. The success of explanation comes down to constructing both dynamically sufficient theory (Lewontin 1974) specifying relevant variables and rules of change, and empirically sufficient descriptions that relate artifacts and patterns among artifacts to those variables suggested to have undergone transformation—the goal of middle-range research.

Archaeological studies of cultural evolution have been investigated under two approaches, which we will discuss below as adaptationism and selectionism. (Though considered a postprocessual paradigm, historical materialism can be treated as a third processual approach.) To differentiate them, it is useful first to distinguish between two kinds of explanation. Etiological explanations purport to explain the occurrence of a phenomenon by reference to its cause. They seek relationships between the phenomenon of interest and antecedent events, processes, or state of the phenomenon. Teleological explanations, in contrast, explain the occurrence of a phenomenon by reference to the phenomenon's effect. They account for purposive, or seemingly goal-directed, processes.

As considered in more detail later, both of these kinds of explanation have a role in evolutionary narrative. However, it is necessary to point out first that one kind of teleological explanation, cosmic teleology (Mayr 1982)—reference to final causes—is denied any place in understanding evolution.

Excepting finalism (cosmic teleology), several kinds of teleological concepts or processes may be parts of archaeological explanation. Mayr (1982) describes teleomatic processes as those which result in outcomes that are strictly a consequence of physical laws. As noted before, such laws, which specify invariant relationships of a physiochemical or mechanical nature, underlie many basic inferences in archaeology, for example, that a pottery vessel is fired clay or that a stone flake is the product of percussive force. Much of the inferential base that we develop in what Schiffer (1988) terms "analytic theory" comes from knowledge of teleomatic processes.

Teleological language is also used to refer to inborn or acquired "programs" that guide physiological processes or behaviors toward some purpose. Mayr (1982) refers to these as "teleonomic processes." Such programs, often genetic, explain ontologic development, for example. Even though enactment of a teleonomic process does not guarantee an expected result, knowledge of the program gives us the ability to predict what the consequence should be. Adapted systems, like the organs of our body or functionally related components of culture, often have been considered in this light, conceived as if programmed for specific results like homeostasis: the purpose of the heart is to circulate blood; the goal of a ritual cycle is to regulate population size in relation to resources. The explanation for the program—or the system—lies in its purpose, in its function. The dog barks, we explain, in order to get into the house.

Functional arguments in archaeology often take this form. The language of systems theory perhaps is the best developed example. We may, of course, invert the structure of the teleonomic argument and seek an explanation of the consequence in the workings of a program and the stimuli that triggered the process. In this instance we have an etiological argument that treats proximate causation—how does the system operate? Seeing its owner through the window, the dog barked.

An alternative to asking why a system works in the fashion it does is to ask why the system has the structure it does rather than another structure. Searching for explanation lies in the history of the system. Answers concern the evolution of the system and are both general and particularistic; the answer cannot be set apart from historical context. Why did the dog bark (rather than meow)? Our explanation will force us to examine the evolution of dog behavior and physiology.

Adaptationism and Selectionism

Evolutionary approaches in contemporary processual thought in archaeology have two forms. The more familiar form is a product of paradigmatic changes of the 1960s, advanced in work by Binford (e.g., 1968), Clarke (e.g., 1968) and others. As it continues to be practiced, the new archaeology operates from a functionalist perspective and derives its theoretical underpinnings most directly from ecological functionalism as elaborated by Julian Steward, but with modification through its connections with systems theory (e.g., Flannery 1968, 1972). The other form of processual thinking—selectionism—has been advanced only since the late seventies and early eighties. It incorporates both a functional and historical perspective, and is modeled in part after evolutionary biology.

For purposes of this discussion we use the terms adaptationism and selection-ism to refer to these processual models. Each purports to account for changes in past human behaviors, although each calls upon different mechanisms to explain change (Dunnell 1980). In adaptationism that mechanism is adaptation, a process whereby humans actively and intentionally direct change in their strategies and tactics of survival. From an evolutionary perspective, adaptation is a product of selection rather than the process fostering change (O'Brien and Holland 1992).

This distinction turns on the role given by each program to behavioral variation and its material referents. In the adaptationist view, phenotypic variation arises in direct response to need—to enhance adaptive fit. A new solution might be devised to meet a problem or a technology might be modified to meet a perceived need. In a critique of this perspective, Rindos (1985:70) describes the adaptationist view of evolution in the following way: "Evolution is a one-step process. The generation of adaptive variation is synonymous with its 'selection' in the evolutionary process. Adaptation is a 'new' response to changed conditions that simultaneously serves to correct the problem that made the adaptation necessary."

Taking this view, human motives or system motives, not variation per se, are the fuel of change. In our lives this perspective is reinforced daily. It is not uncommon to learn that an industry is furiously "innovating" to meet some technical or market challenge. Schiffer (1991) refers to this tendency as a "cultural imperative." As a society, we subscribe to the idea that we can, indeed must, innovate, that problems can be solved by directing, or focusing, the production of variation. To the extent that what is intended as a solution is a product of previous experiences and successes, under adaptationism we are led to expect that change will most always be of a stabilizing or equilibrating sort. The failure of experience in its most marked form, then, will manifest itself as disjunctions in adaptational trajectories, adaptive "shifts," breached thresholds, or system collapse.

In contrast, selectionism views the generation of variation and the selection of variants as separate processes (Rindos 1989:8). Innovations arise independently of the processes of selection. While the production of variants is to a degree constrained by preceding states of the system, the nature of that variation is not determined by the future course of the system. This does not mean that innovation is random (independent of historical conditions), or that it cannot be generated in an attempt to solve a problem. It merely means that the *generation* of variation is *independent* of selection. Again, we need not search too long to find examples of technologies that failed to gain a foothold despite what seem to be advantageous designs, just as we can find failures that resulted from obvious flaws in designs. More to the point, perhaps, are examples of technologies that have been far more successful in contexts unrelated to ones for which they were intended originally.

This means that evolution is "written," so to speak, not by the intentions of individuals but by the differential sorting of behavioral and artifactual variants over time in response to selective agents. All of the collective intentions of early horticulturalists could not explain the evolution of agricultural strategies; neither individuals nor the systems they operated in could foresee the long string of events leading to this transformation (Rindos 1984). The replicative success (Leonard and Jones 1987) of those artifact traits depends, at least in part, upon their contribution to the fitness of individuals possessing those traits as part of their phenotype but almost certainly also to the effectiveness of transmission mechanisms.

Archaeologists of different theoretical persuasions are troubled by what they see as selectionism's apparent denial of human volition. Trigger (1991), for instance, credits what he terms biologistic viewpoints in anthropology (presumably including selectionism) with the idea that the generation of variation is a purely random process and that "cultural selection automatically favors the most adaptive ideas by ensuring the survival of those cultures that happen to act on them" (Trigger 1991:559). This criticism misrepresents the point. Intent plays a significant role in the generation of behavioral and artifactual variation. It is not, however, given a causal role in shaping adaptation. It is not the motivations, goals, or intentions behind the generation of specific variants—artifact forms—that are important; rather, at issue is why a particular variant confers an advantage to those members of a population possessing it at a particular time. Most individuals, presumably, intend to be successful, and they generate their behaviors to that end. As we know, however, only certain behaviors are successful, and to discuss success in terms of the intent of the individuals behind the success makes no more sense than to discuss the failures of other individuals in terms of their unrealized aspirations for success (Leonard and Abbott 1992).

Beyond the logical problems posed by a theory of intentionality are serious methodological problems as well. How are the loci of intent and selection located archaeologically? One way the challenge has been met (and warranted by a normative view of culture) is by shifting the responsibility for the direction of variation to a higher scale, to the cultural system. This is illustrated by the degree of inclusiveness that is part of many adaptationist explanatory narratives. Changes occur in the "adaptive system," which usually means strategies and tactics of subsistence, settlement, and technology at any number of scales. Narratives take the form of "adaptive summaries," wherein an adaptation is treated as some modal tactical set. This tactical set is seen to change over time via directed variation and, on occasion, to undergo significant transformations—leaps to new stable adaptive plateaus.

We are not arguing that modal tendencies do not exist. Certainly, some behavioral alternatives have greater frequencies than others; many traits of artifacts that can be measured quantitatively approximate a normal curve. But it is the alternative qualities and the less well-represented quantities, whose frequencies shift over time, that mark evolution. The transformation of the modal variant, when treated as the essence of an adaptation, is epiphenomenal, however, an artifact of the statistical representation of variation.

Selectionism and Explanation

Methodological essentialism is exemplified in the tendency to regard phenomena (their form, content, or structure) as some average quality, as manifestations of archetypal forms. Variation is conceived (or, at least, represented for analytic purposes) as imperfect representation of the archetype. The effects are evident when we examine two consequences of essentialism.

First, change may go unrecognized. This criticism often is mentioned in reviews of the methods of culture history. In the construction of synthetic units like phases, changes internal to a time interval are masked. The unity of a phase, whether described by stylistic traits or as an adaptation based on functional traits, is emphasized in the imagery used to represent the phase—space-time charts illustrating diagnostic features.

The second, related consequence comes in attempting to cope with differences among phases that seem to express cultural change. Change appears to be step-like, long periods of stability followed by short episodes of change (Plog and Hantman 1990). The processes of change then must be located in the analytically problematic boundary between phases. Similarly, by presenting adaptations in an essentialist form, change necessarily comes to be viewed as the result of saltational processes, significant transformations between equilibrium states.

When typological thinking is replaced by populational thinking, change is reconceptualized. Change is no longer seen as the transformation of the mode but as shifts in patterns of variant representation over time. The investigation of the causes of change turns first to the search for antecedent variation.

How does selectionism improve on "adaptive summaries"? We address this question in this final section by examining two components of the evolutionary narrative, description and explanation. The descriptive component is an attempt to represent the chronological patterns of functional (of adaptive significance) or stylistic (selectively neutral) classes. The imagery is that of seriation or phylogenetic reconstruction. Such descriptions, in turn, rely on two products. One is classification, the means by which artifactual variation is organized into stylistic and functional classes (Dunnell 1978). The other is the determination of true homologies—that sequential components of the archaeological record are derived from populations of genetically related or functionally interdependent individuals.

The second component of the selectionist program is explanation, sets of arguments as to why some traits persist and expand in frequency at the expense of others within a given environmental and historical context. Both proximate and ultimate cause play a role. Together, the description and explanation form what Mayr (1991) or Terrell (1990) would call an evolutionary narrative: how it was in the past and why it changed.

Evolutionary Description

We have seen that selectionist explanations concern both proximate and ultimate causes. Such arguments build both from the dynamic and empirical sufficiency of theory (Lewontin 1974). A dynamically adequate model, however, may not be one that has measurable empirical referents. Thus, to begin to describe an evolutionary event or pattern of events adequately, we are required to consider how the substantive archaeological record expresses variation relevant to potential answers, relevant to the causal processes believed to be significant to the case. This is done through classification. The task turns then to showing the histories of those classes, a step analogous to building an evolutionary phylogeny.

CLASSIFICATION AND MEASUREMENT. Natural selection acts opportunistically on artifactual and behavioral (phenotypic) variation to cause change in the adaptedness of humans. To recognize that variation is present, of course, is an observation that we make about the archaeological record, and thus is a product of the theoretical "eyes" with which we view that record. We operationalize and make explicit those observations through classification.

Classification represents the imposition of order on a phenomenological realm. It is a deductive procedure originating in warranting arguments relating the purpose of the exercise (organizing variation pertinent to hypothesized processes) to the attributes selected. Depending upon the classificatory and measurement criteria selected, as well as the observational scale chosen, variation is manipulated; it can disappear into unity or be enhanced to limitless difference, depending on the choice of scale. Somewhere along this continuum attributes are chosen that convert uniqueness among artifacts into meaningful observations about variation. One particular form of classification, dimensional classification (paradigmatic [Dunnell 1971]), has been advocated by a number of selectionists (e.g., O'Brien and Holland 1990) because of its effectiveness in accommodating pertinent variation.

Classification is not regarded, however, as the only appropriate means to order empirical phenomena. Recently, Neff (1993) argued in favor of grouping procedures. As distinguished from classification, grouping emphasizes the emergence of order from a collection of artifacts. The importance of Neff's arguments warrants some attention.

Neff's criticism centers on the point that classification produces typological units; as theoretical constructs, classes have essences because they are not generated out of an empirical record with real spatial and temporal contexts. Instead, Neff prefers units that are historically contingent, based on the actual variation evident in a set of artifacts. Procedurally, these units emerge as a result of sorting procedures, much as Krieger (1944) would describe typological practice. Justification of this approach rests in the fact that the groups formed can be presumed to relate to the actual processes of transmission and selection in a particular historical setting, especially given archaeologists' past successes in identifying common descent (Neff 1993:31).

While Neff is clear that grouping procedures are to be considered as part of a sampling procedure that is preliminary to the measurement of theoretically relevant processes (e.g., transmission and selection), we believe that Neff misrepresents the methodological role of classification, and in some ways, his own work. First, no assemblage can be stratified for the purpose of sampling without some warranting arguments to support the basis of that sampling design. These warranting arguments are, and should be, theoretically motivated. Indeed, Neff's own persistent concerns are those generated by theory—transmission and selection. These are hardly intuitive concerns.

Second, his claim that grouping procedures are preliminary to the measurement of theoretically relevant processes implies that any given classification is, in effect, a set of hypotheses. Teltser (chapter 4) specifies this relationship between historical types and seriation quite clearly, and Neff seems to appreciate this himself when he concludes that "there is no a priori way to assign meaning to empirical groups; at most the groups constitute guesses as to how underlying processes of interest are expressed in the data" (Neff 1993:32).

While these points may lead to the conclusion that grouping and classification are fundamentally the same and compatible, it is Neff's central criticism, that classes are typological because they have essences, that is perhaps most important. This criticism of classification points precisely to what Dunnell refers to as the "materialist paradox" in chapter 3, and to the reason that it is critical to maintain a distinction between empirical units and theoretical units of measurement, as well as a distinction between the scale at which evolutionary processes occur and the scale at which those processes are manifest. The results of evolutionary processes are generally conceived as empirical units with locations in time and space (e.g., cows, civilizations, or a pottery tradition). The measurement of evolutionary change is made at a finer scale, however, as frequency changes in discrete variants. This is, as Teltser suggests in chapter 1, a methodological expression of the distinction between materialism and essentialism. Indeed, Neff's own work considers the evolution of particular pottery traditions in terms of analytically discrete compositional classes.

Artifact classes do not evolve; indeed, they cannot be conceived as a mutable phenomena if we hope to represent evolution as a change in the frequency of class representation over time. Classes are counting units just as different variants of cows are counting units. We might say that end scrapers evolve over time, but what we are really saying is that, when arrayed chronologically, distinct classes of end scrapers are differentially represented over time. Conceived this way, classification can be viewed as a procedure for partitioning variation so as to provide distinct units for counting. Evolution takes place not in our counting units—classes— but in assemblages (populations) containing representatives of those classes.

Warranting classificatory distinctions is central to any classification exercise. For this discussion, it is useful to make the distinction between stylistic and functional realms, treating the former as variation not subject to selection and the latter as variation affected by selective pressures. As Neff (1993) argues, the choice of attributes in stylistic classification or grouping cannot be justified apart from the empirical record because the specific qualities of style are not universal but rather historically contingent. That is, the nature of stylistic variation depends on the particular representations of stylistic traits in the archaeological record of interest (see Teltser, chapter 4).

For functional variation, however, it is often possible to warrant the choice of classificatory criteria without reference to a particular empirical record because some types of functional actions are reducible to invariant physiochemical or mechanical principles (teleomatic processes). Thus, it is possible to isolate relevant classificatory variables without specific knowledge of their representation in an archaeological case. If we know, for instance, that microcrystalline lithic artifacts are present in an archaeological record, it is quite possible to anticipate the kinds of use-wear damage that might be present and thereby provide a theoretical warrant for such an analysis before any artifacts are actually inspected.

Discussion to this point would suggest that only qualitative variation, the kind of variation that can be categorized nominally, is appropriate for selectionist arguments. Of course, this is not the case. Functionally significant quantities are obvious aspects of most classificatory fields. Volume, mass, length—each may be useful for displaying a historical trend. Once again, however, variation in such traits, rather than exclusively the modal tendency of a distribution of values, must be considered. At issue is not simply that the average value of a functional quantity changes over time but that new modal values have a historical connection in the distribution of values in an antecedent state.

REPRESENTING HISTORICAL PATTERNS. Seriation and phylogenetic reconstructions offer good examples of the manner in which evolutionary patterns can be represented. Each reconstruction attempts to show how a set of classificatory units (e.g., stylistic classes or species) is distributed in time.

The ability to represent such patterns rests on inferences that the entities assigned to the same class at the same or different points of time are related.

Similarity, therefore, is judged to be homologous; that is, similarity arises within a single historical system of information transmission (an inheritance system). Of course, this is precisely the objective of culture history.

Culture history relies on styles that come from geographically circumscribed areas to build a case for homologous similarity. The complexity of stylistic features, and their neutrality with respect to selection, makes the likelihood of convergent evolution very small. The possibility of convergence to similar functional forms (analogous similarity), however, is greater because of the tendency of selection to limit extant variation. Inferential problems are enhanced for the practical matter that functional distinctions often are based on few criteria, sometimes just a single dimension like the volume of a ceramic vessel. It is necessary, therefore, to link the functional record to a stylistic record in order to build a case for homologous functional similarity. Neff (1993, chapter 5) makes a compelling argument for use of compositional criteria (e.g., clay or lithic source) to build inferences about historical relatedness.

Evolutionary Explanation

Evolutionary explanations are historical narratives according to Mayr (1982). They are more than stories about sequentially ordered events, however. As Terrell (1990) thinks of them, narratives of the sorts that historical sciences like archaeology develop require conscious model building. After all, the events contained in a narrative are themselves inferences derived from objects and patterns in an archaeological record, which in turn are ordered sequentially by methods for constructing chronologies, and then are linked to one another by inferred causal processes. As narratives, selectionist explanations attend a concrete archaeological record within a specific historical context; but they also have general, context-free qualities in the fact that individual historical cases are conceptualized in terms of processual uniformities (e.g., ecological relations of a general sort).

The purpose of evolutionary narrative in archaeology is to explain variation in the archaeological record (Teltser, chapter 1). Once again, however, the narrative does not seek out the origins of variation per se, even though origins often can be located in a general way in a particular historical interval. But whether variation is introduced as a consequence of rational intent or mistake, or by other means (as much as some might like to conjecture about innovation for purposes of "filling-out" the narrative), the appearance of variation is significant only so far as it becomes available to other forces that affect its persistence or demise. (This is not meant to deny a place for selectionist study of the evolution of systems that accentuate or regulate the mode and tempo of innovation [e.g., Rindos 1985].) The focus of explanation then is upon that variation which survives at such a frequency and for sufficient time that it is evident archaeologically.

Where change is treated methodologically as the differential persistence of artifactual variants, narratives posit highly plausible arguments as to why archaeological change occurred. Change can assume directional, oscillating, or negligible forms; can be represented by increasing, decreasing, or stable diversity of variants; and can take place at different temporal scales and at varying tempos. For the most part, because of the resolution of the archaeological record, changes relating to strong and/or long-lasting evolutionary forces probably are evaluated most successfully.

Two general processes—transmission and selection—figure in selectionist arguments. Transmission processes refer to modes of social learning by which some kinds of phenotypic traits (e.g., knowledge about the form and manufacture of a tool) are communicated between individuals (Boyd and Richerson 1985). Detecting the operation of transmission is an inference sometimes generated directly out of the traits under inspection, while in other instances it is based on associations with other classes of artifacts in which homologies are more readily inferred. As we have discussed before, detecting cultural transmission is necessary to the description of an evolutionary sequence.

Normally, transmission is treated in archaeological study as having pragmatic utility for constructing sequences but also as constituting a passive process. Beyond inferring the occurrence of transmission, sorting out which modes of transmission may be operating in any archaeological case and whether different modes of transmission are forces of change is a far more difficult problem. Boyd and Richerson (1985), for example, have argued that different transmission processes hold the power to differentially influence trait representation. Although different modes of transmission have consequences for the fidelity of information being communicated (thereby influencing the pool of variability at any time), frequency-dependent transmission may give change a strongly directional character that might be mistaken for an effect of selection.

One area in which deeper understandings of the effects of transmission may prove valuable is in the study of selectively neutral traits. This conclusion is drawn from the general observation that stylistic traits do not behave randomly over time but rather follow a more or less monotonic pattern. How might such trends, described as relating to stochastic processes, be linked with transmission differentials? Imagine, for instance, a case in which a particular style variant is associated with a segment of a population that is increasing in size, a consequence of selection for other (functional) traits which members of that group share. We might anticipate that a corresponding increase in the representation of the style would take place even though the replicative success of the style is not linked in any causal sense to the fitness of members of the population.

The selective neutrality of style (Dunnell 1978) has created conceptual problems for some archaeologists who regard style as having utility, serving to convey information about group affiliation, for example. Commenting on this confusion,

O'Brien and Holland (1992:46) suggest the distinction between style and alternate states of style must be made clear: "neutrality of alternate states of a trait does not imply . . . that possessing the trait carries no selective value." While two groups may identify themselves in terms of dots or triangles (on ceramic vessels, for instance), and while members of one group may be more fit than members of the other, the difference in fitness is not the result of possessing dots rather than triangles. The ability to convey information about one's group affiliation through style may enhance fitness; however, the choice of a particular style is arbitrary, a matter of history and not selection. The issue, O'Brien and Holland (1992) note, turns on choosing the analytic scale appropriate for the question being addressed; style can be functional while particular styles or design elements are neutral (see Graves and Ladefoged, chapter 8).

This brings us to the second class of archaeological traits, functional traits, and the processes that influence their differential survival, collectively termed selection. Selective processes have the potential to influence the representation of alternative functional artifact traits because of the consequences that possessing one alternative rather than another has for fitness—survival and the probability of reproduction.

Out of a pool of functional variation—in behaviors or artifacts—selection fashions adaptations. Conceived in this manner, adaptation is a consequence rather than a force in cultural change or stability; adaptation is a pattern of phenotypic traits. The direction of adaptive change imparted by selection in any particular historical setting is a function of the variation available and of a relevant set of ecological relations obtaining between individuals and their environment. These relations, like competition or mutualism, have universal or theoretical properties. One way in which to link theoretical models and an empirical record for purposes of explanation is in the identification of selective agents. These are external factors that constrain or alter selective conditions such that some individuals rather than others (along with the behaviors and artifactual traits they carry) are favored.

Braun (1990:81) describes several examples. Shifts in the physical or demographic environment may influence the success of competing individuals of different phenotypic form. An expansion of this example might involve the introduction of competition from a previously external cultural group that comes to exert an influence on access to and use of resources. Another example involves an outcome of coevolutionary interactions in which the success of certain cultural practices act to modify their own selection conditions. Of course, innovation and selection of strongly adapted variants may have consequences for selection acting on other functional traits as well.

Inferences to the nature of ecological relations in archaeological cases often are difficult to make. It seems reasonable to assert, however, that those which are most persistent over the long term (like those relating to subsistence) will have the most evident archaeological consequences—historical patterns in the representation of trait frequencies.

In evolutionary biology several kinds of patterns are recognized and a selective mode is described for each. Stabilizing selection refers to processes that limit the diversity of phenotypic variation. Less advantageous variants are lost; new innovations are winnowed away if they do not enhance adaptiveness. Campbell (1965) explains that complex functional structures tend to be maintained by consistent ecological pressures. "Without this, the cumulative occurrence of uneliminated mutations gradually destroys its functionality. . . . The more complex the structure the more statistically likely it becomes that random mutations will lessen rather than increase the adaptive adequacy" (Campbell 1965:40). Directional trends, as for example in the historical increase in the productivity of domesticated plants, are also evident archaeologically. Directional selection describes those processes favoring one tail of a distribution and causing a directional shift in the mode of the distribution over time. Finally, selection may equally favor both tails of the distribution of a functional quantity at the expense of modal values. Over time, two or more variants may assume stable frequencies relative to one another. On the broadest level, this kind of disruptive selection is seen as the cause for groups living in close proximity to move into nonoverlapping niches, by exploiting independent segments of a functional continuum.

This conception of function suggests a means by which to identify those artifactual traits that are potentially adaptive (lead to greater fitness), through so-called "engineering studies." We can reason that out of a group of functional alternatives the artifact class which performs a task most effectively is likely to have the greatest positive effect on fitness, and thus be favored by selection. Schiffer and Skibo (1987), for example, advocate a methodology to detect performance differentials in technology. Where possible, performance assessments are made experimentally since such approaches permit close control over relevant variables. Here the point is to learn which design is optimal according to a set of performance criteria, realizing that an artifact design is often a compromise conditioned by manufacture, use, and maintenance. "By appreciating the patterned differences between the performance characteristics of artifact types, one has a basis for hypothesizing those features of lifeway and social organization that might be responsible for changes" (Schiffer and Skibo 1987:601).

Performance evaluations are powerful tools in understanding the selective processes acting through ecologic relations that govern technologic change. Controlled comparisons (e.g., Maxwell, chapter 6) offer another avenue to explore the history of selection. Instances of evolutionary convergence in independent historical sequences permit one to hypothesize about common selection factors.

In applying these approaches we need to remember that performance differentials or convergent functional forms may assist in identifying the proximate causes of differential trait representation at any particular time. But a potential mistake lies in the assumption that these same proximate causes have held force during an entire evolutionary sequence. Current function need not imply past function; current selective conditions need not imply past selective conditions (Gould and Lewontin 1979; Lewontin 1978). As one example, the forces that favored the representation of circular subterranean structures in the prehistoric North American Southwest are certainly not isomorphic with those favoring the function of kivas in contemporary southwestern societies. Given the cultural capacity to innovate and diversify, co-optation of function is probably a commonplace feature of the archaeological record.

As a final note, we recognize that cultural change that is essentially functional in character is often marked by a complex of correlated changes. The tendency is to regard correlated directional changes as all being responses to the same selective pressures or to consider each class whose states are changing in frequency as being equally influenced by selection. It is probably often the case, however, that the differential persistence of some traits may result from their chance linkage with trait classes or functional complexes that are under strong selective pressure, rather than to any selective relationship of their own. We have referred to this as sorting (Abbott, Leonard, and Jones 1993). Thus when viewing correlated traits, we need to conceptualize problems in terms of adaptive differentials, specifying which traits are the more important vis-à-vis the selective pressures operating at the time.

Summary

Selectionism is a framework for explaining the differential persistence of phenotypic variation. As it pertains to the study of cultural stability and change, selectionism treats phenotypic expressions of two kinds principally, behavior (socially transmitted actions) and artifacts (material products used in or resulting from behavior). In archaeological study, artifacts represent the empirically observable realm of study, and it is the differential representation of variation at all scales among artifacts for which selectionism seeks explanations.

Some, though not all, attributes of artifacts affect the fitness of individuals who use the artifacts. Among alternatives, those artifacts with the highest potential for increasing fitness are most likely to persist and increase in frequency, all things being equal. Guaranteed phenotypic success is not predicted, however. Rather, we say that "on average" association with the effective trait variant will enhance fitness. Success is a statistical property of populations, not a deterministic property of individuals.

Some artifactual variants may increase at the expense of others through no relation to fitness enhancement. We thus distinguish between the replicative success of the artifact and the reproductive success of individuals (Leonard and Jones 1987). In many instances, enhanced replicative success correlates with population increases, therein indicating a strong possibility that selection operates in favoring an artifactual variant. Artifactual traits may increase in frequency, however, not so much for their own fitness effects as for their linkage with other traits that are under strong selective pressure. Study of these possibilities requires as full an exploration of functional complexes as possible in order to identify correctly the nature of selection and the directionality of causes. Some artifactual traits are neutral with respect to selection and behave in an uncorrelated manner with changes in proximate ecologic relations. Finally, change may occur for reasons of chance. Forces of drift segment the range of artifactual and behavioral variability so as to limit which alternatives can be transmitted.

A central premise of selectionism is that the processes responsible for the creation of variation are distinct from those responsible for the differential sorting of variation over time. Cultural systems provide a wide array of variation generating mechanisms, including rational decision making, but none of these guide evolution over the long term. That is accomplished by forces of selection and drift. Far from dismissing it as irrelevant to understanding evolutionary change, conscious decision making must be understood as a significant evolved capacity of humans that has the potential to enhance greatly the pool of phenotypic variation that selection (or drift) may act upon.

Selectionism gives methodological imperative to non-essentialist or populational conceptions of empirical phenomena. This emphasis on extant variation as a fuel of change, which is generated independently of forces that select for variants, distinguishes selectionist approaches from other archaeological perspectives on the evolution of human adaptations. In the interpretation of the archaeological record, the selectionist approach combines description of the historical patterns of differential trait representation and arguments as to how evolutionary forces acted to create those patterns.

The selectionist perspective described here and in other chapters in this book represents an attempt to wed archaeological inquiry into the cultural evolution of humans with the study of organic evolution generally. This point of view is advocated not simply for the insights that might be gained by archaeologists through this paradigmatic association, but to broaden evolutionary theory, to create an inclusive theory of the history of all living things.

Acknowledgments

We would like to thank Patrice Teltser, Michael B. Schiffer, and Charlotte Beck for their frank and helpful comments on this paper.

References

Abbott, A. L., R. D. Leonard, and G. T. Jones
1993   Explaining the Change from Biface to Flake Technology: A Selectionist Appli-
        cation. Paper presented in the symposium: "Convergent Evolution of the Sub-
        fields: Darwinian Models in Anthropology." 92nd Meeting of the American An-
        thropological Association, Washington, D.C., 1993.

Binford, L. R.
1968   Archaeological Perspectives. In *New Perspectives in Archeology,* edited by S. R.
        Binford and L. R. Binford, pp. 5–32. Aldine, Chicago.
1992   Seeing the Present and Interpreting the Past—and Keeping Things Straight. In
        Space, Time, and Archaeological Landscapes, edited by J. Rossignol and L. Wand-
        snider, pp. 43–59. Plenum Press, New York.

Boyd, R., and P. J. Richerson
1985   *Culture and the Evolutionary Process.* University of Chicago Press, Chicago.

Braun, D. P.
1990   Selection and Evolution in Nonhierarchical Organization. In *The Evolution of Po-
        litical Systems: Sociopolitics in Small-Scale Sedentary Societies,* edited by S. Upham,
        pp. 62–86. Cambridge University Press, Cambridge, England.

Campbell, D. T.
1965   Variation and Selective Retention in Socio-Cultural Evolution. In *Social Change in
        Developing Areas: A Reinterpretation of Evolutionary Theory,* edited by H. R. Bar-
        ringer, G. I. Blanksten, and R. W. Mack, pp. 19–49. Schenkman, Cambridge,
        Massachusetts.

Clarke, D.
1968   *Analytical Archaeology.* Methuen, London.

Dunnell, R. C.
1971   *Systematics in Prehistory.* Free Press, New York.
1978   Style and Function: A Fundamental Dichotomy. *American Antiquity* 43:192–202.
1980   Evolutionary Theory and Archaeology. In *Advances in Archaeological Method and
        Theory,* vol. 3, edited by M. B. Schiffer, pp. 35–99. Academic Press, New York.

Flannery, K. V.
1968   Archaeological Systems Theory and Early Mesoamerica. In *Anthropological Arche-
        ology in the Americas,* edited by B. J. Meggers, pp. 67–87. The Anthropological
        Society of Washington, Washington, D.C.
1972   The Cultural Evolution of Civilizations. *Annual Review of Ecology and Systematics*
        3:399–426.

Gould, S. J., and R. C. Lewontin
1979   The Spandrels of San Marco and the Panglossian Paradigm: A Critique of the
        Adaptationist Programme. *Proceedings of the Royal Society of London* B205:581–
        598.

Hanen, M., and J. Kelley
1989   Inference to the Best Explanation in Archaeology. In *Critical Traditions in Contemporary Archaeology,* edited by V. Pinsky and A. Wylie, pp. 14–17. Cambridge University Press, Cambridge, England.

Hempel, C. G.
1966   *Philosophy of Natural Science.* Prentice-Hall, Englewood Cliffs, New Jersey.

Kelley, J. H., and M. P. Hanen
1988   *Archaeology and the Methodology of Science.* University of New Mexico Press, Albuquerque.

Krieger, A. D.
1944   The Typological Concept. *American Antiquity* 9:271–288.

Leonard, R. D., and A. L. Abbott
1992   Theoretical Aspects of Subsistence Stress and Cultural Evolution. Paper presented at a symposium entitled "Resource Stress, Economic Uncertainty, and Human Response in the Prehistoric Southwest." Santa Fe Institute, Santa Fe, New Mexico, February 1992.

Leonard, R. D., and G. T. Jones
1987   Elements of an Inclusive Evolutionary Model for Archaeology. *Journal of Anthropological Archaeology* 6:199–219.

Lewontin, R. C.
1974   *The Genetic Basis of Evolutionary Change.* Columbia University Press, New York.
1978   Adaptation. *Scientific American* 239:212–230.

Mayr, E.
1982   *The Growth of Biological Thought: Diversity, Evolution, and Inheritance.* Harvard University Press, Cambridge, Massachusetts.
1991   *One Long Argument: Charles Darwin and the Genesis of Modern Evolutionary Thought.* Harvard University Press, Cambridge, Massachusetts.

Neff, H.
1993   Theory, Sampling, and Analytical Technique in the Archaeological Study of Prehistoric Ceramics. *American Antiquity* 58:23–44.

O'Brien, M. J., and T. D. Holland
1990   Variation, Selection, and the Archaeological Record. In *Archaeological Method and Theory,* vol. 2, edited by M. B. Schiffer, pp. 31–79. University of Arizona Press, Tucson.
1992   The Role of Adaptation in Archaeological Explanation. *American Antiquity* 57:36–59.

Plog, S., and J. L. Hantman
1990   Chronology Construction and the Study of Prehistoric Culture Change. *Journal of Field Archaeology* 17:439–456.

Renfrew, C.
1982   Explanation Revisited. In *Theory and Explanation in Archaeology: The Southhampton Conference,* edited by C. Renfrew, M. J. Rowlands, and B. A. Segraves, pp. 5–23. Academic Press, New York.

Renfrew, C., M. J. Rowlands, and B. A. Segraves (editors)
1982   *Theory and Explanation in Archaeology: The Southhampton Conference.* Academic Press, New York.

Rindos, D.
1984   *The Origins of Agriculture: An Evolutionary Perspective.* Academic Press, Orlando.
1985   Darwinian Selection, Symbolic Variation, and the Evolution of Culture. *Current Anthropology* 26:65–88.
1989   Undirected Variation and the Darwinian Explanation of Cultural Change. In *Archaeological Method and Theory,* vol. 1, edited by M. B. Schiffer, pp. 1–45. University of Arizona Press, Tucson.

Salmon, M. H.
1982   *Philosophy and Archaeology.* Academic Press, New York.

Schiffer, M. B.
1988   The Structure of Archaeological Theory. *American Antiquity* 53:461–485.
1991   *The Portable Radio in American Life.* University of Arizona Press, Tucson.

Schiffer, M. B., and J. M. Skibo
1987   Theory and Experiment in the Study of Technological Change. *Current Anthropology* 28:595–622.

Spaulding, A. C.
1960   The Dimensions of Archaeology. In *Essays in the Science of Culture in Honor of Leslie A. White,* edited by G. E. Dole and R. L. Carneiro, pp. 437–456. Crowell-Collier, New York.

Terrell, J.
1990   Storytelling and Prehistory. In *Archaeological Method and Theory,* vol. 2, edited by M. B. Schiffer, pp. 1–29. University of Arizona Press, Tucson.

Trigger, B. G.
1991   Distinguished Lecture in Archaeology: Constraint and Freedom—A New Synthesis for Archeological Explanation. *American Anthropologist* 93:551–569.

Watson, P. J., S. A. LeBlanc, and C. L. Redman
1971   *Explanation in Archeology: An Explicitly Scientific Approach.* Columbia University Press, New York.

3

What Is It That Actually Evolves?

Robert C. Dunnell

◆◆ In retrospect, one of the most serious flaws in processual archaeology was its failure to rethink its language of observation, its systematics. Anthropologists and archaeologists disposed toward the use of evolutionary theory seem on the brink of following suit. The issue of units has not generally been addressed; traditional units drawn from the investigators' own culture or from academic lore continue to be used. Even when the importance of units has been recognized, researchers have not bothered to acquaint themselves with modern biological theory in more than a cursory fashion. As a result biology is depicted as having reached a consensus on key systematic concepts when such is not the case. In this chapter I attempt to identify the main issues in current biological debate on systematics and relate them to nascent efforts to use evolutionary theory in anthropology. Following examination of two examples selected to demonstrate the importance of unit definition, specific attention is directed to the traditional archaeological units and their potential in evolutionary applications.

Evolution as Materialist Science

It is easy enough to talk about the archaeological record using words like selection, variation, evolution, and adaptation, and there certainly is nothing particularly new in doing so. Using evolutionary terms and concepts as just another set of interpretive algorithms, however, misses the whole point to evolutionary theory in the first place—it is a *scientific* theory (Dunnell 1987). As a scientific theory, it is intended to generate empirically testable statements about why history has unfolded as it has. Application entails an interactive articulation between the theory and the phenomena to be explained, something not characteristic of the various "isms" that are traditionally employed to create archaeological explanations.

For example, evolution requires a radical departure from archaeological practice in the observation and description of phenomena (Dunnell 1989, 1992a). Evolution explains variation. Consequently, the archaeological record has to be described as variation. Traditional archaeological description, however, is strongly modal; even quantitative methods are typically deployed to suppress variation, as in identifying "significant differences" or creating types (cf. Luedtke 1986). Another consequence of the theory's scientific character is that the terms used to describe the record must also be the terms employed in the theory if the theory is to be able to explain a description (e.g., generally, Hanson 1958 and Whewell 1847; physical science, Crosland 1962; and biology, Lewontin 1974a). Again traditional practice is at variance, most dramatically in Binford's (e.g., 1977, 1981a) notion of "middle range theory." These two examples are, however, problems posed for archaeology simply by scientific explanation, any kind of scientific explanation.

Evolutionary theory poses special problems beyond those of science per se. The most dramatic is the novel ontological position it assumes—materialism. As Haldane (1956:96) put it so succinctly, Darwin not only invented a new science, he invented a new logic as well (cf. Lewontin 1974b). In a materialist view, everything is in the process of becoming—the relation we conceptualize as change. Materialism underlies a genuinely quantitative view of temporal relations, one that is continuously, rather than discretely, variable. Things, kinds, and states are artifacts of observation (e.g., Dunnell 1982; Greenwood 1984; Lewontin 1974a; Sober 1980). On the other hand, application of evolutionary theory (or any theory for that matter) seemingly requires *units,* things on which selection can act, things that vary, evolve, or are adapted. It is thus apparent that materialism greatly complicates the construction of a language of observation. There can be no laws of history because there are no constant terms with which to write such laws (cf. Popper 1963). Alternatively, if units (species or whatever unit) exist, then they cannot possibly evolve. This "materialist paradox" lies at the heart of operational evolutionary theory: units are essentialist constructs but evolution is a materialist theory, so the use of one would seem to preclude the use of the other.

Escaping the materialist paradox requires that we distinguish units along two dimensions. First, we need to consider the "location" of the unit—is it *empirical* (phenomenological of Dunnell 1971), lodged in the phenomenological world, or is it *theoretical* (ideational of Dunnell 1971), residing in the head of the investigator? I have argued the importance of this distinction for more than two decades (Dunnell 1971, 1986) and will not dwell on it here save to point out two features. All units, including theoretical units, usually *refer* to phenomena; the "reality" of a unit has nothing to do with its referent, but rather whether the quality of derives from the phenomenon or from the investigator.

Although the generally atheoretical character of archaeology (e.g., bettis... 1991) does not lead to a wealth of examples, the culture historical notion of artifact type (e.g., Ford 1954; Rouse 1939) supplies a familiar, albeit somewhat oblique, example. The objects that belong to types are empirical, but the rules by which they are associated as a type are supplied by the archaeologist, not the objects. While some archaeologists, notably the culture historians, have displayed remarkable sophistication on this issue, this important distinction is by no means universally appreciated in biology or elsewhere. Archaeological programmatic literature has departed from actual practice (Adams and Adams 1991; Dunnell 1986) and treated types not as classes but as empirical groups (Dunnell 1971; "individuals" in most contemporary biological literature) since the 1950s. This fascination with frankly atheoretical unit construction almost precisely parallels the rise, but not the demise, of numerical phenetics in biology. With a notable exception,[1] this commitment to a method has not been accompanied by a realization of its essentialist ontological entailments, namely that history is a succession of kinds (societies, cultures, phases, or peoples) rather than a sequence of frequencies. Certainly, a principal reason why this distinction remains obscure to many lies in that its utility is confined to materialist science; neither essentialist science (e.g., physics, chemistry) nor common senses (Dunnell 1982) employ such a distinction.

Theoretical units, because, and just because, they are not empirical, resolve the materialist paradox by accommodating divergent (or convergent) continuity as a *change* in frequency of theoretical types. While this notion may seem strange at first, it is something with which we are all familiar. No one argues that inches are "real" or empirical even though size may be. An inch is an arbitrary unit employed to measure size. Centimeters can be made to serve just as well. Using such ideational units allows us to treat size in a quantitative fashion rather than as a discontinuous set of empirical categories such as short and long. Similarly, the standard deviation is a unit specifically designed to "measure" normal distributions; the standard deviation also serves to illustrate the theory dependency of the observational language. The standard deviation does not demark equal units of variation, but rather equal probabilities of a specific value. The solution to the materialist paradox thus hinges on distinguishing empirical units from theoretical ones and employing the latter to describe and explain change.

The second dimension of concern is the scale at which units are formed and its relation to the scale at which processes operate. It is important to distinguish units on which the various processes that constitute a theory operate from units employed to talk about the results of those operations at other scales. A process operating at one scale may have effects at both higher and lower scales. Effects at lower scales are registered in distributions whereas effects at higher scales take the form of kinds. Units employed to talk about effects generated by processes at a lower scale are often termed epiphenomenal. In the classical expression of new synthesis biology, selection and other evolutionary processes operate on individual organisms. Species, populations, and other collections of individuals, where the effects of selection are seen, are epiphenomenal. Altruism, an action benefiting an individual other than ego, presents a classic example. Darwinian selectionism is relentlessly selfish. The existence of altruism among many animals thus suggested "group selection"; that is, the unit of selection is larger than the organism (e.g., Wynne-Edwards 1962). W. D. Hamilton (1964) was able to show mathematically that altruism would be fixed by selection at the scale of organism so long as the altruistic act occurred within viscous populations, that is, populations made up of genetic relatives. Thus the notion of "inclusive fitness" was developed by explaining what initially appeared as a group scale process by processes actually operating at the organism scale. The characteristics of species, or populations of individuals, are understood only by reference to processes operating on their constituent elements, organisms, and not by processes operating on populations or species themselves. When one talks about the evolution of species, one is not talking about a process operating on species, but the results of the operation of one or more processes operating on organisms. Individuals are selected but species evolve. One can, of course, identify the actions on individuals by their effects on aggregates. To do this, however, requires identifying the appropriate aggregate of individuals. This is a major component of the species debate and the primary reason why it is more common today to see demes, or local populations, identified as the evolving units than species per se. Local populations, unlike most species, represent physically *interacting* individuals and thus might be construed to be empirical units.

Application of evolutionary theory requires that units be characterized in two dimensions, their empirical or nonempirical character and their relation to the scale of processes or mechanisms employed in explanation (Fig. 3.1). Much of the continuing debate in biology over species, as well as the long-standing debate in archaeology surrounding types (and to a lesser extent phases/cultures) is tied to a conflation of these two dimensions (mostly under the guise of what is "real") and the work particular units are expected to do.

Units and Evolution in Anthropology

Those writing about the evolution of cultural phenomena still largely ignore both the scale and reality issues. Even when the importance of units is recognized, discussions are often so simplified as to be grossly misleading. A couple of cases serve to illustrate the problem.

	Theoretical	Empirical
+		
=		
-		

Figure 3.1. Kinds of Units Sorted by Construction (Theoretical/Empirical) and Scale in Relation to Processes (+/=/−). The +, =, − symbols denote scales greater than (epiphenomenal), equivalent, and smaller than that of the relevant process(es). If one were to map "species" onto this figure, it would occur in at least four boxes, which is to say that at least four functionally different concepts are involved. Likewise archaeological "type" would map over several boxes indicative of a similar problem.

The Species Concept as a Model

Marks and Staski (1988) are almost unique among anthropologists in giving serious consideration to the role of units in evolutionary theory and how these considerations affect the extension of evolutionary theory to human beings. Marks and Staski predicate their arguments on an equivalence of culture and species. Their understanding of species, however, is defective, not only in terms of substance, but also in the role the concept plays in evolutionary theory. They claim that species "as an individual," a la M. Ghiselin (e.g., 1966, 1987) and E. Mayr (e.g., 1963), is the accepted view of species in biology and imply that it is a settled issue. Nothing could be further from the truth.

As recently as 1992, Panchen identifies at least seven, rather than one, different kinds of species concepts. Rosenberg (1985) identifies at least nine distinct concepts labeled species. Misler and Brandon (1987:405–406), excluding typological (i.e., ideational or theoretical) concepts of species, note that there are "dozens of species concepts" current in biology. Without getting into the bases for such catalogs, at least four radically different *families* of concepts can be recognized conservatively: the so-called biological species concept (e.g., Dobzhansky 1937; Ghiselin 1966; Mayr 1942, 1963); the lineage or evolutionary concept developed by Simpson (e.g., 1961; cf. Wiley 1980); the ecological concept championed by van Valen (1976; cf. Templeton 1989); and a phylogenetic or cladistic concept (e.g., Hennig 1966; Misler and Donoghue 1982). Mayr (1987), the most strident proponent of the "species-as-individual" concept, himself admits that the biological species concept is only one among many. He has abandoned the species-as-individual terminology for the species-as-population (Mayr 1987).

The point is not, however, that the species-as-individual concept is not universally employed in biology or evolution, but that the species question remains one of the mostly actively debated issues in biology. An entire issue of *Biology and Philosophy* (vol. 2, no. 2) was recently devoted to the topic. All major theoretical journals routinely carry articles that treat the concept. Even the pragmatic literature frequently grapples with the implications of different species concepts for such applications as the status of subspecies and the implementation of endangered species legislation (e.g., Cole 1990; Collins 1991, 1992; Echelle 1990; Frost and Hillis 1990; Frost et al. 1992; Highton 1990; Smith 1990). Far from being a solution to any problems in the application of evolutionary theory to human beings, the species concept is part of the problem. Reading the biological literature can be of great value, but simplistic concept borrowing, like that of Marks and Staski (1988), is not helpful.

To make matters worse, the relevance of "species" to evolution is itself a serious question. Darwin's *On the Origin of Species* (1859) is more than a little ambiguous on this point. The title suggests an empirical answer. Yet Darwin repeatedly and unequivocally claims otherwise. Species are for Darwin both theoretical and epiphenomenal: "In short, we shall have to treat species in the same manner as those naturalists treat genera, who admit that genera are merely artificial combinations made for convenience. This may not be a cheering prospect; but we shall at least be freed from the vain search for the undiscovered and undiscoverable essence of the term species" (1859:485).

Darwin's answer to the question posed by *On the Origin of Species* is that species originate in the process of observation (cf. Beatty 1983). The disjunct distribution of organic variability arises because we observe the products of organic evolution in a temporal instant in a spatial field. Darwin's crucial insight is that *kinds* of organisms are the products of a *continuous* process (though not necessarily a gradual one as he supposed). It is thus not surprising that biologists of no less stature than Julian Haldane (1956) find continued use of the species concept in evolution unjustified (a position compatible with, if not historically linked to, the modern cladistic view that regards only ends of branches as species). This *is* the materialist paradox displayed in painfully concrete terms and has played a central role in critiques of evolution both pre-Darwin (e.g., Lyell 1835) and post-Darwin (e.g., Agassiz 1860). Purely typological notions may occasionally approximate empirical units accidentally and vice versa (cf. Kitcher 1987), and this further muddies the water.

While Marks and Staski's (1988) concern with units and selection is commendable, by depicting an increasingly anachronistic view of species as consensus they not only commit themselves inadvertently to an untenable position, but they also attribute a role to the concept of species that is itself under intense debate and scrutiny. In the end, their effort seems more an effort to supply an "evolutionary" rationale for traditional units.

Inattention to Units

Ignoring the role of units is just as disastrous. William H. Durham's (1991) recent book, *Coevolution,* exemplifies this as well as the magnitude of the problems that arise in consequence. Durham develops a theory of cultural evolution on a biological model, one that employs culture as a transmission mechanism "parallel" to genetics. He thus erects a cultural evolution as parallel to, but interacting with, genetic evolution; the bulk of the book is devoted to exploring the interactions thus created. While his examples are rife with assumptions about the units on which evolutionary processes operate, he fails to consider units explicitly with the result that he is neither consistent nor clear on what evolves and why.

His concept of "imposition" illustrates the problem. Crucial to the rationale for creating a separate but equal cultural evolution is the idea that cultural change can and does sometimes operate against the inclusive fitness (defined solely in genetic terms!) of its bearers, a relation Durham terms "opposition." One of his two case studies selected to illustrate opposition, Mundurucu headhunting, turns out to be rather ambiguous as an example of opposition, and he abandons it (Durham 1991:391).

Durham's other example, the spread of the fatal Kuru disease amongst the Fore by means of cannibalism, works as an example of opposition only because he ignores that the Fore were quickly being eliminated and would be extinct (both culturally and biologically) were it not for Australian intervention. In view of this unconvincing evidence for autogenetic opposition, he is compelled to rely on imposition, defined as the coercion or manipulation of a group by an elite or other subgroup, as the sole argument for the occurrence of opposition (Durham 1991: 442–443). Here the matter of units is critical.

To talk about coercion or imposition requires two groups, those coerced and those coercing. If the unit on which evolutionary processes act is larger than the individual organism, and the coerced and the coercers are thus part of the same evolutionary unit, then imposition is a bit like the cells in your feet complaining about their exploitation by your brain cells—"we have to do all the work, we never get to make any decisions, and so forth." Of course, what makes you work is that while your cells are functionally differentiated, each is necessary to the proper functioning of the beast as a whole. If, on the other hand, those coercing and those coerced are different evolutionary units, then imposition is just a culturally biased view of the outcome of interorganismic competition (or symbiosis, depending upon the outcome). Thus, Durham's concept of imposition appears to be the unmarked penetration of his theory by his own cultural values. He has confused folk explanation, variously denominated "intention" or "motivation," with scientific causation. Without imposition, the idea of "opposition" is in dire trouble and without opposition, the need for a coevolutionary theory like Durham's is more than a little questionable. For want of a nail, a shoe was lost, for want of a shoe, a horse was lost. . . .

Units and Evolutionary Theory

It is one thing to show the importance of unit definition through the effects of errors; it is another matter to supply a positive answer to the questions thus posed. A brief survey of the relevant biological literature juxtaposed with the kinds of units identifiable in the archaeological record can serve as a start.[2]

Units of Evolution in Biology

As already indicated, what constitutes an evolutionary individual, the unit or units upon which selection and other evolutionary processes operate, is still a matter of controversy in biology. The issue can be thought of as identifying the scale of the individual(s) in evolution (Gould 1977; Vrba and Eldredge 1984). Lack of consensus on particular units, or the number of units, is not of especial importance because evolutionary biologists do agree more broadly on the characteristics that an evolutionary individual *must* have. Thus, the current controversy over the scale(s) of units and processes is not, for the most part, theoretical, but focused on whether particular entities meet the theoretical requirements of an individual.

Lewontin (1970) set out these requirements more than two decades ago. For selection to operate on a unit, the unit must be: (1) a reproductive entity; (2) a functional entity; and (3) must turn over or respond rapidly in relation to the conditions of selection (cf. Kawata 1987). Most of the controversy about the status of species as an individual has focused, ostensively,[3] on the functional entity requirement. In this it is important to distinguish between structure or pattern— something that groups of individuals clearly do have—and functional integration (Kawata 1987) as required by Lewontin. Removing 10,000 animals from a population or species with hundreds of thousands or millions of animals does little but reduce the size of the population. Removing the head from one animal, however, terminates the animal. Although this example is not as unambiguous as it sounds, it does illustrate the kind of relation that is identified as functional integration.[4] The scale(s) at which selection operates is an empirical question (Smith 1976).

Archaeological Units

While archaeologists have almost uniformly assumed that processes operate on groups of people, societies, or cultures, there is little evidence to support such an assumption generally. As I argued long ago (Dunnell 1978a, 1980; Dunnell and Wenke 1980) the evolutionary individual in the human lineage is no different from that in other social animals until the rise of complex society. The organism is both the unit of reproduction and the functional entity throughout the vast bulk of human history. Only with the appearance of centralized decision making, occupational differentiation, and nonkin-based organization is there evidence for a shift in the scale of the unit on which evolutionary processes operate from the individual bounded by a skin to a larger individual composed of many, functionally differentiated organisms.

It is thus critical to differentiate complex and simple societies and to do so in terms of functional specialization. Functional specialization, or at least "specialization," has been employed in this role for a long time, but usually in the company of, or as an alternative to, other criteria (e.g., social stratification, amount of energy captured, etc.). Evolutionary theory, however, provides a justification for employing a particular criterion in a particular role. In the human case, what evolves varies from one point in the lineage to another. In simple societies, the individual is the organism; in complex societies, groups of functionally differentiated organisms constitute the individual. Indeed, many of the features of the "rise of civilization" (Dunnell 1978a), as well as its periodic "collapses," both ancient (cf. Yoffe and Cowgill 1988) and modern (e.g., Somalia), can be readily understood in terms of changes in the scale of selection.

What kinds of units can be identified in the archaeological record and by what means and how can they be related to the unit requirements of evolutionary theory? We can identify organismic individuals from the physical remains of their bodies. Despite inferential accounts to the contrary (e.g., Gifford 1960; Hill and Gunn 1977), however, there is really very little behavior or cultural information that can be associated securely with individual organisms beyond those data derivable from the bones, or more rarely, other parts of the body. The culturally transmitted component of the organism's phenotype will ordinarily have to be treated from aggregate data. Most of the "cultural" information that archaeologists customarily use represents pooled data derived from a variable number of individuals over variable amounts of time. Tool assemblage composition, pottery type frequencies, faunal remains, and botanical data, to name only the most obvious, are such aggregate data. How those data are aggregated is the crucial question (e.g., Binford 1981b).

The impact of such aggregation likewise differs between simple societies where the organism is an entity on which selection operates and complex societies in which aggregates of organisms constitute the individual and thus are the units of selection. In both cases we need empirical aggregates that can be explained in terms of evolutionary processes acting on individuals, although the precise nature of those aggregates must differ. The most serious problems would appear to

obtain for the analysis of simple societies, yet those problems are easily overesti-
mated by this simple analogy. While the biological component of the phenotype
is constrained by genetics to links with two parents, the cultural "parents" of culturally transmitted components are more numerous if still more or less spatially
localized (e.g., deBoer 1990; Graves 1985; Longacre 1981; Longacre and Stark
1992), leading to the conclusion that some kinds of aggregate data may well be
surrogates at the right scale, if not the precise units desired. What is needed is a
means to identify the appropriate aggregates.

Typically, we have devoted little attention to the nature of archaeologically
identifiable aggregates, much less how those aggregates might articulate with any
theory. The most important counting unit, the *assemblage* in most terminologies,
is a collection of artifacts and observations about which few conventions exist beyond ascertaining whether or not it is temporally "mixed" (cf. Dewar 1992) and
its *use* as a sample representing an empirical unit, variously denominated as an
occupation (Dewar 1992, cf. Dunnell 1971) or component (Rouse 1955; Willey
and Phillips 1958).

While some (e.g., Rouse 1955; cf. Chang 1967) have maintained that components should be "physical" entities, that is, must be empirical, they are almost always *constructed* as types, that is, theoretical units (e.g., Willey and Phillips 1958).
The result has been a circular argument in which phases, ostensibly the theoretical units, are defined as collections of components, while the empirical units,
components, are defined as manifestations of phases; the same kind of circularity
has plagued some uses of "species" in biology for the same reason. Thus in the last
analysis temporal boundaries are established in an ad hoc manner and, some pro-
posals notwithstanding (e.g., Chang 1967), without methodological provisions to
insure their empirical character. Consequently, assemblages are collections of artifacts or observations that are found in close (undefined) spatial proximity (verti-
cal proximity is more sensitive than horizontal proximity) and which display
minimal (undefined) formal variability in "diagnostics" (more variability is toler-
ated in function than in style). Some means to delineate those depositional events
(single objects) that are historically related to one another is needed.

Spatial boundaries of aggregates have attracted no more attention. Even when
there is serious concern about sampling, the spatial population that the sample is
intended to represent is more often than not the "site." "Site" is wholly inadequate
in this role, suffering not only from the fact that it is a theoretical, not empirical,
construct but also one that describes only the present condition of the archaeological record (Dunnell 1992b). It is an archaeologic, not systemic, context concept (Schiffer 1972). Often the "intent" of site is to isolate an archaeological equivalent to an ethnographic "community." The relevance of community is, however,
problematic as a counting unit for both simple and complex societies and neces-

sarily of variable relevance in these contrasting contexts. Again, what is required is some means to associate historically related depositional events.

On the model of the species in evolutionary biology, we need to be able to identify functional differentiation as well as interaction. The evolutionary individual is the largest, functionally differentiated, and interactive aggregate. No traditional archaeological unit matches these requirements, although some, notably "occupation" (sensu Dewar 1992; Dunnell 1971), seem to have similar intent. The scale of units meeting this requirement must vary with context from that more or less equivalent in scale with "household," in the case of simple societies, to "cultures," in the case of complex society. Identifying such units should be a high priority task.

The traditional approach is usually directed at delineating activity areas or similar patterns. Although evolutionary sounding terms are frequently deployed, the inability to test results as well as the lack of theoretical justification has fostered a debilitating pluralism in both function and style. Such imprecision is the inevitable consequence of the use of common sense, our own cultural conventions, as a substitute for theory. Archaeological observations must be "translated" or "decoded" into English; once in English, they are explicable, and so readily so that it may be claimed that there is no need for "general theory" (Dunnell 1982). Reconstructionism, both cultural and behavioral, is perfectly congruent with this methodology, and while it has occupied the New Archaeology for decades, it has yet to produce the anticipated scientific product.

Adding concepts from biology or anthropology to this fund of lore does not change the structure of explanation one whit. Any attempt to apply evolutionary theory must begin from the ground up with a set of units that can be explained by evolutionary processes: one "cannot go out and describe the world any old way we please and then sit back and demand that an explanatory and predictive theory be built on that description" (Lewontin 1974a:12).

Remarkably, the rudiments of the necessary tools are largely in place. As early as the 1930s some archaeologists (e.g., Rouse 1939) saw culture as a transmission process and appreciated the group/class distinction essential to breaking the materialist paradox. Separation of homologous and analogous similarities, those explained by transmission alone and those explained by selection (Dunnell 1978b), has been explored (e.g., Binford 1968). Homologous relations requiring interaction are identifiable by the distribution of neutral traits, or style (Dunnell 1978b). While style has been exploited to a limited degree in this sort of role (cf. Plog 1980), it has been compromised by ad hoc justification and an intuitive commitment to reconstruction (Hill 1970; Longacre 1970). Measurement of functional differentiation or redundancy (Fuller 1981) is likewise within our grasp, but again, a commitment to reconstruction has muddied the effort.

Evolutionary theory can explain why many elements of traditional approaches "work" to the extent they do and why they fail when they do. There are reasons why, for example, the distinction between simple and complex societies has proved so enduring. The theory provides a basis for further concept development as well as choosing among existing alternatives.

We are still a long way from having a satisfactory set of counting units, units that can be *meaningfully* quantified. While formation process research (e.g., Schiffer 1987) is certainly moving the field in the direction of a solution, practical and generally applicable methods (e.g., Jones and Beck 1990, 1992; Madsen and Dunnell 1989; Stafford and Hajic 1992) remain illusive. Still, we are somewhat better off than community ecology when Lewontin (1974a) wrote about its "agony" of not having appropriate units because it lacked the laws those units were to serve but could not write the laws without the units. At least the rough outlines of a demonstrably operational theory exist. Even so, the settling in process, the back and forth adjustment of units and relations, the process of successively more accurate approximations being developed cannot be foregone. Indeed, as I hope I have shown, underestimating the difficulties in generalizing evolutionary theory beyond its historically nonhuman roots and simply borrowing concepts is just as dangerous as ignoring them altogether. Until the matter of units is taken more seriously by evolutionary archaeologists, there is no reason to expect that evolutionary accounts will be anything more than just another story.

Acknowledgments

M. D. Dunnell, D. M. Greenlee, P. A. Teltser, and two anonymous reviewers made valuable comments on earlier drafts of this paper and their assistance is appreciated.

Notes

1. A. C. Spaulding, the modern father of archaeological phenetics (1953), consistently appreciated this consequence and insisted that history is discontinuous and that types were unique to particular samples (e.g., 1978).

2. Madsen and Lipo (1993) have developed components of this position, particularly those focusing on scale, substantially beyond their expression here.

3. The real issue is that the term *species* is currently used to label both theoretical and empirical units as well as concepts intended to describe contemporary variation and explain its cause.

4. This example is sometimes dismissed with a metaphor of trimming branches from a bush, thus suggesting functional integration is intrinsically ambiguous. It is not, of course,

when viewed in terms of structural/functional redundancy, a point that at least some archaeologists have long appreciated (e.g., Fuller 1981).

References

Adams, W. Y., and E. W. Adams
1991   *Archaeological Typology and Practical Reality: A Dialectical Approach to Artifact Classification and Sorting.* Cambridge University Press, Cambridge, England.

Agassiz, L.
1860   *Contributions to the Natural History of the United States of America,* vol. 3. Little, Brown, Boston.

Beatty, J.
1983   What's in a Word? Coming to Terms in the Darwinian Revolution. In *Nature Animated,* edited by M. Ruse, pp. 79–111. Reidel, Dordrecht.

Bettinger, R. L.
1991   *Hunter—Gatherers: Archaeological and Evolutionary Theory.* Plenum, New York.

Binford, L. R.
1968   An Archeological Perspective. In *New Perspectives in Archeology,* edited by S. R. Binford and L. R. Binford, pp. 5–32. Aldine, Chicago.
1977   *For Theory Building.* Academic Press, New York.
1981a   *Bones. Ancient Men and Modern Myths.* Academic Press, New York.
1981b   Behavioral Archaeology and the Pompeii Premise. *Journal of Anthropological Research* 37:195–208.

Chang, K. C.
1967   *Rethinking Archaeology.* Random House, New York.

Cole, C. J.
1990   When Is an Individual Not a Species? *Herpetologica* 46:104–108.

Collins, J. T.
1991   Viewpoint: A New Taxonomic Arrangement for Some North American Amphibians and Reptiles. *Herpetological Review* 22:42–43.
1992   Evolutionary Species Concept: A Reply to Van Devender et al. and Montanucci. *Herpological Review* 23:43–46.

Crosland, M.
1962   *Historical Studies in the Language of Chemistry.* Dover, New York.

Darwin, C.
1859   *On the Origin of Species.* John Murray, London.

deBoer, W. R.
1990   Interaction, Imitation, and Communication as Expressed in Style: The Ucayali Experience. In *The Uses of Style in Archaeology,* edited by M. W. Conkey and C. Hastorf, pp. 82–104. Cambridge University Press, Cambridge, England.

Dewar, R. E.

1992   Incorporating Variation in Occupation Span into Settlement Pattern Analysis. *American Antiquity* 56:604–620.

Dobzhansky, T.

1937   *Genetics and the Origins of Species.* Columbia University Press, New York.

Dunnell, R. C.

1971   *Systematics in Prehistory.* Free Press, New York.

1978a   Natural Selection, Scale, and Cultural Evolution: Some Preliminary Considerations. Paper presented at the 77th Annual Meeting of the American Anthropological Association, November 14–18, Los Angeles.

1978b   Style and Function: a Fundamental Dichotomy. *American Antiquity* 43:192–202.

1980   Evolutionary Theory and Archaeology. *Advances in Archaeological Method and Theory*, vol. 3, edited by M. B. Schiffer, pp. 35–99. Academic Press, New York.

1982   Science, Social Science, and Common Sense: The Agonizing Dilemma of Modern Archaeology. *Journal of Anthropological Research* 38:1–25.

1986   Methodological Issues in Americanist Artifact Classification. *Advances in Archaeological Method and Theory*, vol. 9, edited by M. B. Schiffer, pp. 149–207. Academic Press, New York.

1987   Comment on "History, Phylogeny, and Evolution in Polynesia" by P. V. Kirch and R. C. Green. *Current Anthropology* 28:444–445.

1989   Aspects of the Application of Evolutionary Theory in Archaeology. In *Archaeological Thought in America*, edited by C. C. Lamberg-Karlovsky, pp. 35–49. Cambridge University Press, Cambridge, England.

1992a   Is a Scientific Archaeology Possible? In *Metaarchaeology*, edited by L. Embree, pp. 75–97. Kluwer Academic Publications, Dordrecht.

1992b   *The Notion Site. In Space, Time, and Archaeological Landscapes,* edited by J. Rossignol and L. A. Wandsnider, pp. 21–41. Plenum Press, New York.

Dunnell, R. C., and R. J. Wenke

1980   An Evolutionary Model of the Development of Complex Society. Paper presented at the 1980 Annual Meeting of the American Association for the Advancement of Science, San Francisco.

Durham, William H.

1991   *Coevolution. Genes, Culture and Human Diversity.* Stanford University Press, Stanford, California.

Echelle, A. A.

1990   In Defense of the Phylogenetic Species Concept and the Ontological Status of Hybridogenetic Taxa. *Herpetologica* 46:109–113.

Ford, J. A.

1954   The Type Concept Revisited. *American Anthropologist* 56:42–54.

Frost, D. R., and D. M. Hillis

1990   Species in Concept and Practice: Herpetological Applications. *Herpetologica* 46:87–103.

Frost, D. R., A. G. Kluge, and D. M. Hillis

1992   Species in Contemporary Herpetology: Comments on Phylogenetic Inference and Taxonomy. *Herpetological Review* 23:46–54.

Fuller, J. W.

1981   *Developmental Change in Prehistoric Community Patterns: The Development of Nucleated Village Settlements in Northern West Virginia.* Unpublished Ph.D. dissertation, University of Washington. University Microfilms, Ann Arbor.

Ghiselin, M. T.

1966   On Psychologism in the Logic of Taxonomic Controversies. *Systematic Zoology* 15:207–215.

1987   Species Concepts, Individuality, and Objectivity. *Biology and Philosophy* 2:127–143.

Gifford, J. C.

1960   Type-Variety Method. *American Antiquity* 25:341–347.

Gould, S. J.

1977   *Ever Since Darwin.* W. W. Norton and Co., New York.

1982   Darwinism and the Expansion of Evolutionary Theory. *Science* 216:380–387.

Graves, M. W.

1985   Ceramic Design Variation with a Kalinga Village: Temporal and Spatial Processes. In *Decoding Prehistoric Ceramics,* edited by B. A. Nelson, pp. 9–34. Southern Illinois University Press, Carbondale.

Greenwood, D. J.

1984   *The Taming of Evolution: The Persistence of Nonevolutionary Views in the Study of Humans.* Cornell University Press, Ithaca, New York.

Haldane, J.B.S.

1956   Can a Species Concept Be Justified? In *The Species Concept in Paleontology,* edited by P. C. Sylvester-Bradley, pp. 95–96. The Systematics Association, Publication No. 2., London.

Hamilton, W. D.

1964   The Genetical Theory of Social Behavior. *Journal of Theoretical Biology* 7:1–52.

Hanson, N. R.

1958   *Patterns of Discovery: Inquiring into the Conceptual Foundations of Science.* Cambridge University Press, Cambridge, England.

Hennig, W.

1966   *Phylogenetic Systematics.* University of Illinois Press, Urbana.

Highton, R.

1990   Taxonomic Treatment of Genetically Differentiated Populations. *Herpetologica* 46:114–124.

Hill, J. N.

1970   *Broken K Pueblo: Prehistoric Social Organization in the American Southwest.* Anthropological Papers of the University of Arizona, vol. 18. University of Arizona Press, Tucson.

Hill J. N., and J. Gunn (editors)
1977   *The Individual in Prehistory: Studies of Variability in Style in Prehistoric Technologies.* Academic Press, New York.

Jones, G. T., and C. Beck
1990   An Obsidian Hydration Chronology of Late Pleistocene—Early Holocene Surface Assemblages from Butte Valley, Nevada. *Journal of California and Great Basin Archaeology* 12:84–100.
1992   Chronological Resolution in Distributional Archaeology. In *Space, Time and Archaeological Landscapes,* edited by J. Rossignol and L. A. Wandsnider, pp. 167–192. Plenum, New York.

Kawata, M.
1987   Units and Passages: A View for Evolutionary Biology and Ecology. *Biology and Philosophy* 2:415–434.

Kitcher, P.
1987   Ghostly Whispers: Mayr, Ghiselin, and the "Philosophers" on the Status of Species. *Biology and Philosophy* 2:184–192.

Lewontin, R. C.
1970   The Units of Selection. *Annual Review of Ecology and Systematics* 1:1–18.
1974a   *The Genetic Basis of Evolutionary Change.* Columbia University Press, New York.
1974b   Darwin and Mendel—the Materialist Revolution. In *The Heritage of Copernicus: Theories Pleasing to the Mind,* edited by J. Neyman, pp. 166–183. MIT Press, Cambridge, Massachusetts.

Longacre, W. A.
1970   *Reconstructing Pueblo Societies.* University of New Mexico Press, Albuquerque.
1981   Kalinga Pottery: An Ethnoarchaeological Study. In *Patterns of the Past: Studies in Honor of David Clarke,* edited by I. Hodder, G. Isaac, and N. Hammond, pp. 49–66. Cambridge University Press, Cambridge, England.

Longacre, W. A., and M. T. Stark
1992   Ceramics, Kinship and Space: A Kalinga Example. *Journal of Anthropological Archaeology* 11:125–136.

Luedtke, B. E.
1986   Flexible Tools for Constructing the Past. *Man in the Northeast* 31:89–98.

Lyell, C.
1835   *Principles of Geology.* 4 vols. John Murray, London.

Madsen, M. E., and C. P. Lipo
1993   Units of Evolution within a Darwinian Approach to Anthropology: Definitions and Implications for the Subfields. Paper presented at the Annual Meeting of the American Anthropological Association, November 20, 1993. Washington, D.C.

Madsen, M. E., and R. C. Dunnell
1989   Role of Microartifacts in Deducing Land Use from Low Density Record in Plowed Surfaces. Paper presented at the 54th Annual Meeting of the Society for American Archaeology, Atlanta, Georgia.

Marks, J., and E. Staski

1988   Individuals and the Evolution of Biological and Cultural Systems. *Human Evolution* 3:147–161.

Mayr, E.

1942   *Systematics and the Origin of Species*. Columbia University Press, New York.

1963   *Animal Species and Evolution*. Belknap Press of Harvard University Press, Cambridge, Massachusetts.

1987   The Ontological Status of Species: Scientific Progress and Philosophical Terminology. *Biology and Philosophy* 2:145–166.

Misler, B. D., and M. J. Donoghue

1982   Species Concepts: A Case for Pluralism. *Systematic Zoology* 31:491–503.

Misler, B. D., and R. N. Brandon

1987   Individuality, Pluralism, and the Phylogenetic Species Concept. *Biology and Philosophy* 2:397–414.

Panchen, A. L.

1992   *Classification, Evolution and the Nature of Biology*. Cambridge University Press, Cambridge, England.

Plog, S.

1980   *Stylistic Variation in Prehistoric Ceramics*. Cambridge University Press, Cambridge, England.

Popper, K.

1963   *The Poverty of Historicism*. Revised edition. Routledge and Kegan Paul, London.

Rosenberg, A.

1985   *The Structure of Biological Science*. Cambridge University Press, Cambridge, England.

Rouse, I. B.

1939   *Prehistory of Haiti: A Study in Method*. Yale University Publications in Anthropology, No. 21. New Haven, Connecticut.

1955   On the Correlation of Phases of Culture. *American Anthropologist* 57:165–178.

Schiffer, M. B.

1972   Archaeological Context and Systemic Context. *American Antiquity* 37:156–165.

1987   *Formation Processes of the Archaeological Record*. University of New Mexico Press, Albuquerque.

Simpson, G. G.

1961   *Principles of Animal Taxonomy*. Columbia University Press, New York.

Smith, H. M.

1990   The Universal Species Concept. *Herpetologica* 46:122–124.

Smith, J. M.

1976   Group Selection. *The Quarterly Review of Biology* 51:277–283.

Sober, E.

1980   Evolution, Population Thinking, and Essentialism. *Philosophy of Science* 47:350–383.

1987   Optimist/Pessimist. *Behavioral and Brain Sciences* 10:88–89.

Spaulding, A. C.
1953   Statistical Techniques for the Discovery of Artifact Types. *American Antiquity* 18:305–313.
1978   Artifact Classes, Association, and Seriation. In *Archaeological Essays in Honor of Irving B. Rouse,* edited by R. C. Dunnell and E. S. Hall, pp. 27–40. Mouton, The Hague.

Stafford, C. R., and E. R. Hajic
1992   Landscape Scale. In *Space, Time, and Archaeological Landscapes,* edited by J. Rossignol and L. Wandsnider, pp. 137–161. Plenum, New York.

Templeton, A. R.
1989   The Meaning of Species and Speciation: A Genetic Perspective. In *Speciation and Its Consequences,* edited by D. Otte and J. A. Endler, pp. 3–27. Sinauer, Sunderland, Massachusetts.

van Valen, L.
1976   Ecological Species, Multispecies, and Oaks. *Taxon* 25:233–239.

Vrba, E. S., and N. Eldredge
1984   Individuals, Hierarchies, and Processes: Towards a More Complete Evolutionary Theory. *Paleobiology* 10:146–171.

Whewell, W.
1847   *Philosophy of the Inductive Sciences.* Parker, London.

Wiley, E. O.
1980   Is the Evolutionary Species Fiction?—A Consideration of Classes, Individuals and Historical Entities. *Systematic Zoology* 27:76–80.

Willey, G. R., and P. Phillips
1958   *Method and Theory in American Archaeology.* University of Chicago Press, Chicago.

Wynne-Edwards, V. C.
1962   *Animal Dispersion in Relation to Social Behavior.* Oliver and Boyd, Edinburgh.

Yoffe, N., and G. L. Cowgill (editors)
1988   *The Collapse of Ancient States and Civilizations.* University of Arizona Press, Tucson.

4

Culture History, Evolutionary Theory, and Frequency Seriation

Patrice A. Teltser

◆◆ Frequency seriation, a method to order artifact assemblages chronologically, has an interesting history in Americanist archaeology. After archaeologists abandoned the painstaking business of cataloging artifact assemblages according to trait lists and gave up their obsession for creating chronologically sensitive artifact typologies, an interest in frequency seriation persisted. The focus of interest shifted from debate over issues of classification and the meaning of artifact typologies (e.g., Ford 1952, 1954a, 1954b, 1954c; and Spaulding 1953a, 1953b, 1954a, 1954b) to its quantitative aspects, providing the context for some of the earliest applications of multivariate techniques and computers in archaeology (e.g., Ascher and Ascher 1963; Hole and Shaw 1967). For the most part, these discussions focused heavily on ordering algorithms and technique (e.g., Cowgill 1968, 1972; Dempsey and Baumhoff 1963; Drennen 1976; Hole and Shaw 1967; Johnson 1968; LeBlanc 1975; see Marquardt 1978 for a review of this literature), although there are a few notable exceptions in which other aspects of the method were considered (e.g., de Barros 1982; Deetz and Dethlefsen 1965; Dunnell 1970, 1981; Rouse 1967). A continued interest in seriation no doubt derives from the quantitative nature of the method but also because it works and because the results can be (and usually were) corroborated by independent chronological methods such as radiocarbon and stratigraphy.

For some of the same reasons, the method of frequency seriation has captured the interest of evolutionary archaeologists. Unlike the interest in ordering algorithms that dominated discussion from the 1960s through the early 1980s, recent interest focuses attention on the model of frequency seriation itself, the explanatory principles underlying this model, and why it works. These issues have arisen in the context of discussions regarding evolutionary definitions of style and function (e.g., Dunnell 1978; O'Brien and Holland 1990, 1992) and the consequences of those definitions (Neiman 1990). The purpose of this chapter is to expand on these general notions and to consider the method of frequency seriation in light of the theoretical underpinnings of culture history and evolutionary theory. Interestingly enough, this kind of treatment requires a return to and resolution of some of the original issues regarding classification and measurement raised by culture historians.

In a proximal sense, seriation works because it employs a scaling technique to rank units (e.g., assemblages) along a single dimension (Marquardt 1978). When those assemblages are measured in terms of criteria that are reliable chronological indicators, a relative chronology will result. Although the techniques employed for ordering are important, the dimension along which assemblages are ordered (time, in this case) ultimately depends on the kind of information measured (units of measurement) on those assemblages. The relation between seriation as a method for chronological ordering and units of measurement has been emphasized by many authors (Brainerd 1951; Dunnell 1970; Marquardt 1978; Meighan 1977) and ultimately hinges on the relationship between explanatory concepts underlying the frequency seriation model and units of measurement.

Frequency seriation is interesting from an evolutionary perspective for two reasons. First, the method is based on explanatory concepts about the nature of formal similarity and phylogenetic relationships. From an evolutionary perspective demonstrating phylogeny and descent with modification is important on an explanatory level. Evolutionary change occurs within historically related populations, and any method that demonstrates such relationships in space and time is potentially important for evolutionary studies.

A second reason why frequency seriation has captured the attention of evolutionary archaeologists is that it produces a relative chronology in a way that treats time as a continuous dimension, and change is expressed in terms of change in variant frequencies through time. This is consistent with the way that change is expressed in an evolutionary framework and stands in marked contrast to the way change is expressed in transformational models. The differences between selectionist and transformational models of change, which will be discussed further, lead to very different conclusions regarding the specific phenomenological focus of inquiry and from that, the appropriate scale of analysis.

As I argue below, when first formalized by culture historians in the early twentieth century, frequency seriation was compatible with the explanatory principles of American anthropology but inconsistent with the typological structure of the frameworks in which most anthropologists operated. Here I make an analytic distinction between the content and structure of explanatory frameworks, where content refers to the range of causal mechanisms included within a theoretical framework to account for variation, and structure refers to the way variation is partitioned within that framework. In retrospect, the explanatory content of early twentieth-century anthropology was not so much wrong as it was incomplete, and inadequate for explaining the full range of variability in the archaeological record. On the other hand, even though the products of seriations analyses could not be used directly for culture historical purposes, the empirical results of specific seriation analyses (e.g., Phillips et al. 1951) had important empirical and theoretical consequences for the way in which long-standing archaeological questions were addressed. Unfortunately, because the explanatory content of culture history is insufficient, these questions could not be addressed in a satisfactory manner.

Ultimately, I hope to point out in this chapter how evolutionary theory subsumes certain aspects of archaeological method and theory—in this case frequency seriation. However, it is important to point out that evolutionary theory is not only capable of accounting for the reason seriation works but does so in the context of a more inclusive theory that also provides deterministic accounts for behavioral change. Put in slightly different terms, the explanatory principles that account for why seriation works provide only the "genealogical" information of evolutionary change and do not provide the "ecological" information required to account for evolutionary change (Neff 1992).

Methodological Implications for the Scale of Evolutionary Change

Perhaps one of the most important aspects of an evolutionary framework is the scale at which change is identified. In its broadest sense, evolutionary theory defines change as the differential persistence of alternative traits through time. Change is conceived in terms of frequency changes of analytically discrete variants rather than the transformation of a variant. Ultimately, what is at issue is the appearance, disappearance, or change of historical entities that have locations in space and time (e.g., Mississippian society, Aztec civilization). Despite whatever coherent and discrete systemic properties such entities may have, in an evolutionary framework they are conceived as continually evolving and highly variable populations composed of behaviorally unique individuals. New behaviors are introduced; some are transmitted and persist while others do not. To the extent that most anthropological models of evolution focus on transformation of societal forms, an evolutionary framework is distinctive because it shifts the scale of analysis from society, or some systemic entity, to the individuals (and their behaviors) that comprise those entities.

This shift in the scale of analytic interest specifies the reason it is important to maintain a distinction between the theoretical status of units of measurement (e.g., societies, cultural systems, or pottery types) and empirical entities that may be assigned as members of those units (Dunnell 1986b). For example, the cultural system or society is an important analytic unit in anthropology, enabling the analysis and integration of component activities. When such units are used as theoretical units to measure change, however, the only way change can be monitored is by comparison of systems at different points in time. This is a transformational view of change where differences are substituted for change (Dunnell 1982:13; see also Leonard and Jones 1987).

The point here is not to deny the utility of a systemic view of culture but to point out that analytic units useful in a synchronic framework are not necessarily useful in an evolutionary framework. Furthermore, confusing an empirical unit of observation for a theoretical unit of measurement may be relatively harmless in a synchronic framework. When change is at issue, however, the confusion leads to a very different scale of analysis and a very different kind of methodology. This very methodological issue of concern was played out in the context of the Ford-Spaulding debate for units at the scale of artifact.

Spaulding assumed the position that artifact types were empirical units. This position engendered a methodological strategy that searches for and discovers meaningful units. At the scale of artifact, Spaulding's (1953b) "Statistical Techniques for the Discovery of Artifact Types" embodies such a methodology. At the scale of population, meaningful units are discovered by searching for "jointedness" (Spaulding 1982), presumably cultural boundaries.

For Ford, artifact types were units of measurement, conceived by the archaeologist to measure chronological change (Dunnell 1986b; Rouse 1939). This position engenders a methodological strategy of trial and error (Ford 1962:15). The utility of his types was determined by whether they conformed to a battleship-shaped curve, or what Krieger (1944) referred to as a test for historical significance.

In the parlance of contemporary evolutionary theory, the difference between the search-and-discovery and the trial-and-error approaches reflects a difference between an essentialist and materialist framework (Dunnell 1982). If taken a step further, the difference is also epistemological. Time or chronology is only one of many possible dimensions of variability. When types are used as units of measurement, the dimensions that define specific classes are specified theoretically for the solution to a specific problem. Whether a set of classes measures what it is supposed to measure is determined by testing the classification to determine whether the theoretical assumptions of that classification are obtained in a specific case. Theoretical assumptions are usually embodied in a model of some sort, and arriving at a set of meaningful units is a matter of defining units that conform to the model within certain tolerance limits. The inclusion of "provisional types" in a typology (e.g., Phillips et al. 1951:140–149) is entirely consistent with this approach (i.e., tests of historical significance were inconclusive). This is epistemologically different from relying on a particular technique to determine whether empirical entities have been correctly identified.

Even though Spaulding's approach to unit construction found fewer pragmatic applications than did Ford's, it was far more consistent with the typological aspects of the theoretical framework in which culture historians operated. This inconsistency is instructive, and consequently, it is useful to take a brief look at the difference between the typological structure of culture history and the more materialist basis of frequency seriation as a method.

Seriation and Culture History

Early twentieth-century anthropologists were concerned with identifying and describing Native American cultures, relying on discrete ethnic units as the primary unit of observation, description, and analysis. Activities of archaeologists reflected this interest. For example, the trait lists generated through application of the Midwestern Taxonomic Method (McKern 1939) as a means to identify cultural units were not all that different in conception from the earlier culture element distributions (Kroeber 1939b; Wissler 1914). Culture areas of North America applied equally well to the ethnographic (Kroeber 1939a) and archaeological records (compare to Willey 1966).

For archaeologists the task of creating cultural units was expanded because they were interested in temporal as well as spatial relations. The Midwestern Taxonomic Method was explicit about its emphasis on what we would now refer to as phenetic similarity; that is, units were created solely on the basis of similarity without reference to temporal or phylogenetic relationships. The method was valid, but the product was unsatisfactory because it did not provide chronological relationships among its synthetic units. Nevertheless, history was conceived in terms of the same kind of discrete cultural units. The notion of culture as shared ideas provided the explanatory principle for a method to identify internally homogeneous cultural units using shared traits to infer shared ideas and cultural relatedness. Similarity in form was inferred to be a measure of and direct result of cultural relatedness (Rouse 1939, 1956).

The correlation between cultural units defined archaeologically (e.g., phases) and ethnographic societies was recognized as ambiguous (e.g., Rouse 1955; Willey and Phillips 1958), but this was not a central concern until much later (e.g., Chang 1967). The tradition of Americanist anthropology in the first half of the century relied far more heavily on the notion of culture (e.g., Kroeber 1916, 1919) than on the notion of social relations that characterized British social anthropology (see also Dunnell 1986a). The concept of culture was not without its problems (e.g., Kroeber and Kluckholn 1952) but was generally conceived in terms of shared ideas. For archaeologists the notion of shared ideas was demonstrated through shared traits. The point is that prior to the introduction of cultural ecology and functionalism, archaeologists and ethnologists were pursuing very similar goals and using very similar methods based on the same explanatory principles.

Using formal properties of artifacts and their associations to tell time has a long history in archaeology, extending to Thomsen's three-age chronology of stone, bronze, and iron (see Rouse 1967 for a historical review). The development of frequency seriation, although arising out of those efforts, was an American invention. In the context of early stratigraphic excavations in the American Southwest, (e.g., Kroeber 1916; Nelson 1916) archaeologists observed that different pottery types were most abundant in different levels and those levels, representing different time periods, could be characterized by distinctive pottery types. Although Kroeber did little archaeological work, it appears that he was the first to give theoretical expression to the notion of popularity curves in the context of Zuni potsherds (1916) and his classic work on women's fashion (1919). The chronological significance of such patterning was later demonstrated by Kidder (1924) through additional stratigraphic excavation and analysis.

Frequency seriation was formalized on two separate occasions. Ford (1962; Phillips et al. 1951) was responsible for the first formalization and stated that historical types display a battleship-shaped distribution through time (see also Robinson [1951] who described the distribution of historical types as lenticular). The basis of this description was the notion of popularity curves (Kroeber 1919) and that of culture as shared ideas. Cowgill (1972) and Dunnell (1970) were responsible for the second formalization, substituting monotonic increasing and decreasing, or unimodal, curves for battleship-shaped curves. This curve described what Dunnell (1970) referred to as the "frequency of occurrence rule." While the second formalization was more explicit than the first, both were *post hoc* explanations for distributions that had been empirically derived rather than deduced from a specific body of theory (Dunnell 1970:309; 1981:68).

The second formalization also incorporated an explicit statement regarding the epistemological basis of seriation. Dunnell (1970) specified that the ordering obtained in a seriation is formal and the chronology is inferred. Chronological inference is made on the basis of several assumptions that generate the frequency of occurrence model, and any given seriation tests whether those assumptions are operative for a specific empirical case. The conditions under which the assumptions are operative have been discussed by several authors (Dunnell 1970; Ford 1962; Phillips et al. 1951; Rouse 1939) and specify that the assemblages (1) are from the same cultural tradition, (2) represent comparable periods of time, and (3) are from the same local area.

As a method, frequency seriation has three important aspects. First, unit construction requires a materialist strategy. Artifact typologies play the role of nominal scale measurement devices, defined to solve a particular problem. If one set of classes does not pass the test of historical significance, the classes are not historical types. Second, even though frequency seriation provides only ordinal relationships, discrete assemblages are ordered as samples along a temporal continuum. In this way, time is treated as a continuous dimension. Third, change is expressed in terms of frequency changes of artifact types through time.

These aspects of frequency seriation, although consistent with the chronological goals of culture history, produced a product that was inconsistent with the internally homogeneous and discrete cultural units anthropologists ultimately sought. In short, culture historians operated within two different but incompatible kinds of frameworks. On the one hand, frequency seriation provided a method in which artifact typologies were treated as theoretical units of measurement. Assemblages of artifacts were conceived as samples along a temporal continuum. When assemblages were measured in terms of historical types, variation among assemblages was meaningful and represented change. On the other hand, the kind of synthetic units required by culture historians (e.g., periods and phases) conceived of cultures or societies as "real" phenomena to be discovered. In this framework, artifact assemblages were regarded as samples of internally homogeneous entities. Variation among artifact assemblages was either ignored or it represented differences in kind (i.e., differences between kinds of cultures). So long as this view was held, transformational models of change were destined to emerge and to appear most appropriate.

Ultimately, the latter framework of sequential, internally homogeneous units was upheld (compare, for example, the chronological framework provided by Phillips et al. 1951 with Phillips 1970). In practice, seriation seems to have played an exploratory role; it is difficult to find a case where researchers actually attempted to refine an existing seriation sequence. Once a sequence of types, or the period to which a type corresponded, was known, types could be used as index fossils to assign assemblages to discrete phases or cultural units. In the American Southwest, where one can find the origins of the seriation method, it was not long before access to dendrochronology allowed archaeologists to bracket their ceramic types with absolute dates. This allowed archaeologists to use pottery styles in an index fossil manner. The index fossil methodology never challenged the notion that "types are real" but most likely encouraged it while reinforcing transformational notions of change. Not until much later did some archaeologists realize that seriation had the potential to provide a more precise chronology (e.g., LeBlanc 1975).

Even though seriation did not provide discrete cultural units, the implications of seriation results for describing and characterizing change were not completely lost. Ford's later efforts to read meaning into seriation curves themselves were clearly less than successful (e.g., Ford 1966). However, when comparing the kind of information provided by seriation and sequences of phases (i.e., between the two conflicting frameworks of culture history), Ford noted that "it should now be clear how a quantitative chronology differs from an impressionistic succession of 'cultural periods'. . . . The graph shows that change was taking place in each period and allows a much better measure of the passage of time than the mere use of a name does" (Ford 1962:39).

In retrospect, the empirical results of specific seriations had important theoretical implications. That importance is illustrated by the seriation results from the Lower Mississippi Valley survey (Phillips et al. 1951). One of the primary goals of that work was to provide an understanding of pre-Mississippian cultures and the development of the Mississippian culture in the lower Mississippi Valley (Phillips et al. 1951:v). Up to that point, understanding Mississippian development was conceived as a problem that required locating a heartland (or core area or nuclear area) from which Mississippian society expanded (Smith 1984). Contrary to expectations, the lower Mississippi Valley seriations demonstrated cultural continuity and *in situ* development throughout that vast region. That is, their results did not help to "nucleate" a Mississippian heartland but presented evidence for a more complex situation. As Smith (1984:30) notes, more than fifty years of research "has witnessed the initial development and acceptance, subsequent elaboration, and finally the reappraisal and rejection of the [heartland-migration] explanatory framework."

In this context, the search for a heartland (locating spatial and temporal precedence for a certain constellation of essential traits) can be seen as a method to explain variability in the archaeological record that was derived from the typological aspects of the culture history framework. Once located, subsequent space-time distributions could be explained in familiar diffusionist terms (e.g., expansion of a cultural system, migration, or both). Variability could be explained in terms of local environmental effects on the expression of a prototype.

This strategy failed for two reasons, but not for lack of good scholarship. First, the wrong method was applied to a question that was fundamentally evolutionary; and second, which I discuss in the next section, the theoretical content of culture history could only account for the origin and distribution of traits in terms of culture as shared ideas. This kind of explanation, seen as diffusionist in its most extreme form, was applied to nearly everything from pottery styles to agriculture, settlement patterns, house forms, and burial customs.

This sort of explanation was insufficient for several reasons, as changes in American anthropology and dissatisfaction with culture history began to make clear as far back as the 1930s (e.g,. Steward and Setzler 1938; Tallgren 1937). In particular, interest in how human populations interact with their environment, concerns that we would now regard as functional issues, made it apparent that tracking the origin and distribution of traits did not explain why some traits persisted and others did not, or the emergence of similarities that could not be accounted for by shared ideas (e.g., independent invention).

In short, culture history produced frequency seriation as a means to tell time. Seriation was based on an empirical generalization regarding the distribution of historical types and required that artifact types be treated as units of measurement. The explanatory content of culture history could accommodate seriation ("frequency of occurrence rule") through the notion of "popularity curves" or culture as shared ideas. At the same time, the products of seriation were at odds with the internally homogeneous cultural units archaeologists were seeking to identify. Even though a seriation sequence could be periodized into more familiar cultural units, the results of specific seriation analyses, such as that from the lower Mississippi Valley, suggested that the kind of expectations generated from the more typological aspects of the explanatory framework were not accurate. Even though seriations were capable of providing history and context, culture history provided no additional theoretical content (apart from the notion of culture as shared ideas) to explain other causes for the patterning of variation in the archaeological record.

Much of what was later to become associated with the New Archaeology can also be seen as an attempt to compensate for the theoretical and explanatory deficiencies of culture history. While explicitly concerned with more functional issues, much of that work has proven to be predominantly synchronic in perspective, unable to accommodate change in other than transformational terms. To the extent that evolutionary theory is a framework to understand variation (e.g., Dunnell 1980), it is interested not only in the origins and histories of traits, but equally interested in understanding why some traits persist at any given time and place (e.g., functional concerns). This touches on the issue of the explanatory content of evolutionary theory and how it explains why seriation works.

Seriation and Evolutionary Theory

Evolutionary theory applies to biological populations of phenotypically variable individuals who have the capacity to reproduce and transmit information to succeeding generations. Depending on a variety of historically contingent factors (collectively referred to as the selective environment), reproduction and transmission are differential.

Transmission of information is a critical element (see, for example, Neff 1992). It is implied by the notion of differential persistence and further implies that the phenomena of concern in evolutionary explanations are historically and empirically related. Information transmission explains why offspring resemble their parents and why similarity in form can be used to infer relatedness (cultural or genetic). When information is extended to include nongenetic information and transmission is expanded to learning, this aspect of the evolutionary process has much in common with the notion of culture as shared ideas transmitted in the context of human interaction (e.g., acculturation, trade, migration, and diffusion). It is important to point out, however, that the notion of learned behavior is part of the more inclusive concept of shared ideas. Perhaps more importantly, however, evolutionary theory incorporates the notion of information transmission (and the mechanisms that can account for it) into a more inclusive theoretical framework that also provides a deterministic account for the differential persistence of behavior and analogous similarity (i.e., convergence).

When artifacts are conceived as part of the behavioral aspect of the human phenotype (e.g., Leonard and Jones 1987), the differential persistence of variants can be explained in one of two ways. Those variants that directly affect an individual's potential to reproduce are defined as functional, while those that are neutral with respect to selection are defined as stylistic. These definitions imply that stylistic and functional traits will have different distributions in time and space (Dunnell 1978). The differential persistence of functional variants can be explained in terms of deterministic processes in that they are constrained by environmental parameters and the selective environment. Such distributions are predictable only to the extent that environmental constraints and selective pressures are known (Teltser 1988:30). Once known, deterministic processes account for the direction of change in parameter values (Sober 1984:116). Time, history, and context are important on an explanatory level because different traits will affect reproductive success only in relation to the context in which they occur.

Because stylistic variants are neutral with respect to selection, no external constraints or forces exist to determine the direction in which they change. This is why several authors have treated the differential persistence of neutral variants as a direct analogue of random genetic drift (e.g., Neiman 1990; O'Brien and Holland 1990, 1992). In strictly biological terms (where transmission is implied by reproduction), differential persistence is explained in terms of "sampling error" during reproduction (or, more accurately, gamete formation). Here, sampling error is confined to the fact that actual frequencies in one generation can generate a probability distribution for expected frequencies in the next generation, but in any one sample, actual frequencies will depart from expected frequencies. The departure is always more pronounced when population size is small. In historical situations there is only one sample, the results of which determine the probability distribution for the next generation, and so forth. Consequently, in the absence of selective pressures, the frequency of a given variant has equal probability of increasing or decreasing at any given point in time. This is a stochastic process that is Markovian in nature because the frequency of a variant is dependent on its frequency in the immediately preceding time period.

To the extent that all processes with a random component are predictable at the scale of population, stochastic processes can produce patterned distributions through time. This has been demonstrated by Gould et al. (1977) in their work comparing the shape of real and random clades (also the product of stochastic processes), both of which produced distributions not unlike the monotonic battleship-shaped curves we recognize from frequency seriations. In applying the process of drift to populations of social learners, Neiman (1990) simulated similar distributions, pointing out that in general, the distribution of neutral traits is lenticular, beginning and ending with frequencies of zero and reaching a maximum frequency near their midpoints.

In both cases the distributions are not strictly monotonic. That is, there is some degree of erratic increase and decrease even though the distributions are lenticular. Neiman argues that this appears to be a regular feature of Markovian processes, not necessarily a function of the simulation or poor sampling of the fossil/archaeological records (Neiman 1990:166). It is important to point out, however, that the distributions generated by simulation are empirical distributions (lenticular) and should be expected to diverge from ideal distributions (e.g., monotonic). Furthermore, Neiman's own work shows that as population increases, the lenticular distributions display less of their erratic increases and decreases and the resulting distributions are appreciably smoother. This is to be expected for a random process at the scale of population. Neiman's same work also shows that when discard rates (a context-specific behavioral process) and time averaging (a feature of archaeological/fossil assemblages) are accounted for in the composition of assemblages, the resulting distributions again lose many of their erratic increases and decreases (Neiman 1990:182–193). Consideration of these kinds of processes does not necessarily compensate for "poor sampling" of the archaeological record but accounts for the nature of archaeological data as representing aggregate behavior and that any one assemblage is a discrete sample along a temporal continuum.

It is also interesting to note that in simulating the distributions of neutral variants, most variants are relatively short-lived and disappear within two or three transmission episodes (Neiman 1990: 162). This aspect of the simulation appears to be due to the stochastic nature of the transmission of neutral traits. Since no external constraints (i.e., selective pressures) drive the frequency of neutral traits up or down and all new variants necessarily begin with a frequency of one, new variants will have a lower "probability" of being replicated or transmitted. Clearly, some variants do display monotonic distributions through time. In this context, historical types (i.e., those with monotonic distributions as used in seriation) can be seen as a special class of stylistic types. Given a materialist strategy to unit construction, it is possible to define a set of classes that conform to that distribution.

The role of unit construction cannot really be discussed apart from the manner in which chronological inference is established from a seriation. As discussed above, the order obtained in a seriation is strictly formal and the chronological relations among assemblages are inferred. It is possible to obtain an order that approximates the model but is not a chronology. Chronological inference is based on a series of assumptions established by the seriation method as well as on whether the conditions specified by those assumptions hold for a particular case. As stated above, these conditions specify that the assemblages are (1) from the same cultural tradition, (2) of comparable duration, and (3) from the same local area. The first two conditions address matters of assemblage comparability and can be verified internally to the seriation (Dunnell 1970:315); that is, if either of these assumptions is violated, it will be impossible to produce an order that approximates the seriation model.

The third condition is specified to control the effects of spatial variation. Since information transmission occurs across space as well as through time, the same processes (e.g., human interaction) that account for the differential persistence of neutral traits through time should be expected to have significant expression across space. Indeed, the effects of spatial variation in seriation have long been recognized (Deetz and Dethlefsen 1965; Phillips et al. 1951). Hence, assuming that variation is continuous through time but not space is not only logically inconsistent and empirically false (Dunnell 1970: 314), it is also antithetical to the theoretical underpinnings of evolutionary theory. This led Dunnell (1970:314) to conclude some years ago that even though many seriations are no doubt chronologies, because the third condition is logically impossible to satisfy, any given seriation cannot be demonstrated to be a chronology since the method itself lacks the logical basis for such inference.

The resolution to this problem lies in creating units of measurement that are more sensitive to change through time than space. Consequently, demonstrating that the order obtained by a seriation is a chronology can only be based on independent assessments (e.g., chronometric dating methods) or additional seriations based on different sets of classes. Narrowly conceived, the chronological inference based on any seriation (or perhaps more accurately, an inference that the classes used are historical types) is a hypothesis that has not been rejected.

Summary and Conclusions

The theoretical basis of seriation lies in the nature of the transmission of stylistic or neutral information. Analytically, this information is conceived in terms of discrete variants. By definition, stylistic variants are not constrained by external forces (i.e., selective forces) to drive their frequencies up or down. That is, the differential persistence of neutral traits cannot be accounted for by deterministic processes such as natural selection but only by the transmission process itself. This has been shown to be a stochastic process analogous to random genetic drift, in which the frequency of a variant is dependent on its frequency in the immediately preceding time period.

Simulations of stochastic processes among populations of social learners show that some but not all neutral variants display monotonic distributions through time. At the scale of population, most neutral variants are introduced into the behavioral repertoire and either fail to be transmitted or are transmitted only a few times. In this context, historical types can be seen as a special class of stylistic classes.

When stylistic or neutral information is conceived in terms of discrete variants, a particular style can be seen as a complex constellation of attributes whose probability of being "reinvented" is extremely low (Teltser 1988:30). The differential persistence of such variants can only be explained in terms of the transmission process; that is, the distribution of a given style can only be accounted for through human interaction and can therefore be used to track phylogenetic relationships regardless of the shape of its particular distribution.

When principles regarding the transmission of neutral information are employed to derive a chronology, specific data considerations must be met. Two of the three conditions address comparability of archaeological assemblages used in a seriation. The third addresses elimination of spatial variation. Operationally, these conditions are not trivial or easily resolved with regard to chronological inference (see for example, Dunnell 1981). While it is beyond the scope of this chapter to consider these conditions in detail, it is important—if not critical—to point out that these conditions are anthropological and archaeological in nature, and have little to do with classic neo-Darwinian evolutionary theory. Issues of assemblage comparability, such as duration and discard rates, are matters that concern the formation of the archaeological record in terms of human behavior. Likewise, controlling for spatial variation is a logical outcome of expanding the notion of inheritance to include nongenetic mechanisms of information transmission.

In conclusion, seriations produced more than forty years ago still provide the backbone for many regional chronologies. The theoretical basis of seriation lies in the nature of the transmission process for stylistic or neutral information. Using these principles to create a method for chronological inference requires additional assumptions. Determining whether the conditions of these assumptions hold for a given case requires the same kind of testing used in any scientific methodology, and this has fairly rigorous data requirements. There are, of course, other methods for telling time (e.g, radiocarbon). In the past, archaeological research programs have not required that time be treated as a continuous dimension, or that phylogenetic relationships be established, or that change be modeled as frequency changes through time. Consequently, the kind of information provided by seriation has hardly seemed worth the effort of its fairly rigorous data re-quirements. Indeed, creating chronologically sensitive artifact typologies was a painstaking business and to create them without the conflation of stylistic and functional attributes could prove even more demanding. In an evolutionary framework, however, the kind of information potentially provided by seriation—phylogenetic reconstruction—is fundamentally relevant and meeting these re-quirements in one way or another will be necessary. Finally, one of the character-istics of a progressive research program is the cumulative nature of empirical *and* theoretical knowledge. New explanatory frameworks do not always replace ear-lier frameworks so much as they serve to incorporate and subsume them within a larger and more inclusive theory. Here, an argument is made to show how frequency seriation, a method of chronology building invented by culture histori-ans, can be subsumed by evolutionary archaeology. At the same time, this exam-ple also illustrates how building an evolutionary archaeology is more than simple theory borrowing of biological models, and requires instead expanding that the-ory to include inherently anthropological and archaeological issues. For culture historians, in the absence of independent chronometric methods where only for-mal attributes of artifacts could be used to tell time, the problem of chronology was approached from a materialist framework. The success of this method is at-tributed to the use of explanatory concepts that are subsumed by information transmission of neutral variants within an evolutionary framework. That it is compatible with both the metaphysical structure and explanatory content of evo-lutionary theory does not seem fortuitous but an indication of the explanatory power of evolutionary theory to incorporate the best parts of archaeology, accom-modate what we have gotten right, and explain why we have gotten it right.

Acknowledgments

This paper has benefited from comments on earlier versions by Robert Dunnell, Ann Ramenofsky, Michael Schiffer, William Walker, and two anonymous reviewers; and from discussions with G. T. Jones and Fraser Neiman.

References

Ascher, M., and R. Ascher
1963   Chronological Ordering by Computer. *American Anthropologist* 65:1045–1052.
Brainerd, G. W.
1951   The Place of Chronological Ordering in Archaeological Analysis. *American Antiq-uity* 16:301–313.

Chang, K. C.
1967   Major Aspects of the Interrelationship of Archaeology and Ethnology. *Current Anthropology* 8:227–243.

Cowgill, G. L.
1968   Review of Hole and Shaw "Computer Analysis of Chronological Seriation." *American Antiquity* 33:517–519.
1972   Models, Methods, and Techniques for Seriation. In *Models in Archaeology*, edited by D. L. Clarke, pp. 381–424. Methuen, London.

de Barros, P.L.F.
1982   The Effects of Variable Site Occupation Span on the Results of Frequency Seriation. *American Antiquity* 47:291–315.

Dempsey, P., and M. Baumhoff
1963   The Statistical Use of Artifact Distributions to Establish Chronological Sequence. *American Antiquity* 28:496–509.

Deetz, J. F., and E. S. Dethlefsen
1965   The Doppler Effect and Archaeology: A Consideration of the Spatial Effects of Seriation. *Southwestern Journal of Anthropology* 21:196–206.

Drennen, R. D.
1976   A Refinement of Chronological Seriation Using Nonmetric Multidimensional Scaling. *American Antiquity* 41:290–302.

Dunnell, R. C.
1970   Seriation Method and Its Evaluation. *American Antiquity* 35:305–319.
1978   Style and Function: A Fundamental Dichotomy. *American Antiquity* 43:192–203.
1980   Evolutionary Theory and Archaeology. In *Advances in Archaeological Method and Theory*, vol. 3, edited by M. B. Schiffer, pp. 35–99. Academic Press, New York.
1981   Seriation, Groups, and Measurement. In *Manejo de Datos y Metodos Matematicos de Arqueologia*, compilado y organizado por George L. Cowgill, Robert Whallon, y Barbara S. Ottaway. Union Internacional de Ciendias Prehisotricas y Protohistoricas, Mexico.
1982   Science, Social Science, and Common Sense: The Agonizing Dilemma of Modern Archaeology. *Journal of Anthropological Research* 38:1–25.
1986a   Five Decades of American Archaeology. In *American Archaeology Past and Future*, edited by D. J. Meltzer, D. D. Fowler, and J. A. Sabloff, pp. 23–49. Smithsonian Institution Press, Washington, D.C.
1986b   Methodological Issues in Americanist Artifact Classification. In *Advances in Archaeological Method and Theory*, vol. 9, edited by M. B. Schiffer, pp. 149–207. Academic Press, New York.

Ford, J. A.
1952   *Measurements of Some Prehistoric Design Developments in the Southeastern States*. Anthropological Papers 44 (3). American Museum of Natural History, New York.
1954a   Comment on A. C. Spaulding, "Statistical Techniques for the Discovery of Artifact Types." *American Antiquity* 19:390–391.

1954b   Spaulding's Review of Ford. *American Anthropologist* 56:109–112.

1954c   The Type Concept Revisited. *American Anthropologist* 56:42–54.

1962   *A Quantitative Method for Deriving Cultural Chronology.* Pan American Union Technical Manual 1, Organization of American States, Washington, D.C.

1966   *A Comparison of Formative Cultures in the Americas: Diffusion of the Psychic Unity of Man?* Smithsonian Contributions to Anthropology, vol. 11. Smithsonian Institution, Washington, D.C.

Gould, S. J., D. M. Raup, H. L. Sepkoski, T.J.M. Schopf, and D. S. Simberloff
1977   The Shape of Evolution: A Comparison of Real and Random Clades. *Paleobiology* 3:23–40.

Hole, F. A., and M. Shaw
1967   *Computer Analysis of Chronological Seriation.* Rice University Studies 53 (3). Rice University, Houston.

Johnson, L., Jr.
1968   *Item Seriation as an Aid to Elementary Scale and Cluster Analysis.* Museum of Natural History, Bulletin No. 15, University of Oregon, Eugene.

Kidder, A. V.
1924   *An Introduction to Southwestern Archaeology.* Papers of the Southwestern Expedition No. 1, Phillips Academy, New Haven, Connecticut.

Krieger, A.
1944   The Typological Concept. *American Antiquity* 9:271–288.

Kroeber, A. L.
1916   *Zuni Potsherds.* American Museum of Natural History, Anthropological Papers No. 18(1):7–21. New York.

1919   On the Principle of Order in Civilization as Exemplified by Changes of Fashion. *American Anthropologist* 21:253–263.

1939a   *Cultural and Natural Areas of Native North America.* University of California Publications in American Archaeology and Ethnology 38, University of California, Berkeley.

1939b   *Culture Element Distributions. XI. Tribes Surveyed.* Anthropological Records, vol. 7, no. 1, University of California, Berkeley.

Kroeber, A. L., and C. Kluckhohn
1952   *Culture: A Critical Review of Concepts and Definitions.* Papers of the Peabody Museum of American Archaeology and Ethnology, no. 47. Harvard University, Cambridge, Massachusetts.

LeBlanc, S. A.
1975   Micro-seriation: A Method for Fine Chronologic Differentiation. *American Antiquity* 40:22–38.

Leonard, R. D., and G. T. Jones
1987   Elements of an Inclusive Evolutionary Model for Archaeology. *Journal of Anthropological Archaeology* 6:199–219.

Marquardt, W. H.
1978   Advances in Archaeological Seriation. In *Advances in Archaeological Method and Theory*, vol. 1, edited by M. B. Schiffer, pp. 257–314. Academic Press, New York.

McKern, W.
1939   The Midwestern Taxonomic Method as an Aid to Archaeological Culture Study. *American Antiquity* 4:301–313.

Meighan, C.
1977   Recognition of Short Time Periods Through Seriation. *American Antiquity* 42:628–629.

Neff, H.
1992   Ceramics and Evolution. In *Archaeological Method and Theory*, vol. 4, edited by M. B. Schiffer, pp. 141–194. University of Arizona Press, Tucson.

Neiman, F. D.
1990   *An Evolutionary Approach to Archaeological Inference: Aspects of Architectural Variation in the 17th-Century Chesapeake.* Ph.D. dissertation, Yale University, New Haven, Connecticut.

Nelson, N.
1916   Chronology of the Tano Ruins, New Mexico. *American Anthropologist* 18:159–180.

O'Brien, M. J., and T. D. Holland
1990   Variation, Selection, and the Archaeological Record. In *Archaeological Method and Theory*, vol. 2, edited by M. B. Schiffer, pp. 31–79. University of Arizona Press, Tucson.
1992   The Role of Adaptation in Archaeological Explanation. *American Antiquity* 57:36–59.

Phillips, P.
1970   *Archaeological Survey in the Yazoo Basin, Mississippi, 1949–1955.* Papers of the Peabody Museum of American Archaeology and Ethnology, no. 60. Harvard University, Cambridge, Massachusetts.

Phillips, P., J. A. Ford, and J. B. Griffin
1951   *Archaeological Survey of the Lower Mississippi Alluvial Valley, 1940–1947.* Papers of the Peabody Museum of American Archaeology and Ethnography, no. 25. Harvard University, Cambridge, Massachusetts.

Robinson, W. S.
1951   A Method for Chronologically Ordering Archaeological Deposits. *American Antiquity* 16:293–301.

Rouse, I. B.
1939   *The Prehistory of Haiti.* Yale University Publications in Anthropology 21. Yale University Press, New Haven, Connecticut.
1955   On the Correlation of Phases of Culture. *American Anthropologist* 57:713–722.
1956   The Strategy of Culture History. In *Anthropology Today*, edited by A. L. Kroeber, pp. 57–76. University of Chicago Press, Chicago.

1967   Seriation in Archaeology. In *American Historical Anthropology: Essays in Honor of Leslie Spier*, edited by C. L. Riley, and W. W. Taylor, pp. 153–195. Southern Illinois University Press, Carbondale.

Smith, B. D.

1984   Mississippian Expansion: Tracing the Historical Development of an Explanatory Model. *Southeastern Archaeology* 3:13–32.

Sober, E.

1984   *The Nature of Selection*. MIT Press, Cambridge. Massachusetts.

Spaulding, A. C.

1953a   Review of "Measurements of Some Prehistoric Design Developments in the Southeastern States," by J.A. Ford. *American Anthropologist* 55:588–591.

1953b   Statistical Techniques for the Discovery of Artifact Types. *American Antiquity* 18:305–313.

1954a   Reply. *American Anthropologist* 56:112–114.

1954b   Reply to Ford. *American Antiquity* 19:391–393.

1982   Structure in Archaeological Data: Nominal Variables. In *Essays in Archaeological Typology*, edited by R. Whallon and J. A. Brown, pp. 1–20. Center for American Archaeology Press, Evanston, Indiana.

Steward, J. H., and F. M. Setzler

1938   Function and Configuration in Archaeology. *American Antiquity* 4:4–10.

Tallgren, A. M.

1937   The Method of Prehistoric Archaeology. *Antiquity* 11:152–161.

Teltser, P. A.

1988   *The Mississippian Archaeological Record on the Malden Plain, Southeast Missouri: Local Variability in Evolutionary Perspective*. Ph.D. dissertation, University of Washington, Seattle.

Willey, G. R.

1966   *Introduction to American Archaeology Volume 1: North and Middle America*. Prentice-Hall, Englewood Cliffs, New Jersey.

Willey, G. R., and P. Phillips

1958   *Method and Theory in American Archaeology*. University of Chicago Press, Chicago.

Wissler, C.

1914   Material Cultures of the North American Indians. *American Anthropologist* 16:447–505.

5

A Role for "Sourcing" in Evolutionary Archaeology

Hector Neff

◆◆ Evolution is about diversification and diversity. Assume only that there exist transmittable differences among living entities in how effectively they pass on blueprints for structure or action to descendant living entities, and descent with modification ensues automatically. Add the additional assumption that spatial barriers may arise and divide the living entities into subgroups, and a historical branching pattern ensues automatically. If branches disappear faster than new branches appear, diversity declines. This historical branching process is part of what Eldredge (1985) calls the "genealogical" side of evolution.

Diversity and evolution, however, are intertwined in another sense. At particular times and places, living entities that are the products of previous evolutionary diversification aggregate into ecological communities. The diversity of such communities reflects the opportunities for making a living afforded by the physical environment and the potential for interaction with other community members. Over the long run, variation in the nature of opportunities available adds up to selection. Thus, from a genealogical perspective evolution creates diversity—through the historical process of diversification—but from an ecological perspective diversity is a measure of selection since it reflects opportunities for making a living at a particular place and time.

Archaeologists have always studied the diversity of archaeological remains (Jones and Leonard 1989), and there has been a good deal of interest recently in quantitative indices of diversity (e.g., Bobrowsky and Ball 1989; Kintigh 1984, 1989). Some time ago, Meggers et al. (1965:6-7) recognized that contemporary archaeological diversity derives from an evolutionary process of diversification driven by Darwinian mechanisms (see Rindos 1989 for a recent discussion). The existing concern with diversity and diversification constitutes a sort of preadaptation for developing the methods of evolutionary archaeology. What we lack is explicit attention to how the units in which our descriptions are framed could have been affected by evolution (Dunnell 1980). More specifically, if the archaeological record is the product of a selection-driven, ramifying historical process, then developing methods for evolutionary archaeology hinges on describing that record in such a way that we may recognize both the historical process of diversification and the shifting opportunities that created selective pressure in the past.

On a practical level, I suggest we begin by evaluating existing modes of describing archaeological remains for the purpose of determining to what extent they can be tailored to the needs of evolutionary archaeology. In what follows I intend to pursue this task with one particular kind of description, description of patterned chemical variation in pottery.

Compositional Analysis

Compositional description of materials includes mineralogical and chemical characterization. The total range of compositions, chemical or mineralogical, that might be produced with raw materials of a particular type available in a particular region defines a "compositional space." The composition of an artifact made within any particular compositional space is a concrete manifestation of raw material use by an individual in the past, which is a characteristic of a past human phenotype; conversely, compositional characterization of an artifact directly monitors part of a past human phenotype. An analysis of variation in compositional data thus constitutes an analysis of variation in past human phenotypes.

The amount of information gleaned from compositional analysis depends on how compositional space is structured naturally, the precision and appropriateness of the analytical technique, and the appropriateness of statistical and pattern-recognition techniques brought to bear on the compositional data. Obviously, if raw materials are homogeneous over a wide area, or if the chosen analytical technique is incapable of revealing patterned compositional variation, compositional analysis will yield no new information about patterned phenotypic variation. On the other hand, the application of an appropriate technique in an area of geographically patterned raw material variation will directly link past humans with specific, localized resources.

Data Analytic Considerations in Ceramic Provenance Studies

I turn now to the particular case of pottery and to chemical techniques of compositional characterization.

A fundamental concept in ceramic sourcing is the chemical compositional group (Arnold et al. 1991; Bishop et al. 1982). Such groups exist if (1) potters exploited local resources preferentially rather than exploited all resources randomly or uniformly (Arnold 1985) and (2) chemical variation in the source region raw materials is geographically patterned as it is in the case study presented below. If these conditions are met, then the multivariate space defined by elemental concentrations determined for a series of ceramic specimens will have areas of high point density, which reflect localized sources or source zones. The overall clumpiness of the multivariate elemental concentration space reflects the past presence of several localized pottery-making groups. Because the sources used by potters are initially unknown, there is no means to define the relevant analytical units (pottery derived from a common ceramic resource base) beforehand. However, once groups are identified in the data, they can be tied to geographic space by comparison with an analyzed sample of raw materials.

Whether compositional groups are recognizable in chemical data is an empirical question that can be addressed through the application of pattern-recognition techniques in a search for subgroup structure. Groups are described by parameters of location (centroid) and dispersion (variance-covariance matrix), and distinct groups are recognizable as areas of high point density in the multivariate space defined by elemental concentrations. Areas of high point density are identified through application of pattern-recognition techniques (e.g., hierarchical cluster analysis, principal components analysis, and bivariate scatterplots) coupled with group refinement using multivariate probabilistic statistics based on Mahalanobis generalized distance. Mahalanobis distance takes into account variances and covariances in the multivariate group and thus is analogous to expressing distance from a univariate mean in standard deviation units. Like measurements in standard deviation units, Mahalanobis distances can be converted into probabilities of group membership for each individual specimen (e.g., Bieber et al. 1976; Bishop and Neff 1989; Harbottle 1976). For relatively small sample sizes, it is appropriate to base probabilities on Hotelling's T^2, which is a multivariate extension of the univariate Student's t. When raw material analyses are available, likely sources or source zones for the compositional groups can be identified by calculating probabilities of group membership for the raw materials.

Definition of chemical compositional groups by the above means is sample-dependent and thus extensional (Dunnell 1971). This means that confidence in the assignment of any particular specimen to a group varies with membership of the group, and there is always a possibility of misassignment. If boundaries between the compositional groups are somewhat indistinct, the number of questionable assignments may be substantial. This problem may be partially circumvented by identifying the most likely source of each individual analyzed specimen independent of its group affiliation.

One approach to individual specimen sourcing is analogous to the group-sourcing method described above. To source an individual pottery specimen, Mahalanobis distances are calculated between it and a series of raw material analyses; the variance-covariance matrix of the total raw material data set is used to account for variation in point density in the multivariate compositional space. As in the group approach, variation in probabilities among analyzed raw materials indicates variation in the likelihood that the pottery specimen came from different raw material sampling locations. Unfortunately, this approach entails a significant problem in data presentation, since it generates a separate probability surface for every pottery analysis in the data set.

A more efficient approach to individual specimen sourcing is possible if systematic compositional trends along both north-south and east-west axes exist in the raw material data. (Such systematic trends may be expected in sedimentary environments, in which weathering products from several parent materials are mixed in varying proportions.) A variance-covariance matrix calculated from the complete raw material data (i.e., geographic coordinates together with elemental concentrations) constitutes a complete representation of geographic trends in the raw material sample. Best fit geographic coordinates for any single pottery analysis can be estimated by finding those coordinates that minimize the Mahalanobis distance to the centroid of the (complete) raw materials data. These coordinates constitute the best estimate of the unknown pottery specimen's provenance[1] based on the available raw material sample. Adequacy of raw material sampling limits this approach, as does the propensity of potters to alter ceramic composition through tempering and other paste preparation practices.

In summary, linking pottery to raw materials can be pursued either on the level of the pottery compositional group or on the level of individual pottery analysis. Here, I rely primarily on the group approach to sourcing but present in addition the individual specimen provenance coordinates calculated using the second of the two approaches described above. I use the first approach to individual specimen sourcing to check some of the calculated provenance coordinates that seem to conflict with the results of the group-based approach.

Provenance Studies and Evolutionary Archaeology

From the evolutionary perspective that is central to this paper, compositional diversity in archaeological ceramics reflects variation in raw material source usage that was shaped by evolutionary processes in the past. Assuming that traditional practices of ceramic resource procurement and paste preparation were passed down from potter to potter over some span of time in the past, then the pottery made during that time would show continuity in composition (Neff 1993). Conversely, assuming there is sufficient natural variation in ceramic raw materials in a region, diversification of production practices would yield an increase in the diversity of ceramic compositional profiles. Compositional profiles may also disappear as traditional production practices disappear. In short, pottery compositional data record the historical continuity, branching, and extinction of past traditions of ceramic production, thus affording a genealogical perspective on ceramic evolution.

Looked at from a consumption viewpoint rather than a production viewpoint, the record of ceramic compositional diversity within a region reflects the ecological contexts within which selection operated. Selection arises from pottery consumption because consumption provides opportunities for human phenotypes to encompass the suite of characteristics associated with pottery production and because shifts in consumption track shifts in the opportunities for expressing pottery-making traits (Neff 1992). One gauge of consumption is assemblage compositional diversity, which measures the diversity of raw material procurement patterns of the potters whose products were consumed within particular spatial and temporal limits. If all economic interaction takes place within the domestic unit, ceramic composition will reflect local procurement of ceramic resources by potters meeting household consumption requirements. But if additional opportunities for pottery making are available because of regional economic interaction, then some assemblages will contain pottery derived from nonlocal ceramic resource bases, and variation in compositional diversity among assemblages will exist. From this ecological perspective, compositional data record past selective pressures that arose out of variation in the opportunities for making a living through pottery production.

To develop these points further, I now turn to a discussion of compositional patterning in ceramic raw materials and pottery from the central Pacific coastal region of Guatemala. Analyses reported below indicate that between Terminal Formative and Late Classic times, serving-vessel potters in this region broadened their use of ceramic resources. Also, throughout this period one particular zone stands out as consumer of nonlocal ceramic products. I argue that excess consumption of serving vessels in one zone provided opportunities that selected for expanded production of serving vessels and exploitation of new ceramic resources in other zones.

The Ceramic Environment of Pacific Coastal Guatemala

My colleagues and I have devoted considerable effort to characterizing pottery and ceramic raw materials from Pacific coastal and highland Guatemala (e.g., Bove et al. 1992; Neff 1984; Neff and Bishop 1988; Neff et al. 1989; Neff et al. 1992), an effort which has now produced well over 2,000 neutron activation

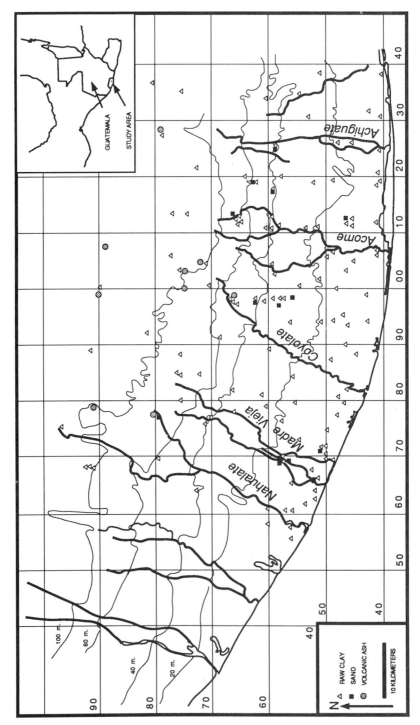

Figure 5.1. Map of the Central Pacific Coast of Guatemala showing major geographic features and sampling locations for clay, sand, and volcanic ash.

analyses. In 1990 we conducted a ceramic raw materials survey of a portion of the Pacific coastal plain encompassing most of the department of Escuintla (Fig. 5.1). Additional raw materials were collected in 1992. The surveys yielded approximately 300 raw material samples, of which 162 clays, 16 sands, and 11 volcanic ashes were analyzed by neutron activation. The raw materials provide a background—a compositional space—against which to project 1,100+ pottery analyses from Escuintla.

The chemical data produced by NAA could be described and mapped onto geographic space as raw elemental concentrations or as any conceivable function of the elemental concentrations. Principal components analysis yields nonarbitrary linear functions of the original elemental data. Using either the variance-covariance matrix or the correlation matrix of the elemental concentrations, principal components analysis identifies the longest axes in the data set (those with the largest eigenvalues). In general, the longer axes are interpretable, while the smaller axes are attributable to "noise" in the data. Here, for example, one expects the several largest components of the raw clay data to display geographic trends, which would help us source chemically characterized pottery. The geographic interpretations of the first four components are particularly clear.

The first principal component, which accounts for about 40 percent of variance in the clay data (Table 5.1), displays a pronounced trend from high values at the eastern edge of the study area to low values at the western edge (Fig. 5.2). High negative coefficients for U, Cs, Sb, Rb, and Th on component 1 combined with high positive coefficients for Ca and Sr suggest that the component expresses the effect of weathering from distinct parent materials (Neff et al. 1992). Near-coast clays from the eastern edge of the study area are fine-textured sedimentary clays incorporating fine grains of mafic sand and relatively high frequencies of plagioclase feldspar. Moving west, sedimentary clays become more felsic, with increasing proportions of K-feldspar relative to plagioclase. Clays from the major north-south trending compositional "valley" in the center of the study area, and compositional basins in the northwest and northeast quadrants (Fig. 5.2) are from primary clay deposits developing in association with rhyolitic pumice and ash deposits derived from recent eruptions in the volcanic chain just north of the study area. Such deposits, not all of which were sampled, are incorporated into the quaternary alluvium along the upper edge of the coastal plain.

The second principal component of the data (Fig. 5.3) differentiates the northeastern quadrant of the study area, an area of very high values, from the rest of the study area, where values are relatively low. Moderate to high positive coefficients for transition metals (Co, Cr, Fe, Sc, Mn, Ti, and V) combined with high negative coefficients for group IA and IIA elements (Cs, Rb, Sr, Ca, K, and Na) suggest that the clays of this region incorporate material derived from relatively mafic parent

Table 5.1. Eight Principal Components Calculated from the Variance-Covariance of the Pacific Coast Raw Clay Data (n=162)

	PC01	PC02	PC03	PC04	PC05	PC06	PC07	PC08
Eigenvalue	0.4371	0.1905	0.1181	0.0707	0.0610	0.0344	0.0309	0.0190
% Variance	41.12	17.93	11.11	6.65	5.74	3.24	2.90	1.79
Cumulative	41.12	59.05	70.16	76.81	82.55	85.78	88.69	90.47

EIGENVECTORS (LARGEST TO SMALLEST)

Element

	PC01	PC02	PC03	PC04	PC05	PC06	PC07	PC08
AS	−0.2006	−0.0021	−0.2271	−0.0583	0.1197	0.5290	0.5284	0.0862
LA	−0.1737	−0.0371	-0.1453	0.0817	−0.1363	−0.1921	0.0152	−0.2400
LU	−0.0624	0.0146	−0.1384	0.1682	−0.1499	−0.0342	−0.0345	0.0598
ND	−0.0947	−0.0328	−0.2046	0.1527	−0.1606	−0.1494	−0.0423	−0.0591
SM	−0.0631	−0.0167	−0.2176	0.1761	−0.1388	−0.0780	−0.0207	0.0384
U	−0.3552	−0.1011	−0.0020	0.0395	0.1674	−0.0720	0.0322	0.4555
YB	−0.0512	0.0078	−0.1612	0.1745	−0.1705	−0.0448	−0.0336	0.0341
CE	−0.1913	0.0264	−0.0433	0.0134	−0.1465	−0.0014	0.0435	−0.0700
CO	0.0752	0.1903	−0.2734	−0.1327	0.0048	0.1574	−0.1618	−0.0238
CR	−0.0594	0.2458	−0.3087	−0.3377	0.6188	−0.4550	0.0405	−0.0991
CS	−0.3077	−0.2493	−0.0854	−0.0548	0.0560	−0.0332	−0.1875	0.1569
EU	0.0048	0.0098	−0.2319	0.1717	−0.1199	−0.1015	−0.0397	0.0175
FE	0.0449	0.1665	−0.1625	−0.0159	0.0859	0.1425	−0.1946	0.0318
HF	−0.1375	0.0747	−0.0069	0.0115	−0.0259	−0.0921	−0.0326	−0.1852
RB	−0.2290	−0.3535	−0.0461	−0.1943	0.1071	0.1085	−0.4145	0.0923
SB	−0.2834	−0.0153	−0.1300	−0.0471	0.0601	0.2166	0.2769	0.0143
SC	0.0433	0.1340	−0.1639	0.0822	0.0678	0.0983	−0.0960	0.1049
SR	0.2595	−0.3644	−0.2307	0.0737	0.0613	−0.1499	0.1530	−0.0455
TA	−0.2773	−0.0266	0.0057	0.0402	−0.0510	−0.0886	0.0575	−0.1095
TB	−0.0195	0.0375	−0.2301	0.1331	−0.0225	−0.0760	−0.0475	0.1633
TH	−0.3893	−0.0432	0.0085	−0.0116	0.0107	−0.1395	0.0831	−0.1636
ZN	0.0041	0.0422	−0.2423	0.1110	0.0436	0.0483	−0.1355	0.1964
ZR	−0.1248	0.0573	−0.0059	0.0480	−0.0424	−0.0917	−0.0755	−0.1664
AL	−0.0580	0.0841	−0.0251	0.0568	−0.0121	−0.0144	0.0050	0.0182
BA	−0.1216	0.0470	−0.0578	0.0381	−0.0651	0.0373	0.2288	−0.4594
CA	0.3374	−0.3616	−0.2970	−0.0755	0.0483	0.0594	0.1558	0.0756
DY	−0.0385	−0.0250	−0.2710	0.2420	−0.1664	−0.0493	−0.0307	0.0519
K	−0.1403	−0.3044	0.0226	−0.1709	0.0032	0.3088	−0.3515	−0.2994

Table 5.1. *Continued*

	PC01	PC02	PC03	PC04	PC05	PC06	PC07	PC08
MN	0.0018	0.1288	−0.2089	−0.7091	−0.5779	−0.1023	0.0435	0.1474
NA	0.1290	−0.4415	−0.1463	−0.0707	0.0457	−0.1251	0.0933	−0.2502
TI	0.0190	0.1604	−0.1790	0.1351	0.0730	0.1514	−0.1904	−0.0827
V	0.0781	0.1957	−0.2437	−0.0074	0.0793	0.2964	−0.2096	−0.2970

SCALED FACTOR LOADING MATRIX (LARGEST TO SMALLEST COMPONENT)

Element

	PC01	PC02	PC03	PC04	PC05	PC06	PC07	PC08
AS	−0.1326	−0.0009	−0.0780	−0.0155	0.0296	0.0981	0.0928	0.0119
LA	−0.1148	−0.0162	−0.0499	0.0217	−0.0337	−0.0356	0.0027	−0.0331
LU	−0.0412	0.0064	−0.0476	0.0447	−0.0370	−0.0063	−0.0061	0.0082
ND	−0.0626	−0.0143	−0.0703	0.0406	−0.0397	−0.0277	−0.0074	−0.0082
SM	−0.0417	−0.0073	−0.0748	0.0468	−0.0343	−0.0145	−0.0036	0.0053
U	−0.2348	−0.0441	−0.0007	0.0105	0.0413	−0.0134	0.0057	0.0628
YB	−0.0339	0.0034	−0.0554	0.0464	−0.0421	−0.0083	−0.0059	0.0047
CE	−0.1265	0.0115	−0.0149	0.0036	−0.0362	−0.0003	0.0076	−0.0096
CO	0.0497	0.0831	−0.0940	−0.0353	0.0012	0.0292	−0.0284	−0.0033
CR	−0.0392	0.1073	−0.1061	−0.0898	0.1528	−0.0844	0.0071	−0.0137
CS	−0.2034	−0.1088	−0.0293	−0.0146	0.0138	−0.0062	−0.0329	0.0216
EU	0.0032	0.0043	−0.0797	0.0456	−0.0296	−0.0188	−0.0070	0.0024
FE	0.0297	0.0727	−0.0558	−0.0042	0.0212	0.0264	−0.0342	0.0044
HF	−0.0909	0.0326	−0.0024	0.0031	−0.0064	−0.0171	−0.0057	−0.0255
RB	−0.1514	−0.1543	−0.0158	−0.0517	0.0265	0.0201	−0.0728	0.0127
SB	−0.1874	−0.0067	−0.0447	−0.0125	0.0148	0.0402	0.0486	0.0020
SC	0.0287	0.0585	−0.0563	0.0218	0.0167	0.0182	−0.0169	0.0145
SR	0.1716	−0.1591	−0.0793	0.0196	0.0151	−0.0278	0.0269	−0.0063
TA	−0.1833	−0.0116	0.0019	0.0107	−0.0126	−0.0164	0.0101	−0.0151
TB	−0.0129	0.0164	−0.0791	0.0354	−0.0055	−0.0141	−0.0083	0.0225
TH	−0.2574	−0.0189	0.0029	−0.0031	0.0027	−0.0259	0.0146	−0.0225
ZN	0.0027	0.0184	−0.0833	0.0295	0.0108	0.0090	−0.0238	0.0271
ZR	−0.0825	0.0250	−0.0020	0.0128	−0.0105	−0.0170	−0.0133	−0.0229
AL	−0.0383	0.0367	−0.0086	0.0151	−0.0030	−0.0027	0.0009	0.0025
BA	−0.0804	0.0205	−0.0199	0.0101	−0.0161	0.0069	0.0402	−0.0633
CA	0.2230	−0.1578	−0.1021	−0.0201	0.0119	0.0110	0.0274	0.0104
DY	−0.0255	−0.0109	−0.0931	0.0643	−0.0411	−0.0091	−0.0054	0.0072

Table 5.1. *Continued*

	PC01	PC02	PC03	PC04	PC05	PC06	PC07	PC08
K	−0.0927	−0.1329	0.0078	−0.0454	0.0008	0.0573	−0.0617	−0.0413
MN	0.0012	0.0562	−0.0718	−0.1885	−0.1427	−0.0190	0.0076	0.0203
NA	0.0853	−0.1927	−0.0503	−0.0188	0.0113	−0.0232	0.0164	−0.0345
TI	0.0126	0.0700	−0.0615	0.0359	0.0180	0.0281	−0.0334	−0.0114
V	0.0516	0.0854	−0.0837	−0.0020	0.0196	0.0550	−0.0368	−0.0410

rocks. Mineral content reinforces this interpretation (Neff et al. 1992). Principal component 2 should facilitate easy recognition of pottery made from raw materials procured in the northeast quadrant of the study area.

The third principal component (Fig. 5.4) identifies several peaks and a broader zone of high values trending northwest from the center of the study area. Based on the component coefficients (Table 5.1), high values indicate depletion of rare earths, some transition metals, and Ca combined with slight enrichment of K. The plateau in the central zone is dominated by residual clays developing on geologically recent pumice and ash. This is also true of the peak between the two northern tributaries of the Nahualate River and of some of the clays near the peak along the northeast edge of the study area. Pottery made from these clays, or to which volcanic ash temper has been added, is expected to show high scores on component 3.

The fourth principal component surface (Fig. 5.5) has a peak in the north-central area and generally higher values in the eastern half of the study area. The transition metals Mn and Cr make major negative contributions to this dimension (Table 5.1). The clays developing on volcanic ash tend to have low scores on this dimension.

Geographic trends are also present in principal components beyond the first four and in individual elemental concentrations, texture, fired color, and mineralogy (Neff et al. 1992). However, the first four principal components of the chemical data depicted in Figures 5.2 to 5.5 subsume the clearest regional trends. The existence of these trends suggests that compositional groups representing circumscribed production zones should be recognizable with the pattern-recognition and group-evaluation techniques discussed above.[2]

Geographic trends in the compositional data also make it possible to source individual specimens by the two techniques discussed previously. In support of this expectation, when individual raw clay analyses are removed successively from the data set, and the Mahalanobis distances from the remaining points are calculated

Principal Component 1 Surface

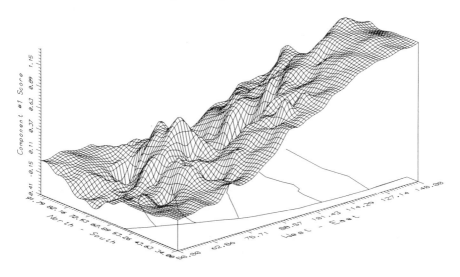

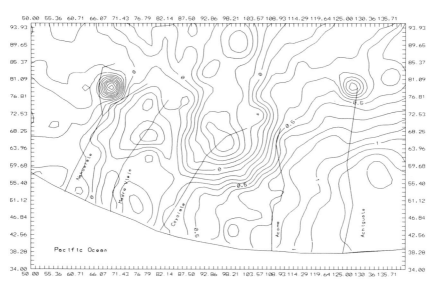

Figure 5.2. Regional Trends in scores on principal component 1 of the 162-specimen raw clay data set. Top: Orthographic projection surface. Bottom: contour map, contour interval 0.1.

Principal Component 2 Surface

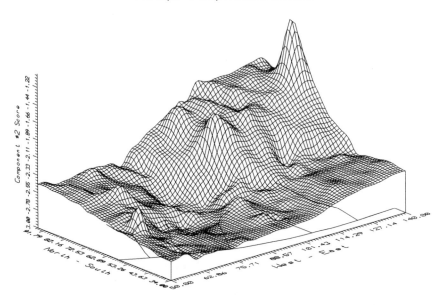

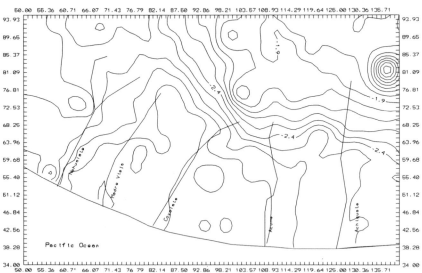

Figure 5.3. Regional Trends in scores on principal component 2 of the 162-specimen raw clay data set. Top: Orthographic projection surface. Bottom: contour map, contour interval 0.1.

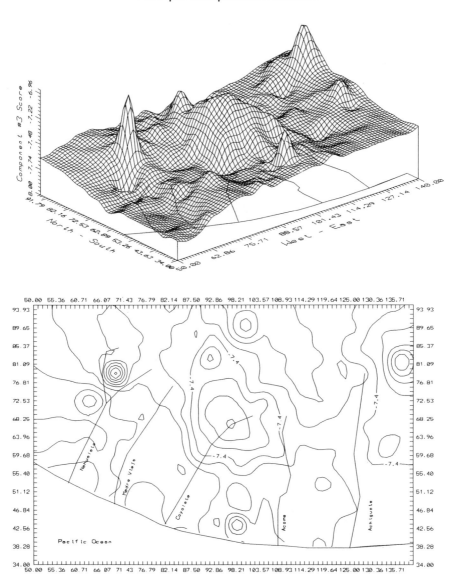

Figure 5.4. Regional Trends in scores on principal component 3 of the 162-specimen raw clay data set. Top: Orthographic projection surface. Bottom: contour map, contour interval 0.1.

Principal Component 4 Surface

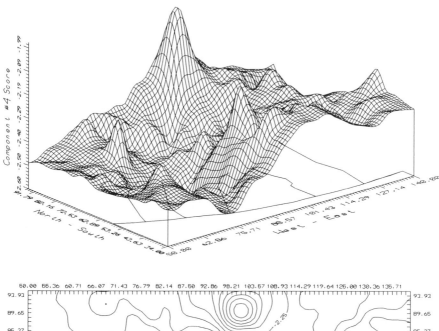

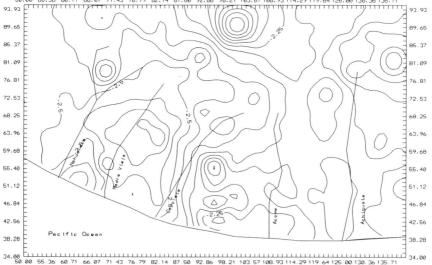

Figure 5.5. Regional Trends in scores on principal component 4 of the 162-specimen raw clay data set. Top: Orthographic projection surface. Bottom: contour map, contour interval 0.05.

(the first approach to individual specimen sourcing), the zone of peak probability (lowest Mahalanobis distance) consistently includes the true point coordinates.

Furthermore, when the raw clay analyses are removed and geographic coordinates are recalculated using the minimum Mahalanobis distance criterion (the second approach to individual specimen sourcing), the calculated coordinates lie within zones of high probability identified by the first approach. The average distance of the calculated location from the true location is 13.5 km; deviations from the true value show no systematic directional bias, either east-west or north-south; and principal component score surfaces based on the recalculated coordinates differ only slightly from the true surfaces shown in Figures 5.2 to 5.5. In light of these observations, individual pottery sample provenances calculated by the minimum Mahalanobis distance criterion are expected to fall in the general area of their true provenance.

The Formative–Classic Serving-Vessel Tradition of the Guatemalan Central Pacific Coast

Potters first began exploiting the ceramic resources of the Escuintla coast (Fig. 5.6) around 1600 or 1700 B.C., when Barra tradition pottery made its appearance between the Coyolate and Madre Vieja rivers (Arroyo 1991, 1992). So from about 1700 B.C. until sometime after the Spanish conquest potters were sampling the same ceramic environment that we sampled during our recent raw material survey. By sampling and analyzing the potters' samples and comparing the results to our own raw material analyses, we directly monitor one aspect of human interaction with the natural environment.

My focus here is on a serving-vessel tradition that emerged by the end of the Late Formative period (around 200 B.C.). During Terminal Formative–Early Classic times, this tradition was characterized by slipped and burnished bowls, plates, and cylindrical vessels in either red-orange (including Usulutan) or black-brown variants, often with some kind of plastic decoration (Parsons 1967). Middle and Late Classic representatives of the serving-vessel tradition fall into the same general shape categories as the earlier serving vessels, although details of workmanship differ. Later serving vessels include an orange or cream-slipped ware known as "Tiquisate" (Hatch 1989; Parsons 1967), a red-painted ware known as "Patulul Orange-Brown" (Parsons 1967), and black-brown vessels in shape and decorative variants that parallel the Tiquisate and Patulul wares. A large subcategory of Tiquisate ware vessels have a distinctive, light-colored paste; we refer to these as Tiquisate White ware. The Middle–Late Classic serving-vessel tradition is argued to have descended from the earlier red-orange and black-brown tradition (Hatch 1989). Among the many neutron activation analyses we have generated of coastal Guatemalan pottery are 292 analyses pertaining to the Terminal Formative–Early

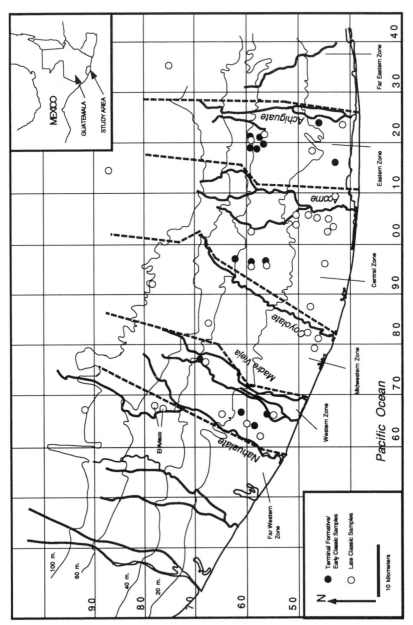

Figure 5.6. Map of the Central Pacific Coast of Guatemala showing archaeological Terminal Formative–Early Classic and Late Classic archaeological sites represented in the analyzed sample of serving vessels.

Classic (TF/EC) end of the serving-vessel tradition and 346 analyses that represent the Middle–Late Classic end of that tradition. Locations of sites represented in the analyzed serving-vessel sample are shown in Figure 5.6.

In what follows, I compare how earlier (TF/EC) and later (Late Classic) serving-vessel potters exploited the ceramic resources of the region sampled during our own 1990 survey. The basis of this comparison is a consideration of the evidence pertaining to the origins of raw materials used in all the analyzed serving vessels.

Compositional Patterning in Terminal Formative–Early Classic Serving Vessels

Four chemical subgroups of Terminal Formative–Early Classic serving vessels were recognized by pattern recognition and by group validation techniques already mentioned (see also Bieber et al. 1976; Bishop and Neff 1989; Harbottle 1976). To some extent, the chemical groups coincide with differences in nonplastic constituents, one group including specimens with abundant glassy volcanic ash shards (the ash-tempered group) and the other three including specimens with nonplastic constituents dominated by crystalline grains found in sands and silts of the coastal plain quaternary alluvium. Part of the multivariate compositional distinctiveness of the three groups can be illustrated by projecting the pottery analyses onto the first two principal components of the analyzed clay data (Fig. 5.7). None of the four groups shows high enough values on component 2 to have been derived from clays procured in the northeastern corner of the study area (see Fig. 5.3 above). The positions of the three nonash tempered groups on component 1, the east-west dimension of the clay data, suggest that they reflect procurement of argillaceous sediments in the western, central, and eastern zones. The proveniences that dominate in each group support this interpretation, with the eastern group dominated by eastern zone proveniences, the central group dominated by central zone proveniences, and the western group dominated by western proveniences. The compositional overlap between the nonash tempered groups in principal component space disappears in canonical discriminant space (not shown).

The likely zone of origin of each pottery compositional group can be assessed directly by incorporating information on raw clay compositions. Probability surfaces obtained by calculating Mahalanobis distances (and associated probabilities) between raw clay analyses and the pottery group centroids indicate the most likely zones of origin for the groups,[3] and the individual specimen provenances calculated using the minimum Mahalanobis distance technique can be displayed on the same map with each group's probability surface (Figs. 5.8 and 5.9).

Both the group and individual specimen approaches to sourcing indicate different origins for the groups provisionally referred to as "eastern" and "western." Raw clay probabilities suggest the coastal plain east of the Coyolate River as the

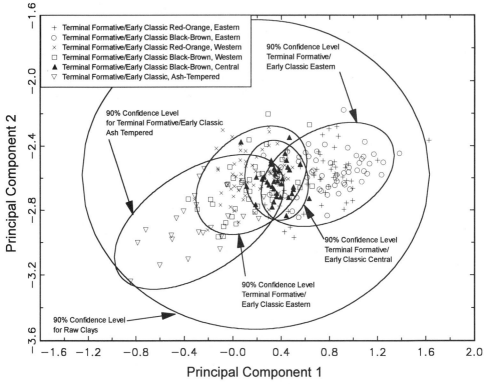

Figure 5.7. Plot of scores for Terminal Formative–Early Classic serving vessels on principal components 1 and 2 of the raw clay data.

likely origin for the eastern group (Fig. 5.8, top) and the coastal plain west of the Coyolate River as the likely origin for the western group (Fig. 5.8, bottom). The calculated provenances for both groups suggest a shift west for the eastern group (Fig. 5.8, top) and a shift north and west for the western group (Fig. 5.8, bottom). Most importantly, there is little overlap between the point swarms for the two groups, and the high probability areas for the two groups show no overlap at all.

The relatively large high probability zone and the discordant results from the two sourcing methods cast some doubt on any specific inferences about where the eastern group originated. The easternmost Terminal Formative–Early Classic contexts (around the site of Balberta), from which most of the eastern group members are derived, fall within the zone of high probability, but only two individual calculated provenances fall east of the Acomé River (Fig. 5.8, top). The high probability zone extends some distance west, almost to the Coyolate River, and the main point swarm of calculated provenances is centered along the Coyolate,

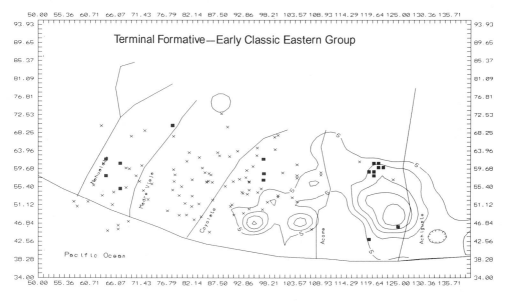

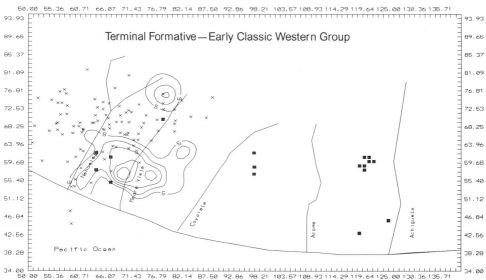

- ■ Terminal Formative—Early Classic Archaeological Site
- × Calculated Serving Vessel Provenance
  (Contour lines indicate calculated probabilities that raw clays belong to the pottery compositional groups.)

Figure 5.8. Contour maps with elevations representing the probability that raw clay analyses belong to the Terminal Formative–Early Classic eastern group (top) or the Terminal Formative–Early Classic western group (bottom). Probabilities of membership are based on thirty-two elements (listed in Table 5.1). Plotted points indicate calculated provenances for all speciments in each group.

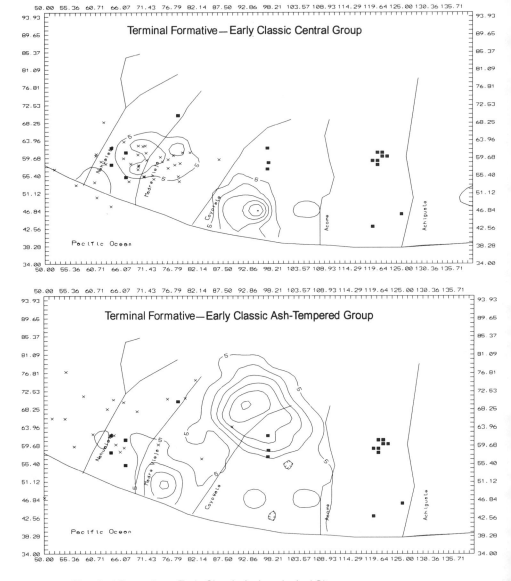

- ■ Terminal Formative—Early Classic Archaeological Site
- × Calculated Serving Vessel Provenance
  (Contour lines indicate calculated probabilities that raw clays belong to the pottery compositional groups.)

Figure 5.9. Contour maps with elevations representing the probability that raw clay analyses belong to the Terminal Formative–Early Classic central group (top) or the Terminal Formative–Early Classic ash-tempered group (bottom). Probabilities for top map based on thirty-two elements (listed in Table 5.1); probabilities for bottom map based on scores on principal components 1 through 8 of the clay data (Table 5.1). Plotted points indicate calculated provenances for all speciments in each group.

which might suggest that the group represents exploitation of ceramic resources lying mainly to the west of the Acomé River. The main cloud of points representing calculated provenances extends about 10 km west of the Coyolate River. Calculated provenances between the Madre Vieja and the Nahualate rivers appear to be erroneous results reflecting uneven raw material sampling; individual probability maps generated for these outlying specimens (the alternate approach to individual specimen sourcing) placed all peak probability zones east of the Madre Vieja River with most falling between the Coyolate and Acomé rivers. These results suggest that the production zone for the eastern group probably extends west of the Acomé River but probably not as far west as the individual calculated provenances would suggest. A better raw material sample might clarify these ambiguities.

Better agreement exists between the two sourcing approaches for the western group (Fig. 5.8, bottom). Most of the high probability zone and all but seven calculated provenances lie west of the Madre Vieja River. Although the calculated provenances are slightly offset from the highest probability zone, both sourcing approaches suggest that the bulk of specimens in the western group are derived from ceramic raw materials procured on the coastal plain west of the Madre Vieja River. Spot checking of the individual provenances by the alternate individual sourcing technique tends to move individual provenances into the lower coastal zone of peak probability for the group. Despite some uncertainty regarding the exact location and extent of the western group source zone, inference of west-to-east movement based on membership in this group would seem to be on firm ground.

Zones of high probability for the central group overlap with both the eastern and western high probability zones, although the calculated provenances fall exclusively west of the Coyolate River (Fig. 5.9, top). The peak probability zone lying just east of the Coyolate River is more often favored by the alternate approach to individual sourcing. On the basis of this partially contradictory evidence, a large section of the coastal plain lying within about 15 km of the coast and west of the Acomé River must be considered a potential source zone for vessels with this intermediate composition. Occurrences of this composition east of the Acomé River constitute tentative evidence of west-to-east movement.

The ash-tempered group is relatively heterogeneous and would probably be divisible into subgroups with a larger sample. Raw clays from a wide area of the coastal plain show above 5 percent probability of membership in this small, heterogeneous group, with peak probabilities found in a zone lying about 25 km inland along the Coyolate River (Fig. 5.9, bottom)[4]; primary clays developing on rhyolitic volcanic ash predominate in this zone. Calculated provenances for the individual ash-tempered specimens are found across a wide area of the coastal plain west of the Coyolate River but largely outside the zone of high probability;

the alternate approach to individual sample sourcing produces better agreement with the group approach. The contradictory sourcing results from the two approaches may be due in part to the effect of volcanic ash tempering: if the group consists of diverse clays to which volcanic ash has been added, the pottery group variance-covariance structure might most easily accommodate ash-derived clays from the piedmont, whereas the composition of individual pottery specimens predicts geographic coordinates in the zone of sedimentary clays found on the coastal plain farther south. Production centers making these ash-tempered specimens may have been located along the upper edge of the coastal plain, where both sedimentary clays and volcanic ash were available. The group may also include some pottery specimens made from primary clays developing in association with the upper coastal plain ash deposits. Although the group appears not to be related to any raw material sources found east of the Acomé River, the effect of volcanic ash temper would have to be examined in greater detail before this could be used confidently as a basis for inferring west-to-east movement of vessels.

Compositional Patterning in Middle–Late Classic Serving Vessels

Applying pattern-recognition and group refinement procedures to the Late Classic serving-vessel data yields three discrete groups and one anomalous, chemically variable group. Separation between the three main groups is best illustrated by a scatterplot of principal components 1 and 4 of the clay data (Fig. 5.10). Positions of the three groups on principal component 1 suggests an east-west compositional gradient, just as in the Terminal Formative–Early Classic data, with the Tiquisate White ware group lying at the extreme western end. Consistent with the observed lower scores of western clays on principal component 4 (Fig. 5.5), the Late Classic western group tends to lie below the eastern group on component 4 (Fig. 5.10). On several principal components, including components 1 and 4 (Fig. 5.10), there is a tendency for the eastern and western groups to segregate further into subgroups dominated by northern (interior) proveniences on one hand and southern (near coast) proveniences on the other hand. The Tiquisate White ware group also subdivides into two "proto-groups." Different symbols are used for the "proto-groups" in Figure 5.10, but, because of the fuzziness of the distinction between coastal and interior specimens in the available sample and the small sizes of these proto-groups, they are treated as single groups for purposes of comparison with the raw clays. The tendency toward subgroup differentiation beyond the basic east-west distinction may reflect expansion of the range of exploited ceramic resources in both the eastern and western zones, as discussed in more detail below.

Association of the eastern nonwhite group with the eastern half of the study area is supported both by the probability surface and by individual calculated provenances (Fig. 5.11, top). But the fact that a much larger part of the study area

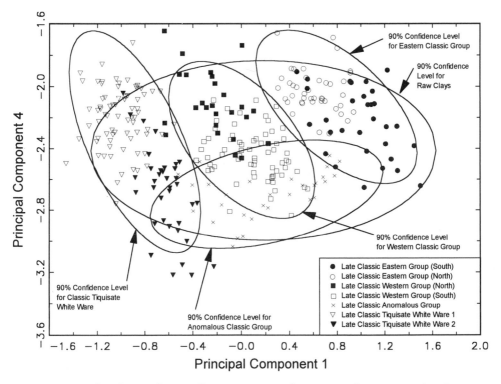

Figure 5.10. Plot of scores for Late Classic serving vessels on principal components 1 and 4 of the raw clay data.

lies above the 5 percent probability contour suggests that a larger number of production centers (most presumably lying east of the Coyolate) using a wider variety of ceramic resources is represented in the Late Classic eastern group than in the earlier eastern group. The large number of points lying east of the Acomé River, in a zone nearly devoid of TF/EC eastern group individual provenances (Fig. 5.8, top) identifies this as one area where extensive ceramic production may have been initiated during the Middle Classic period. As with the Terminal Formative–Early Classic eastern group, quite a few calculated provenances lie west of the Coyolate River. In this case, however, spot checking with the alternate individual provenancing technique confirms a western provenance in most cases. Thus, the production zone represented by the eastern nonwhite group may extend west of the 5 percent probability contour at the Coyolate River.

Judging from both the probability surface and the calculated provenances, the presumed western group originated west of the Coyolate River. The correspondence between the individual and group-based approaches is especially convinc-

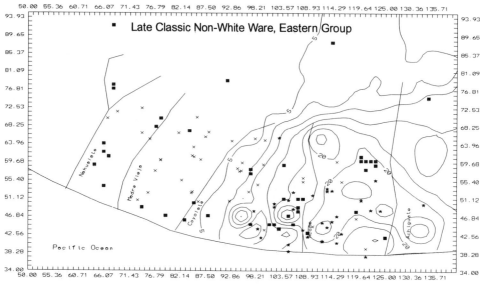

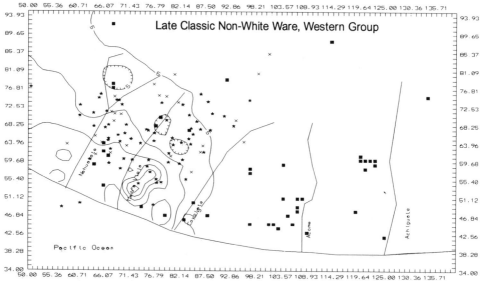

- ■ Middle - Late Classic Archaeological Site
- × Calculated Provenance for Late Classic Serving Vessel (Northern Proto-group)
- ⋆ Calculated Provenance for Late Classic Serving Vessel (Southern Proto-group)
  (Contour lines indicate calculated probabilities that raw clays belong to the pottery compositional groups.)

Figure 5.11. Contour maps with elevations representing the probability that raw clay analyses belong to the Late Classic nonwhite eastern group (top) or the Late Classic nonwhite western group (bottom). Probabilities of membership based on thirty-two elements (listed in Table 5.1). Plotted points indicate calculated provenances for all speciments in each group.

ing in this case, with only a few calculated provenances falling below the 5 percent probability contour. Compared with the TF/EC western group, a larger area lies above the 5 percent probability contour, and individual calculated provenances are spread over a wider area west of the Coyolate River. A broader range of raw material sources thus seems to be represented in the Late Classic western group than in the earlier western group.

A heterogeneous subset of Late Classic analyses is labeled "anomalous" (Fig. 5.10). Specimens in the group are spread across a range of values on principal component 1 and plot toward the low end of component 4. A distinguishing feature of specimens in this group is high manganese concentrations, which accounts for the low scores on component 4. High manganese was encountered in some deeply buried clays in the sedimentary zone lying just inland from the beach, so it is possible that these specimens are the result of low-frequency use of such clays, perhaps by potters in a number of locations along the coast. Although a specific source zone cannot be identified for this group, its distinctive compositional profile offers further evidence of ceramic resource use diversification between Early Classic and Late Classic times.

The most obviously innovative ceramic resource procurement pattern in the Late Classic sample, however, is associated with Tiquisate White ware vessels. Like the main eastern and western groups, the Tiquisate White ware group shows a tendency to subdivide into two overlapping subgroups, which are differentiated by symbols in Figure 5.10. As a whole, Tiquisate White ware is quite divergent from other clays and pottery from the study area, so much so that the majority of specimens lie outside the 90 percent confidence level for all coastal clays on the third largest dimension of variance in the clay data (Fig. 5.12). The distinctiveness of the Tiquisate White ware composition compared to other clays and pottery is even more marked on a bivariate tantalum-scandium plot (Fig. 5.13).

The two subgroups of Tiquisate White ware, designated Tiquisate White ware 1 (TiqWW1) and Tiquisate White ware 2 (TiqWW2), have distinct nonplastic inclusions in the paste that are observable under low-power magnification. While TiqWW1 specimens have a dense paste with very sparse nonplastic grains, TiqWW2 has a noticeably larger and more variable nonplastic component. In thin section, the sparse inclusions in TiqWW1 turn out to be mainly quartz, plagioclase feldspar, mica, and volcanic glass shards. The dark particles in TiqWW2 pastes include dark mineral grains along with rounded volcanic rock fragments incorporating plagioclase feldspar. Free grains of feldspar are also more common in TiqWW2, and a number of examples have abundant volcanic glass and pumice that appear to have been added as temper. The majority of examples of both pastes are light-colored and refire to a buff color, but TiqWW2 includes a few reddish examples. Chemically, the abundant nonplastics in the paste of TiqWW2 contribute larger amounts of sodium and calcium (Fig. 5.14), which slightly

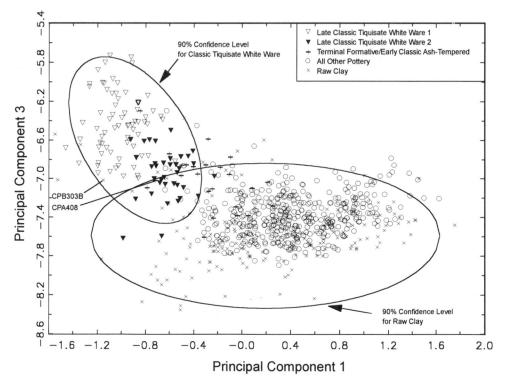

Figure 5.12. Plot of scores for all serving vessels and raw clay on principal components 1 and 3 of the raw clay data with Late Classic Tiquisate White ware and other ash-tempered analyses differentiated by symbols.

dilute concentrations of other elements (e.g., Fig. 5.13). The two pastes clearly form a single continuum of elemental concentrations (Figs. 5.10, 5.12, 5.13, and 5.14) and cannot be separated consistently with multivariate probabilistic statistics. Consistent differentiation can, however, be achieved with the combination of low-power microscopic examination and chemistry.

Tiquisate White ware analyses fall at the extreme low end of principal component 1 (Figs. 5.10 and 5.12), implying a source in the western part of the study area. Although no likely Tiquisate White ware source clays were located during the original 1990 ceramic raw materials survey, an additional targeted survey in February 1992 located a clay deposit at 79 north 69 east that is macroscopically indistinguishable from TiqWW1 pastes. The deposit is a residual clay developing on one of the geologically recent rhyolitic volcanic ash flows that jut out onto the upper part of the coastal plain just northeast of the Late Classic archaeological site of El Arisco (77 north 68 east; see Fig. 5.6). Figures 5.12 and 5.13 show that a bulk analysis of this clay, CPB303B, falls within the range of Tiquisate ware variation on several key dimensions. CPB303B also shows a 33.7 percent probability of membership in the aggregated Tiquisate White ware group and 45.7 percent probability of membership in the more restricted TiqWW1 group; since none of the other 161 clay analyses have greater than 0.4 percent probability of membership in the aggregated group or greater than 0.3 percent probability of membership in the more restricted group, and the vast majority have below .0005 percent probability of membership in both groups, this is the only possible candidate for a source of TiqWW1 clay so far located within the study area. These clay probability data are depicted graphically in Figure 5.15 (peak probabilities at 79 north 69 east are not as high as reported above because a weighted average of the ten nearest points is used to calculate grid corner elevations on the probability surfaces).

Individual calculated provenances for the TiqWW1 group shown in Figure 5.15 clearly identify the northwestern corner of the study area as the only possi-

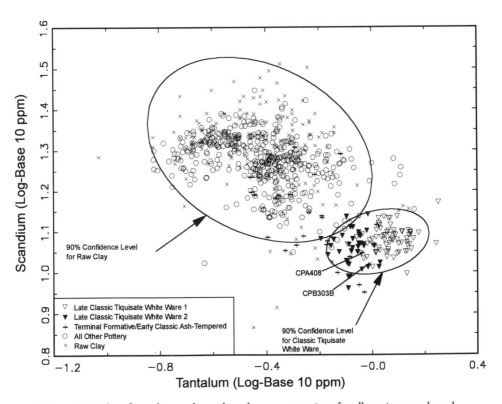

Figure 5.13. Plot of tantalum and scandium log-concentrations for all serving vessels and raw clay with Late Classic Tiquisate White ware and other ash-tempered analyses differentiated by symbols.

ble source zone. (A number of calculated provenances are off the map toward the west.) Dispersal of the calculated provenances toward the north and west from El Arisco reflects chemical variation in the El Arisco source (the basis for calculating provenance coordinates) coupled with the low intensity of raw material sampling in this area (see Fig. 5.1). The alternative approach to individual specimen provenance determination clearly identifies the El Arisco source as the only possible origin of TiqWW1 specimens. The exact extent of the El Arisco source itself remains to be determined. In any case, however, since 100 percent of the analyses from El Arisco have a TiqWW1 compositional profile, there seems little doubt that El Arisco was an important center of Tiquisate White ware production and that the source zone for TiqWW1 lies in the northwestern corner of the study area.

The TiqWW2 group also appears to come from the western part of the study area, but a source zone on the coastal plain south of the TiqWW1 source at El Arisco is suggested by the individual calculated provenances in Figure 5.15. The alternate approach to individual specimen sourcing yields a somewhat different

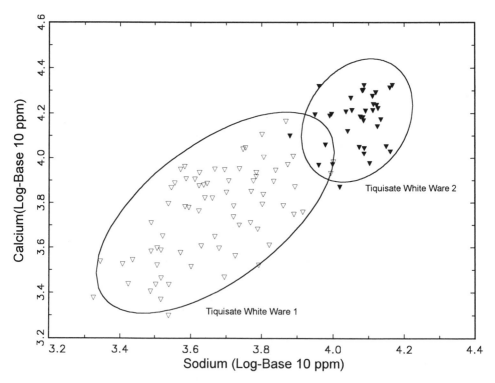

Figure 5.14. Plot of sodium and calcium log-concentrates for two subgroups of Late Classic Tiquisate White ware. Ellipses represent 90 percent confidence level for membership in the two subgroups.

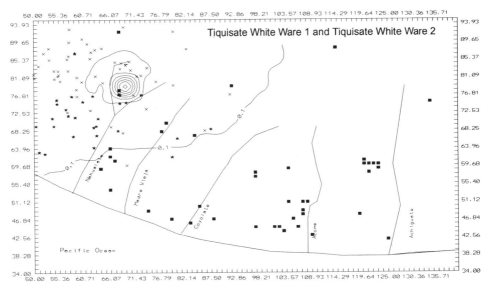

Figure 5.15. Contour map with elevations representing the probability that raw clay analyses belong to the Late Classic Tisquisate White ware group (combined TiqWW1 and TiqWW2). Probabilities of membership based on thirty-two elements (listed in Table 5.1). Plotted points indicate calculated provenances for TiqWWI and TiqWW2.

picture: most peak probabilities are on the piedmont along the Madre Vieja River, with secondary high probability zones sometimes appearing downstream along the Madre Vieja and Nahualate. A dual affiliation with piedmont residual clays and downstream sedimentary clays is consistent with the nonplastic constituents in TiqWW2 specimens: the presence of volcanic sand and silt in many specimens indicates sedimentary derivation, and the common presence of added volcanic ash temper provides a link with volcanic ash deposits on the piedmont. The group also includes some specimens with textures and nonplastic constituents similar to the residual clays encountered on the piedmont and more widely on the coastal plain west of the Nahualate River, where most of the calculated provenances cluster (see Figs. 5.1 and 5.15). In short, the compositional characteristics of TiqWW2 seem to be imparted by volcanic ash temper and/or ash-derived residual clay, both of which are available in a number of locations in the western half of the study area.

The association between Tiquisate White ware and volcanic ash-derived clays suggests a possible compositional link with earlier ash-tempered serving vessels of the TF/EC period, a link suggested also by the overlap in zones identified as likely to contain sources of both TiqWW2 and earlier ash-tempered serving vessels (compare calculated provenances in Figs. 5.9 and 5.15). When earlier ash-tempered serving vessels are projected against the Tiquisate White ware groups, three specimens stand out as most compositionally similar. All are from sites located along the lower reaches of the Nahualate River, and all are bichrome orange ware bowls. One red-on-cream bowl matches the aggregated Tiquisate White ware group at a probability level of 24 percent (all others are far below 1 percent). The same vessel matches the TiqWW2 at a level of 93 percent but fails to provide a convincing match for TiqWW1. One Usulutan (wavy-line resist) bowl and one red-on-orange bowl, both from sites west of the Madre Vieja River, also show greater than 60 percent probability of matching TiqWW2. Thus, ceramic resource and paste preparation practices consistent with production of Tiquisate White ware were practiced in low frequency in the western part of the study area before the Middle–Late Classic appearance of Tiquisate White ware, although the specific clay source near El Arisco used for the most distinctive of these vessels cannot yet be documented.

Diversification of Serving-Vessel Production During the Classic Period

The compositional data just presented fit a model of diversification in serving-vessel production. Ceramic resource procurement and paste preparation practices that were followed during Terminal Formative and Early Classic times yielded serving-vessel compositions that subdivide into four chemical groups. Three of these groups can be linked to argillaceous sediments sampled during our raw materials survey. The fourth TF/EC group, which is relatively small, results from low-frequency procurement of primary clays developing on volcanic ash and/or addition of vitric volcanic ash to sedimentary clays.

Use of sedimentary clays continued into the Late Classic period, although the two major compositional profiles (eastern and western) are linked to a broader range of clays than the earlier groups, suggesting expansion of serving-vessel production throughout the study area. This pattern might be due partly to the larger number of sites represented in the Late Classic sample, but the fact that there is a much larger number of Late Classic sites than earlier sites (Bove 1989; Shook 1965) would lead one to expect serving-vessel production to have taken place at a larger number of locations; an expanding population during the Classic period provides the ecological context for diversification, as discussed in the following section.

The most obvious shift in the serving-vessel tradition that occurred during the

Classic period is that paste preparation involving volcanic ash or ash-derived clays became much more frequent. Part of the continuum of Late Classic ash-related compositions (represented by TiqWW2) overlaps with earlier ash-tempered compositions from the western part of the study area. Expanded use of ash or ash-derived clays is expressed most clearly in the appearance of a visually and chemically distinct paste represented by the TiqWW1 group. The source of clay for vessels with this paste was not exploited prior to the appearance of Tiquisate White ware. This result is clearly not due to sampling of a larger number of Late Classic sites, since vessels of TiqWW1 composition occur at nearly all sites west of the Acomé River. Because vessels in this compositional group manifest the same range of forms, surface treatment, and decoration as vessels in other Late Classic compositional groups, they are clearly part of the serving-vessel tradition traceable to Late Formative times. (The definitive Tiquisate cream slip is present in all compositional groups.) However, based on the distinctive visual and compositional properties of TiqWW1 pastes combined with the restricted occurrence of suitable raw materials, TiqWW1 vessels may be considered to represent a new branch of the local serving-vessel tradition. Recovery of clays compositionally indistinguishable from TiqWW1 near the site of El Arisco demonstrates that this branch of the serving-vessel tradition differentiated within the northwestern part of the study area.

The Ecological Basis of Diversification of Serving-Vessel Production

Consumption of serving vessels derived from different production zones left a record of varying compositional diversity in the excavated assemblages from the Guatemalan central Pacific coast. As argued previously, variation in assemblage compositional diversity monitors variation in opportunities for making a living through pottery production, opportunities that were created by ecological circumstances at particular places during the times over which the assemblages accumulated.

Assemblage Compositional Diversity

The calculated provenances for individual analyzed specimens afford one means of examining serving-vessel consumption patterns. Plotting calculated provenances for all analyses from a particular site or zone (regardless of compositional group affiliation) provides an indication of how widespread were the production centers supplying that site or zone.

Distortions in calculated provenance are, of course, inevitable, given that raw material sampling is uneven and inadequate in some areas (especially the edges of the study area) and that additional compositional variation is introduced by tempering and other paste preparation practices. Even for the raw clays them-selves, which were unaltered by paste preparation, the average deviation between true and calculated provenances was 13.5 km. Taking this as a minimum estimate of the error expected in calculating pottery provenances, the approach would ap-pear best suited for revealing general differences between relatively large geo-graphic units. Even more worrisome, although there is no directional bias in the raw clay deviations, paste preparation might introduce a systematic directional bias into the calculated provenances for pottery. On the positive side, examining consumption patterns in this way is completely independent of the extensionally defined pottery source groups and thus is unaffected by any mistakes in group assignment.

Calculated provenances for the total TF/EC serving-vessel sample lie predomi-nantly west of the Coyolate River (Fig. 5.16). For sites located east of the Coyolate (Fig. 5.16, top), this implies a tendency to have looked west for sources of serving vessels; sites located east of the Acomé River apparently imported a large propor-tion of serving vessels from production centers located farther west. Sites in the western zone (west of the Madre Vieja), in contrast, appear to have derived almost all serving vessels from local production centers lying along the Nahualate (Fig. 5.16, bottom). Aside from the specific inference about directionality of exchange relations of eastern sites, the data presented in Figure 5.16 suggest that eastern zone sites (Fig. 5.16, top) consumed vessels made over a broader area of the coastal plain than sites located west of the Coyolate (Fig. 5.16, bottom).

Unfortunately, there is probably some westward bias in the data displayed in Figure 5.16 (top). For example, many of the eastern group vessels have calculated provenances west of the Coyolate (Fig. 5.8, top), but both the group sourcing ap-proach and the alternate individual sourcing approach suggest that virtually all vessels in this group originated east of the Coyolate. Thus, many of the prove-nances lying west of the Coyolate in Figure 5.16 (top) may in fact have originated farther east, and the apparent magnitude of west-east vessel movement may be substantially inflated.

Variation in assemblage compositional diversity can also be examined by map-ping variation in the frequencies of source-related compositional groups. A con-venient way to map assemblage compositional diversity is with pie charts, which express richness by the number of different slices and evenness by the relative sizes of the slices. This approach circumvents the possible problem of paste preparation-induced directional bias in the calculated provenances. On the other hand, an approach relying on group frequencies suffers from the possibility of fre-quency distortion due to group misassignments and uncertainty in geographic at-tribution of the source groups. The primary concern here is whether the pattern suggested by the group frequency data reinforces or contradicts the pattern sug-gested by the individual calculated provenances.

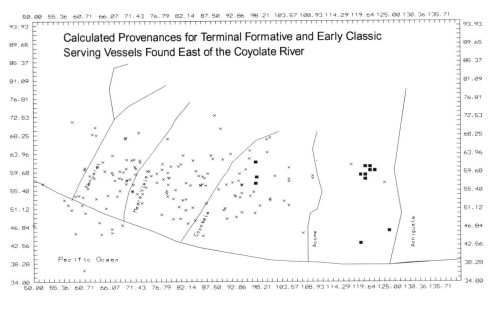

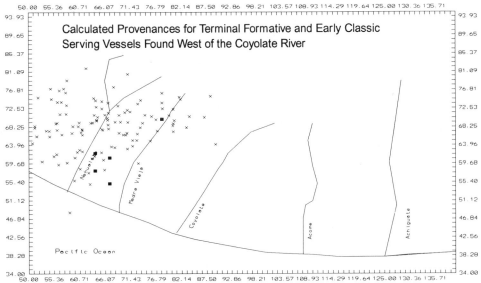

- ■ Terminal Formative—Early Classic Archaeological Sites in the
  Eastern Zone (Top) or Western Zone (Bottom) Sample
- × Calculated Provenance for Terminal Formative—Early Classic Serving Vessel

Figure 5.16. Calculated provenances for all Terminal Formative–Early Classic vessels
found east of the Coyolate River (top) and west of the Coyolate River (bottom).

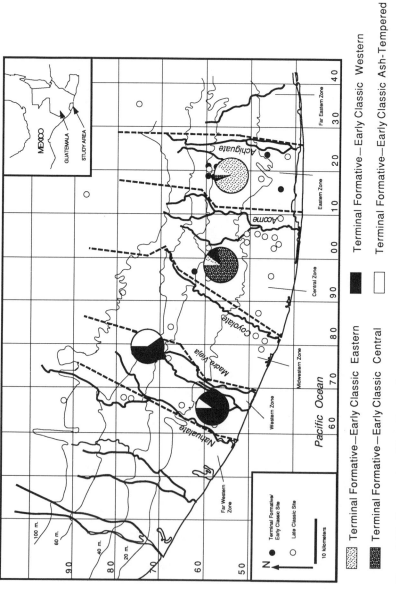

Figure 5.17. Frequencies of four Terminal Formative–Early Classic serving-vessel compositional groups in four site clusters (the northwestern cluster consists of a single site, La Noria).

Terminal Formative–Early Classic Eastern

Terminal Formative–Early Classic Central

Terminal Formative–Early Classic Western

Terminal Formative–Early Classic Ash-Tempered

The analyzed TF/EC pottery comes from sites falling into four geographic clusters (Fig. 5.17). With the possible exception of the northwestern cluster, compositional evenness in all site clusters can be characterized as low, in that the analyzed pottery tends to be dominated by a single compositional group with minor representation of other groups. The central and eastern clusters are richer than the two western clusters, apparently as a result of movement of western group pots eastward combined with some movement of pots back and forth between the central and eastern zones. The ash-tempered group makes up a minor proportion of the analyzed specimens from each geographic cluster, possibly indicating low-frequency local production and distribution of ash-tempered specimens in several zones. Evenness in the northwestern cluster appears greater than in other zones, but this probably results from inadequate sampling, with only five specimens from a single site making up the total analyzed collection from this cluster. Of the well-sampled geographic clusters, the central zone cluster is highest in both richness and evenness, although the eastern cluster is equally rich and only slightly less even. The group frequency data thus identify the central and eastern zones as regions of greatest opportunity for potters during TF/EC times. Furthermore, although the calculated provenances (Fig. 5.16) may inflate the magnitude of west-east vessel movement, the existence of such a pattern is clearly reinforced by the group frequencies data.

Calculated provenances for Late Classic serving vessels found east of the Coyolate River are distributed widely across the study area, from east of the Achiguate River to west of the Nahualate River (Fig. 5.18, top). The lower coastal region lying east of the Acomé River may have seen its first substantial serving-vessel production after the Early Classic period, since calculated provenances in this area, which are fairly numerous in the Late Classic sample, are virtually absent in the TF/EC sample (Figs. 5.8, 5.9, and 5.16). Still, the bulk of individual serving vessels at eastern sites appears to have originated west of the Coyolate; moreover, as discussed previously with respect to the Late Classic eastern compositional group, the alternate approach to individual specimen sourcing does not contradict this conclusion. Judging from the greater dispersion of calculated provenances west of the Coyolate, the western production centers supplying eastern sites must have proliferated between Early Classic and Late Classic times (compare Figs. 5.16, top, and 5.18, top). Initiation of Tiquisate White ware production focused on volcanic ash-derived raw material accounts for part of this difference, but a larger number of production centers is also suggested for the nonash tempered western group (note the relatively broad area above the 5 percent contour in Fig. 5.11, bottom). In short, Late Classic people at sites located east of the Coyolate consumed compositionally diverse serving vessels produced at many locations scattered throughout the study area.

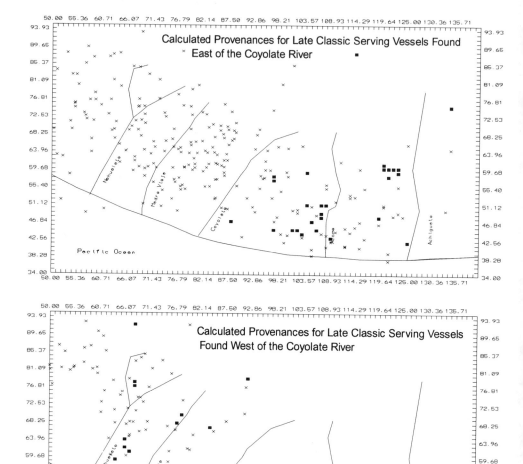

- Middle - Late Classic Archaeological Sites in the
  Eastern Zone (Top) or Western Zone (Bottom) Sample
× Calculated Provenance for Late Classic Serving Vessel

Figure 5.18. Calculated provenances for all Late Classic vessels found east of the Coyolate River (top) and west of the Coyolate River (bottom).

In marked contrast, Late Classic serving vessels found west of the Coyolate are linked almost exclusively to local raw material sources (Fig. 5.18, bottom). Most calculated provenances lie along the Nahualate River, with those in the northwestern quadrant indicating calculated provenances for Tiquisate White ware. (Some calculated provenances are off the map to the west.) The calculated provenances thus indicate that Late Classic people at sites lying west of the Coyolate River consumed locally produced serving vessels and had virtually no access to the output of centers located east of the Coyolate.

The Late Classic group frequencies (Fig. 5.19) reinforce and augment the apparent contrasts evident in the calculated provenance data. Site clusters in the Late Classic sample parallel the four TF/EC clusters but with additional clusters in the extreme northwestern corner of the study area, near the coast just west of the Coyolate River, and at the north-central site of El Castillo.

Considerably more variation in evenness from place to place is evident in the Late Classic group frequencies than in the earlier sample. One extreme is represented by the far northwestern cluster, where all analyzed specimens (a total of twenty-two from two sites) pertain to a single compositional group, the TiqWW1 group. (This is partly an artifact of sampling, since only Tiquisate ware was sampled from these two sites.) The near-coast western zone sample is richer than before, with four out of five compositional groups represented; evenness remains low, however, since two groups, both locally made in the western zone, dominate the assemblages. Both richness and evenness are very low in the eastern zone, where only two groups are represented, and one of these (the eastern nonwhite group) accounts for the vast majority of specimens. The two midwestern clusters are also relatively rich, with four of five compositional groups represented in both; of these clusters, the inland (northwestern) is the more even, although this difference may reflect the small sample sizes in both clusters. Evenness is high at El Castillo, where two compositional groups making up over half the assemblage (TiqWW1 and western nonwhite) originate some distance west and south of the site. Both richness and evenness reach a distinct maximum along the lower reaches of the Acomé River; the eastern and anomalous nonwhite groups, which may originate not too far from these sites, make up less than half the total, while the remainder of specimens in these assemblages pertain to three compositional groups that originate west of the Coyolate River.

In summary, the Late Classic serving-vessel consumption data demonstrate that the earlier west-to-east flow of serving vessels continued and intensified during the Late Classic period. Compositional diversity reaches a peak along the lower reaches of the Acomé River, reflecting the diverse origins of vessels consumed in this area. In marked contrast, Late Classic assemblages from the far northwestern and western zones of the study area are dominated by a few locally originating groups (only one in the case of the far northwestern zone, Fig. 5.19).

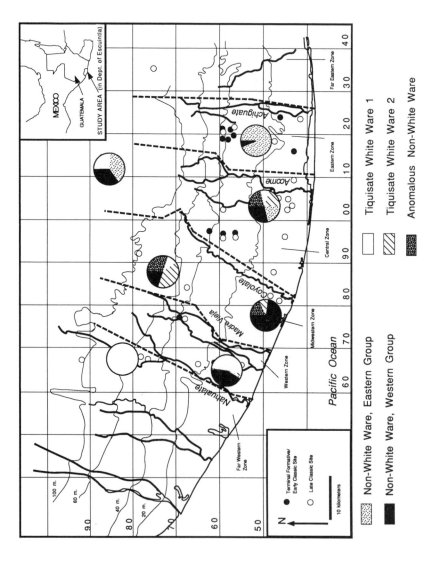

Figure 5.19. Frequencies of five Late Classic serving-vessel compositional groups in seven site clusters (the north-central cluster consists of a single site, El Castillo).

Selective Pressures That Shaped the Serving-Vessel Tradition

The contrasts in compositional diversity between TF/EC assemblages and Late Classic assemblages provide a partial description of the selective environment that shaped serving-vessel production. Certain parts of the study area created richer opportunities for potters than others, and opportunities varied through time. Judging by the group-frequency data (Figs. 5.17 and 5.19), TF/EC compositional diversity is comparatively low in all zones, indicating that local consumption furnished the major source of opportunity for potters. In the Late Classic analyzed sample the contrast between high diversity zones and low diversity zones is much more dramatic, suggesting expanded opportunities for potters available through nonlocal consumption of their products. Thus, for example, vessels in the TiqWW1 group, which were produced in the far northwestern part of the study area, make up a sizable proportion of assemblages at least as far east as the Acomé River, while western nonwhite, which also originated west of the Coyolate River, is found in high proportions in assemblages along the lower Acomé River and at the piedmont site of El Castillo.

Based on the individual calculated provenances (Figs. 5.16 and 5.18), people living east of the Coyolate River tended to import serving vessels from the west during both TF/EC and Late Classic times (although the flow seems to be inflated in the TF/EC data). The group frequencies data (Figs. 5.17 and 5.19) suggest that sites in the central zone, between the Coyolate and Acomé rivers, were the biggest consumers of nonlocal vessels during both time periods. These geographic contrasts in serving-vessel consumption may be related to the widespread, highly productive sandy loam soils of the central zone (Simmons et al. 1959), which would have favored an emphasis on agricultural production at the expense of other activities, such as pottery making. Not only would the zone's inhabitants have concentrated on agriculture rather than other pursuits, but the very high population densities made possible by high agricultural productivity would have enhanced the zone's role as a net consumer of many goods, including pottery. Judging from the extreme density of Late Classic remains within the central zone (Bove, personal communication, 1992), population must have peaked during the Late Classic period, at the same time that serving-vessel compositional diversity reached a maximum.

I argue that the ecological conditions just described, which are inferred largely from assemblage compositional diversity data, helped bring about evolutionary diversification within the coastal Guatemalan serving-vessel tradition. A growing population of nonpotters, particularly in the central zone, opened up new opportunities for the expression of pottery-making phenotypes in other zones, where conditions were particularly favorable for exploiting these new opportunities. Potters in some zones were well situated to exploit the expanded opportunities simply because of proximity to the zones of high opportunity. For example, the calculated provenance data (Fig. 5.11) suggest that serving-vessel production was either initiated or greatly expanded during the Middle–Late Classic period on the lower coast just east of the Acomé River, adjacent to a major zone of Late Classic population concentration just west of the river.

Expanded opportunities for potters drove diversification of serving-vessel production elsewhere on the coastal plain as well. In the northwestern part of the study area, special raw materials became the focus of exploitation by potters who made what we recognize today as Tiquisate White ware. The general compositional pattern associated with exploitation of volcanic ash-derived clays of the western zone was present in low frequency during TF/EC times. However, selection associated with population growth and variation in agricultural productivity favored a dramatic expansion of this resource procurement pattern by Middle–Late Classic times. That Tiquisate White ware potters were exploiting nonlocal demand for pottery is manifest in the widespread distribution of TiqWW1 and TiqWW2 compositional profiles (Fig. 5.19).

In short, a ramifying, selection-driven historical process underlies the observed patterning in the ceramic compositional data. Of course, there is more to coastal Guatemalan serving-vessel evolution than this. For one thing, we need to identify the precise local conditions that favored increased reliance on serving-vessel production among potters who produced the new Tiquisate White ware pastes. Precise identification of the source materials constitutes a major step in this direction. It seems likely that the relevant conditions included the firing properties of the El Arisco clay, which yielded light-colored, very fine, durable vessels that must have been comparatively easy to transport. In this and other respects, Tiquisate ware evolution seems to parallel the evolution of Plumbate pottery, which took place 100 or so kilometers west of Escuintla over approximately the same span of time (Neff 1984; Neff and Bishop 1988). Common features of the selective environments in the two cases would be illuminated through detailed comparative study of the two archaeological sequences. Interestingly enough, the low frequency but widespread occurrence of Plumbate within the region discussed here indicates that Plumbate potters also exploited opportunities for serving-vessel producers that were created by the ecological conditions of the central Guatemalan Pacific coast.

Conclusion

The foregoing presentation is intended not as a definitive account of serving-vessel evolution on the Guatemalan coast but as an illustration of the potential contributions of compositional analysis to evolutionary archaeology. The fundamental tenet of evolutionary archaeology is that the archaeological record was created by a process whereby variation in inherited instructions for creating human phenotypes was differentially perpetuated through history. This formulation requires us to pay equal attention to what Eldredge (1985) calls genealogy and ecology. Ceramic compositional data pertain to genealogical issues, since they demonstrate continuity and diversification within ceramic traditions, but also to ecological issues, since they show how pottery consumption created selective pressures that favored success of certain phenotypic expressions rather than others.

Acknowledgments

The National Science Foundation supported both fieldwork and analytical work on this project (BNS89-11580, BNS88-01707, and BNS91-02016).

A compositional approach to pottery of the Guatemalan central Pacific coast is the brainchild of Frederick J. Bove, who began sampling pottery for analysis in 1981. To my good fortune, Fred took me on as a collaborator in 1987. Our subsequent ceramic raw materials survey and sampling of Late Formative–Late Classic pottery provided the data on which this paper is based. It would have been impossible for me to write this chapter without Fred's guidance, help, and encouragement over the past six years.

I wish to thank numerous other individuals who contributed time and expertise to the research on which this paper is based. I am especially fortunate to have had the collaboration of three experts in neutron activation analysis: Ronald L. Bishop, Michael D. Glascock, and M. James Blackman. Brenda Lou worked tirelessly directing the laboratory work in Guatemala and participated in all phases of field investigations. Barbara Arroyo, Jim Cogswell, Sindy Hays, Carlos Herman, Enrique Linares, Sara Meadors, Sonia Medrano, Sergio Rodas, and Claudia Wolley provided invaluable assistance in the field and laboratory analysis phases of the project as well. Fraser Neiman provided detailed and helpful suggestions on aspects of the statistical analysis. Finally, I thank Patrice Teltser for inviting my participation in the 1992 SAA symposium at which a preliminary version of this paper was presented, and for encouraging me to complete a final version for publication.

Notes

1. "Provenance" is used here as a synonym for "source," while the alternative spelling, "provenience," is used to refer to the location where an artifact was found archaeologically.

2. Discussion of the sourcing results is illustrated in the following sections by projecting the pottery data into the principal component space defined by the clay analyses. The principal components derived from raw material analyses describe compositional variation on a regional level. Compositional groups identified among the pottery analyses are assumed to represent intensive sampling (by ancient potters) of more restricted ceramic resource zones within this region, and there is no reason to expect the pottery compositional

groups to be elongated along axes parallel to the principal components of the raw clay data (i.e., they need not have the same variance-covariance structure). Nevertheless, with the exception of one compositional group derived from a localized, compositionally unique clay source (Tiquisate White ware 1), all the compositional groups discussed in this chapter fall completely within the range of variation of the raw clay data; this is true whether one looks at elemental concentrations or principal component scores.

3. Whenever possible, probabilities are calculated from the thirty-two available elemental concentrations. When small group size (and resulting singularity of the group variance-covariance matrix) precludes this approach, dimensionality is reduced by calculating probabilities from scores on the first eight principal components of the raw clay data.

4. Because of the small size of the TF/EC ash-tempered group, membership probabilities for the clays had to be calculated from scores on the first eight principal components of the clay data rather than elemental concentrations. (These components represent more than 90 percent of the variance in the clay data, as shown in Table 5.1.) Still, the small size and heterogeneity of the group contribute toward inflated probability estimates when probabilities are based on the sample size corrected Hotelling's T^2.

References

Arnold, D. E.

1985   *Ceramic Theory and Cultural Process.* Cambridge University Press, Cambridge, England.

Arnold, D. E., H. Neff, and R. L. Bishop

1991   Compositional Analysis and "Sources" of Pottery: An Ethnoarchaeological Approach. *American Anthropologist* 93:70–90.

Arroyo, B.

1991   *Informe preliminar del proyecto Tecojate.* Unpublished preliminary report submitted to the Institute of Anthropology and History, Guatemala.

1992   *Proyecto Tecojate: Informe preliminar de la segunda temporada.* Unpublished preliminary report submitted to the Institute of Anthropology and History, Guatemala.

Bieber, A. M., Jr., D. W. Brooks, G. Harbottle, and E. V. Sayre

1976   Application of Multivariate Techniques to Analytical Data on Aegean Ceramics. *Archaeometry* 18:59–74.

Bishop, R. L., and H. Neff

1989   Multivariate Analysis of Compositional Data in Archaeology. *Archaeological Chemistry IV,* edited by R. O. Allen, pp. 576–586. Advances in Chemistry Series 220, American Chemical Society, Washington, D.C.

Bishop, R. L., R. L. Rands, and G. R. Holley

1982   Ceramic Compositional Analysis in Archaeological Perspective. In *Advances in Archaeological Method and Theory,* vol. 5, edited by M. B. Schiffer, pp. 275–330. Academic Press, New York.

Bobrowsky, P. T., and B. F. Ball
1989   The Theory and Mechanics of Ecological Diversity in Archaeology. In *Quantifying Diversity in Archaeology,* edited by R. D. Leonard and G. T. Jones, pp. 4–12. Cambridge University Press, New York.

Bove, F. J.
1989   Reporte Preliminar de las Investigaciones en las Regiones de Tiquisate y La Gomera/Sipacate, Costa Sur de Guatemala. In *Investigaciones Arqueologicas en la Costa Sur de Guatemala,* edited by D. S. Whitley and M. P. Beaudry, pp. 38–81. UCLA Institute of Archaeology, Monograph 31, Los Angeles.

Bove, F. J., H. Neff, B. Lou, and S. Medrano
1992   Terminal Formative and Early Classic Ceramic Traditions of Pacific Coastal Guatemala. In *Chemical Characterization of Ceramic Pastes in Archaeology,* edited by H. Neff, pp. 189–202. Prehistory Press, Madison.

Dunnell, R. C.
1971   *Systematics in Prehistory.* Free Press, New York.
1980   Evolutionary Theory and Archaeology. In *Advances in Archaeological Method and Theory,* vol. 3, edited by M. B. Schiffer, pp. 35–99. Academic Press, New York.

Eldredge, N.
1985   *Unfinished Synthesis.* Oxford University Press, Oxford.

Harbottle, G.
1976   Activation Analysis in Archaeology. In *Radiochemistry,* vol. 3, edited by G.W.A. Newton, pp. 33–72. The Chemical Society, London.

Hatch, M. P. de
1989   Observaciones sobre el desarollo cultural prehistórico en la costa sur de Guatemala. In *Investigaciones Arqueológicos en la costa sur de Guatemala,* edited by D. S. Whitley and M. P. Beaudry, pp. 38–81. UCLA Institute of Archaeology, Monograph 31, Los Angeles.

Jones, G. T., and R. D. Leonard
1989   The Concept of Diversity: An Introduction. In *Quantifying Diversity in Archaeology,* edited by R. D. Leonard and G. T. Jones, pp. 1–3. Cambridge University Press, New York.

Kintigh, K. W.
1984   Measuring Archaeological Diversity by Comparison with Simulated Assemblages. *American Antiquity* 49:44–54.
1989   Sample Size, Significance, and Measures of Diversity. In *Quantifying Diversity in Archaeology,* edited by R. D. Leonard and G. T. Jones, pp. 25–36. Cambridge University Press, New York.

Meggers, B. J., C. Evans, and E. Estrada
1965   *Early Formative Period of Coastal Ecuador: The Valdivia and Machalilla Phases.* Smithsonian Contributions to Anthropology, vol. 1. Smithsonian Institution, Washington, D.C.

Neff, H.

1984   *Developmental History of the Plumbate Pottery Industry in the Eastern Soconusco Region, A.D. 600 through A.D. 1250.* Unpublished Ph.D. dissertation, University of California, Santa Barbara.

1992   Ceramics and Evolution. In *Archaeological Method and Theory,* vol. 4, edited by M. B. Schiffer, pp. 141–193. University of Arizona Press, Tucson.

1993   Theory, Sampling, and Technical Studies in Archaeological Ceramic Analysis. *American Antiquity* 58:23–44.

Neff, H., and R. L. Bishop

1988   Plumbate Origins and Development. *American Antiquity* 53:505–522.

Neff, H., R. L. Bishop, and F. J. Bove

1989   Compositional Patterning in Ceramics from Pacific Coastal and Highland Guatemala. *Archeomaterials* 3:97–109.

Neff, H., F. J. Bove, B. L. Lou P., and M. F. Piechowski

1992   Ceramic Raw Materials Survey in Pacific Coastal Guatemala. In *Chemical Characterization of Ceramic Pastes in Archaeology,* edited by H. Neff, pp. 59–84. Prehistory Press, Madison.

Parsons, L. A.

1967   *Bilbao, Guatemala: An Archaeological Study of the Pacific Coast Cotzumalguapa Region,* vol. 1. Milwaukee Public Museum, Publications in Anthropology, 11.

Rindos, D.

1989   Diversity, Variation, and Selection. In *Quantifying Diversity in Archaeology,* edited by R. D. Leonard and G. T. Jones, pp. 13–23. Cambridge University Press, New York.

Simmons, C. S., J. M. Torono T., and J. H. Pinto Z.

1959   *Clasificación de Reconocimiento de los Suelos de la República de Guatemala.* Instituto Agropecuaria Nacional, Guatemala City.

Shook, E. M.

1965   Archaeological Survey of the Pacific Coast of Guatemala. In *Handbook of Middle American Indians,* vol. 2, edited by G. R. Willey, pp. 180–194. University of Texas Press, Austin.

6

The Use of Comparative and Engineering Analyses in the Study of Prehistoric Agriculture

Timothy D. Maxwell

◆◆ The study of the historical record of a trait is often believed necessary for determining the effects of natural selection and resulting adaptations (O'Brien and Holland 1992). Although an understanding of patterns of succession and of persistence of varying traits assists in the recognition of adaptation, archaeologists frequently encounter situations where study of the frequency distribution of traits through time is not possible. This poses a dilemma for those presuming that the identification of adaptation requires examination of a trait's history. As argued below, other methods for determining when natural selection and adaptation have occurred can be used productively.

Today, archaeologists have varied notions of what constitutes an adaptation. In their evaluations of the concept of adaptation in archaeology, several authors discuss the contrast between use of the term in archaeological and biological studies (Dunnell 1980; Leonard and Jones 1987; O'Brien and Holland 1992; Rindos 1984). They point out that in most current archaeological research, adaptation is perceived as a problem-solving mechanism that results in some form of transformation within the archaeological culture under study. In other words, populations are seen to respond to changes, usually environmental, through adaptation to a new set of conditions. In this view, adaptation is implied through the addition of new and better techniques, or the modification or subtraction of existing ones, for contending with changed conditions. These responses are seen as important transformations in the evolutionary sequence of the archaeological culture. The continued presence of the new transformational state is offered as vindication that an adaptation has been identified.

In contrast, biological studies of adaptation conventionally assume that traits are adaptations only if they have evolved because there was selection for organisms that carried the trait. Unlike the previous strategy, this strategy recognizes that new or modified traits can appear and persist for reasons other than adaptation. For archaeologists using approaches grounded in the evolutionary biological framework, commonly known as a selectionist perspective, the question of whether the appearance of a new trait is a problem-solving technique or not is ultimately immaterial. What matters is that subsequent selective agents will determine whether a new or modified trait becomes an adaptation. Additionally, variation in the expression of traits at any one time is to be expected, and it is possible that a particular trait or variant, which may be inconsequential at one moment, can provide increased benefits for its bearers as environmental conditions change through time. As a result, particular traits can be frequent but may not be adaptations. Unlike the previous approach, an additional methodological step is required before adaptation can be confirmed—determining exactly what selective conditions led to the persistence of a particular trait. The methodological value of this approach lies in the ability of other researchers to make independent evaluations of the postulated causes for adaptation.

To many archaeologists the difference between the two perspectives seems subtle, but it is not. For a more thorough discussion see Dunnell 1989; Leonard 1990; Leonard and Jones 1987; O'Brien and Holland 1989, 1992; Rindos 1984, 1989. Briefly though, in the first approach, adaptation is considered to be a process that allows humans to readjust to changes in the local environment. In some manner, populations amend their behavior or technology to track environmental or social change, and these transformations are thought to be synonymous with adaptation. That the long-term persistence of a given trait then represents adaptation is justified by the belief that Y replaced X because it was more adapted. Accepting this belief, however, creates a difficult situation for archaeologists wishing to provide rigorous explanation, for adaptation then becomes both mechanism and result. Any explanation must conflate the result with the mechanism, neglecting any clear intermediary link between cause and effect (Leonard and Abbott 1992). Therefore, no independent method exists for evaluating the resulting interpretation. Besides being tautological, this position can be justifiably criticized as "adaptationism," where one "assumes without further proof that all aspects of the morphology, physiology, and behavior of organisms are adaptive optimal solutions to problems" (Lewontin 1979:6).

In the selectionist viewpoint, the mechanism for achieving adaptation is distinctly viewed as natural selection, and adaptation is only one possible outcome that can result from the interplay between trait variation and changing conditions. The selectionist perspective, therefore, presumes that not all traits have the requisite history to be adaptations; in other words, the traits were not shaped by natural selection (Leonard and Reed 1993; O'Brien and Holland 1992:38). As in archaeology, recognition of an adaptation is a difficult problem for biologists. It is methodologically demanding to prove that a feature or trait is the direct result of natural selection—a problem that even Darwin encountered (Mayr 1988:137). The problem is compounded because a trait can contribute to adaptedness but not be under selective control (Lewontin 1978; O'Brien and Holland 1992:46). Here, adaptedness refers to the morphological, physiological, and behavioral equipment of a species that permits it to compete successfully with other species and to tolerate the extant physical environment (Mayr 1988:137). Lastly, a trait may be neutral, offering no gain in adaptedness, and may or may not be correlated with a trait that does. Despite these problems, the selectionist approach provides criteria for determining when an adaptation has occurred and those interpretive results can be evaluated by other researchers.

The difference between the two approaches illustrates that the concept of adaptation is generally not addressed in adequately disciplined fashion by archaeologists. For most archaeologists, adaptation is typically assumed when a transition to a new state of long-term structural or morphological change is discerned in the archaeological record—an assumption that makes easy demands on an incompletely applied theory of adaptation. If long-term persistence is the criterion for recognizing adaptation, it does not matter whether we use Lamarckian, Darwinian, or Cultural Evolutionary concepts for the causes of change. Using persistence as an axiomatic principle would lead to the same interpretive result. Such a research tactic is unlikely to lead to any advances in developing a general understanding of evolutionary change.

For most biologists, evolutionary biology may be conceived as having two major tasks: (1) determining the genetic and ecological mechanisms of evolutionary change, and (2) determining the actual history of evolution (Futuyma 1986: 286). The latter approach, or determining the actual history of species evolution, is largely the province of paleontology and biological systematics. This bipartite approach is believed necessary because so much of the understanding of species development rests on the ability to detect evolutionary history and an understanding of the methods by which the historical evolution of organisms can be inferred is important. Given this concern in biology, O'Brien and Holland (1992: 43) argue that archaeologists may have little or no hope of knowing whether they have identified adaptations unless the traits under study can be ordered chronologically.

Leonard and Jones (1987:213) also discuss the importance of constructing and chronologically ordering the distribution of traits for determining the effects of selection. The differential persistence through time of the traits selected for study leads to discernment of their replicative success (Leonard and Jones 1987:214). They argue that each trait has replicative success that may or may not affect the Darwinian fitness of its bearer. Success can then be gauged by frequency changes in the representation of traits through time. The trait can then be examined for links to selective agents that may be conditioning its diachronic frequency representation.

Archaeologists often confront a situation of inadequate chronological information when examining regional data. Small nonresidential sites, particularly lithic artifact scatters or farming features and facilities, may contain no datable materials. Also, it is not unusual for some regions to have a brief occupational history, perhaps limited to two or three hundred years. Given a situation where undatable sites are known to have occurred within a short time span, it may become impossible to determine the frequency distribution through time for a selected trait. Traits that appear to occur throughout the history of the region may have actually been limited to a period of much shorter duration. If migration into the region is suspected, examination of precursor traits might be useful in evaluating the historical or evolutionary trajectories of traits, but the geographical origins of migrant populations may be unknown or there may be competing candidate regions. Furthermore, as populations expand or migrate into new regions, no necessary continuity between new and previous behaviors exists (Rouse 1986).

This is a frustrating predicament for those requiring historical data for analyzing adaptation. One may suspect that a particular trait is an adaptation; however, without knowing the chronological framework for the appearance of the traits, diachronic approaches to the study of adaptation are inapplicable. Given the difficulties of constructing chronological sequences for trait distributions in these situations, how can one proceed? What necessary methodological procedures might be taken to isolate possible selective agents and assess the adaptive significance of a trait?

Two approaches can help solve this dilemma—engineering and comparative analyses. Used in combination, these analyses can help the archaeologist understand the prevalence and maintenance of traits, regardless of their histories. Engineering studies can be useful in determining whether a trait has served to improve adaptedness (Futuyma 1986; Lewontin 1978; O'Brien and Holland 1992; Rindos 1984; Sober 1984). Such analyses often can provide critical information on function. Demonstrating function can be difficult, but adaptation has been strongly implicated by the correspondence between the form of a structure and the design that an engineer might specify for a particular function (Gans 1974).

Secondly, the comparative method is often practical for gaining insights into selection and adaptation by correlating the differences and similarities among groups of organisms with environmental factors. Futuyma (1986:252–253) argues that the comparative method is most powerful when it draws upon patterns of convergent evolution for its inferences. For example, one might infer that leaflessness in plants is often an adaptation to xeric conditions because of the predominant lack of leaves in many unrelated desert plants (Futuyma 1986). The distinct advantage to this approach is that analysis of temporal patterning is unnecessary. Phylogenetic analysis, however, has proved a useful adjunct to comparative studies. In practice, biologists find it important to count the number of times a trait has independently arisen during phylogeny and to figure out if each of these evolutionary events occurred in a particular selective context (Clutton-Brock and Harvey 1984). Still, along with a consideration of functional design, the comparative method can yield predictions that constitute tests of hypotheses about adaptation.

A Case Study

The problem of inadequate chronological information is relevant to the lower Rio Chama region of northwestern New Mexico. The region contains several types of agricultural fields, including rock-bordered fields with and without rock mulch, checkdams, linear borders, reservoirs, rock piles, and floodwater fields (Anschuetz et al. 1986; Bandelier 1890–1892; Bugé 1984; Cordell et al. 1984; Hibben 1937; Lang 1980). One field type in particular, however, the gravel- or cobble-mulched field, occurs in a high frequency not found elsewhere in the Southwest. These fields are constructed by placing gravel, or a mix of gravel and cobbles, upon field plots. While little systematic surveying and recording has been performed, general aerial reconnaissance and the observations of several archaeologists suggest that cobble-mulched fields are the predominant type of field in the region. Systematic studies are just beginning (Anschuetz 1992; Lightfoot 1990; Maxwell and Anschuetz 1992), but the data already on hand indicate considerable variation in the structural design of this field type. The internal structure of the fields ranges from uniform, symmetrical compartments formed of regularly spaced rocks, to sinuous informal rock borders delineating rectilinear partitions, to unbordered gravel-covered plots. The fields are found in a variety of topographic settings. Most appear to be on terraces near permanent streams. Despite their ubiquity throughout the region, and due to the absence of chronometric samples, the fields cannot be readily dated except to the very broad time range of A.D. 1200 to A.D. 1500.

Given the preponderance of this type of field, its limited geographical distribution, and its complexity, one might reasonably ask if the rock-mulch technology is an adaptation. As pointed out earlier, the necessary analysis also subsumes the possibilities that the field type or rock mulch technology increased the adaptedness of local populations without being under selective control, or simply occurred through the process of drift and was not the product of selection.

Analysis Methods

Engineering Analysis

An engineering analysis focuses on the determination of function. An initial assumption, as outlined by Williams (1966:258), who quotes Pittendrigh (1958), is that "some feature of the organism—morphological, physiological, or behavioral . . . serves some proximate end (food getting, escape, etc.) that the observer feels that he can discern fully by direct observation and without reference to the history of the organism." Although full discernment may be idealistic, this approach does provide a reasonable framework for elucidating the operational behavior of a selected trait.

The effectiveness of rock mulch in increasing moisture infiltration and inhibiting evaporation has been amply demonstrated. Research by Alderfer and Merkle (1943) shows that bare-soil plots lose 40 to 60 percent of incoming rain to runoff, while rock-mulched plots lose only 3 to 10 percent. The rock also inhibits the formation of soil crust (Corey and Kemper 1968), further enhancing infiltration (Poesen 1985). Also, the soil is protected from raindrop splash that can dislodge soil particles that then clog soil pores. With increased clogging, water infiltration declines and erosion increases. The large pores in a rock-mulched field allow incident precipitation to move rapidly to lower layers (Lightfoot 1990:131).

Soil water conservation studies by Lamb and Chapman (1943:577) show that a 65 percent stone cover results in a significant reduction in evaporation rate, an increase in water absorption, and a maintenance of relatively high water-holding capacity. Corey and Kemper (1968:18) report that in tests using two different soil types—a clay loam and a fine sand—gravel mulch proved to be the most effective surface treatment for evaporation control and soil-moisture maintenance. Fairbourn (1973:926) reports an 18-mm-per-day constant-rate evaporation in gravel-mulched fields compared with an 88-mm-per-day evaporation rate on bare-soil control plots. After four days, the water loss on the gravel field was still less than a single day's loss of moisture from the control plot. After seventeen days, the gravel-mulched soil had 1.9 times more water than the unmulched soil. Fairbourn also reports that the gravel-mulched fields stored 60 percent of total winter precipitation (October through May) whereas the bare-soil control plots stored only 40 percent of total winter precipitation. Choriki et al. (1964) found that over a two-year period there was a 30 to 40 percent increase in soil water stored in rock-mulched soil as compared to unmulched soil.

Since the soil moisture percolates downward rather than being drawn upward through the capillary action associated with evaporation, an ancillary action connected with the conservation of the soil moisture is the inhibition of salinization (Lightfoot 1990:138). Salts dissolve and move downward instead of upward, where they would be left on the surface as evaporate deposits.

Another function of the gravel mulch is related to temperature. Soil temperatures affect the rate at which roots take up water and nutrients from the soil (Othieno and Ahn 1980) and have a significant impact on plant production. Agronomic field experiments show that the higher temperatures associated with rock mulch accelerate seed germination and plant development. Fairbourn (1973: 927) reports that a 2 to 3°C increase in soil temperature under gravel-mulched fields resulted in significant differences in plant growth patterns. Fairbourn (1973) found that, in contrast to corn-stalk-mulched plots, the gravel-mulch treatment hastened germination and emergence of young corn by two to three days. He also notes that "plant growth rates were higher and mature plants were larger for all crops on gravel mulches when compared with other treatments. Corn tasseled 4 to 7 days earlier on gravel-mulched fields compared to all other treatments" (Fairbourn 1973:927). Corresponding findings were made by Hakimi and Kachru (1978) who found that maize root length in rock-mulched fields was 1 percent greater at 62 days of growth than in bare fields. At 118 days, there was a 19 percent greater length. Plant height at 25 days was 10 percent greater in the mulched fields and 23 percent higher at 62 days. By 118 days, however, plant height was 7.3 percent lower, but the corn was nearing maturation and a greater part of maize growth was going into the ears and not into plant height, providing 37 percent greater yield from the mulched plots.

Fairbourn (1973) concludes that conservation of soil water and increased soil temperature were the primary factors responsible for higher crop yields in gravel-mulched fields. In assessing the effectiveness of gravel mulches in conserving soil moisture, Fairbourn (1973:925) concludes, "Large pores of the gravel permit rapid infiltration of water to the soil but retard evaporation. Water moves back to the atmosphere almost entirely by vapor phase across the gravel pores. Thus, the gravel acts as a one-way water valve for the soil."

As the above experiments show, rock mulching increases crop yields through moisture and temperature regulation. It seems safe to take a uniformitarian perspective and assume that the rock mulch functioned in the same manner prehistorically. Still, this provides little confirmation that the technology represents an adaptation. To call a trait an adaptation is to say something about its origin and continued appearance in regard to particular environmental conditions. It is for this reason that adaptations stand in contrast to fortuitous benefits (Sober 1984: 199). At this point, a comparative analysis is helpful.

Comparative Analysis

Although every introductory text on evolution offers some testimony for selection and its influence on adaptation, most examples illustrate the selective value of individual genes, gene combinations, and gene arrangements, as revealed through experimental populations or other experimental procedures. At times it has also been possible to establish in the field a correlation between gene frequencies and certain environmental factors, but the effect of selection would be far more convincing if one could demonstrate a selective value for specific components of the phenotype (Mayr 1988:137). Endler (1986) and Wade and Kalisz (1990) also argue that emphasis on multivariate experimental analyses of selection are insufficient for identifying the causal agents of selection. They believe that to understand the relationship of phenotype to fitness we first require knowledge of the ecological relationships to choose those phenotypic traits that may be associated with fitness (Wade and Kalisz 1990:1949) and thus to have additional information for identifying the causes of selection. As argued by Leonard and Jones (1987:213), artifacts of any scale, agricultural fields in this case, can be considered as an expression of human behavioral variability and a component of the human phenotype. Consequently, the evolutionary context of artifacts or technology can be examined using the same processes as those found in biology (Dunnell 1989; Leonard and Jones 1987).

By examining the farming techniques used in a region similar to the Rio Chama, it should be possible to gain some idea of the environmental conditioners that led to the widespread use of rock-mulched fields in the lower Rio Chama. Adaptation occurs through the relative fitness of traits, and the fitness of traits is mediated by the environment. Hence, a comparative mode of analysis is effective. As argued by Mayr (1988:154), the methodology for establishing adaptive significance generally consists in establishing a tentative correlation between a trait and a feature of the environment and analyzing in a comparative study other populations exposed to the same feature of the environment, to see whether they have acquired the same traits.

In this regard, the modern physical environment in the Zuni region has important correspondences to the lower Rio Chama. Although climatic variation on a local scale is important, the data do not currently exist to supply more than a general overview. As is commonly recognized, extrapolation of modern climate into the past is also problematic.

Temperature regimes are similar in both areas—the Zuni area has a mean annual temperature of 10.0°C while the Rio Chama averages 9.4°C. Growing season temperatures at Zuni average 18.3°C and in the lower Rio Chama they average 17.9°C. Each region also has a growing season length between 140 and 160 days (Tuan et al. 1973:Fig. 38). In each region, the last date for a spring killing frost is between May 10 and May 30, and the date of first killing frost is between September 30 and October 10 (Tuan et al. 1973:Figs. 39 and 40).

Monthly precipitation patterns are also analogous. In the Zuni area the mean annual precipitation is 594 mm and 543 mm in the lower Rio Chama. Zuni, however, receives more snowfall. Precipitation during the growing season at Zuni is around 310 mm and in the lower Rio Chama, 323 mm. However, early growing season precipitation (May through June) in the lower Rio Chama has twice the variance as that in the Zuni area. The soils of each region also have similar Available Water-Holding Capacity (AWHC). The major soil association in which fields are found in the lower Rio Chama has been classified by Maker et al. (1973) as Pojoaque-Rough Broken Land. Most of these soils are forming in unconsolidated old alluvium that is predominantly coarse to medium-textured and gravelly (Maker et al. 1973:33). Maker et al. (1973:44–45) describe it as a sandy clay loam to a sandy loam with moderate permeability and an AWHC of 100 to 127 mm (4.0 to 5.0 in). A much wider variety of soil associations has been identified in the Zuni region (Maker et al. 1974). These associations range from alluvial soils of deep, fine-grained loams with high AWHC and generally low permeability to eolian soils derived from wind-blown sands and silts. These soils are moderately deep, fine sandy loams, are highly permeable, drain rapidly, and have moderate AWHC of 100 to 140 mm (4.0 to 5.5 in). Upland soils range from a shallow to moderately deep, fine sandy loam, also with a moderate AWHC of 100 to 140 mm (4.0 to 5.5 in). Cobble sources, similar to those found along the lower Rio Chama, are also found in the major washes at Zuni, although such deposits decrease in frequency outside the drainages.

Despite the many environmental resemblances, few rock-mulched fields have been recorded in the Zuni region. In general, the archaeology of early and late prehistoric farming in the region is characterized by fieldhouses, terraces, and checkdams. The general farming strategy, therefore, seems to have made use of small, mulch-free plots and small-scale water control features, and irrigation perhaps after A.D. 1300 (Ferguson and Hart 1985:26; Kintigh 1984:231).

Although there exist general environmental correspondences between the two regions, contrasts in at least two variables—precipitation and temperature—suggest that they can be identified as potential selective agents. Three differences in precipitation patterns are: (1) the Zuni region receives more winter moisture than the lower Rio Chama; (2) the variance in the early growing season rainfall is two times greater in the lower Rio Chama area than the Zuni area; and (3) the lower Rio Chama receives its peak summer rainfall one month later than Zuni. These periods of potential moisture deficits in the lower Rio Chama occur during critical periods in the growth cycle of maize—germination and tasseling—and moisture stress during either period can lead to stunted plants and low crop yields. Studies have shown that moisture stress reduces the height of maize plants, delays development, and causes some yield reduction, depending upon the timing, length, and degree of the stress period (Classen and Shaw 1970; Denmead and Shaw 1960; Robbins and Domingo 1953).

Additionally, the mean annual temperature in the lower Rio Chama is cooler by .4°C. Studies by Walker (1969) have shown that even a 1°C soil temperature difference during the early growth period of maize can result in a maximum 20 percent change in the dry weight biomass of seedlings. Other studies (Knoll et al. 1964; Lehenbauer 1914; Willis et al. 1957) have shown that corn seedling growth increased linearly as soil temperature increased, while Ketcheson (1970) used heating cables to heat soil and found that germination was advanced, emergence improved, and growth and yield increased. Studies that involved raising the early season soil temperature also showed that emergence time was decreased (Adams 1967). In contrast, lower temperatures reduced water permeability of corn root tissue and induced water stress in the shoot tissue, which in turn, retarded cell extension (Kleinendorst and Brouwer 1970, 1972). These experimentally observed consequences of increased temperature on plant growth within rock-mulched fields demonstrate that rock mulch would offset any disadvantage associated with cooler temperatures.

Conclusions

Assuming that precipitation and temperature are conditioners for agricultural production, engineering studies suggest that rock mulches can compensate for low values in either variable. The rock mulch would, therefore, offer an advantage in crop production to farmers living in regions with periods of low or variable rainfall and low temperatures. When compared to the Zuni region, such an environmental situation is found in the lower Rio Chama, and the distribution of field types across regions shows a correlation with these conditions.

It would be helpful to have additional knowledge of competing agricultural technologies that may have been used in each region. As stated previously, other farming strategies are documented, but the scale of their implementation is unknown. Rock-mulched fields are simply more visible, and though they cover hundreds, and perhaps thousands, of acres, other important farming strategies may also have been used. Since natural selection requires variation for its operation, it would be advantageous to know how the function of rock-mulched fields compares with the functions of other field types used in the Rio Chama and how agricultural productivity would be comparatively influenced. Current knowledge of the frequency distribution of field types in the region, however, indicates that the rock-mulched fields have greater replicative success than other field types (Leonard and Jones 1987).

Despite the lack of historical study believed by other researchers to be necessary, it is posited here that adaptation in this case is consequently substantiated through the comparison of the environmental settings and by the identification of technological functions. As this study demonstrates, it is not always necessary to structure our observations of phenomena in a strictly diachronic framework. After all, the mechanism of natural selection lies outside history—history serves to suggest that adaptation may have occurred. With the approach taken here, one must first decide the level of detail appropriate to the problem and the scale at which we might safely ignore variation. Presumably, an argument can be made that the target scale is being affected by some selective agent that may be acting upon its constituent components. Once defined, one also may be secure in ignoring variation below those constituent parts. Certainly an area that we must begin exploring as a discipline is whether there are specific scales that are appropriate for examining the effects of selective pressures (Reed and Maxwell 1990).

For example, one can easily compare coat coloration between polar bears and brown bears and see that the camouflage value of coat color provides an advantage to the individuals in their respective environments. It might also be easily predicted that given the inability to camouflage itself, brown bears found in an arctic environment would rapidly become extinct. If the panda bear were also included in such a study, its distinctive markings might suggest that a phenomenon other than crypsis occurred during its evolution. A detailed analysis of environment would still be dictated since there may be distinct characteristics of the local environment that exerted selective pressures on panda bear coloration, but at this point, other selective processes such as sexual selection might also be examined. The issue is that this scale of analysis requires neither diachronic data nor knowledge of the range of variation on a local scale. The differences in the prevalence and maintenance of traits in each population can be understood regardless of the details of their prior history.

Referring to the original question of the adaptive significance of rock mulch, can it be determined that the use of rock mulch is the consequence of selection and not a chance event? It is difficult to prove conclusively that any trait is the incidental result of stochastic processes. Such conclusions can perhaps arise when rival hypotheses regarding selection are dismissed. Also, it is clear that selection and chance are not mutually exclusive alternatives—there are stochastic perturbations during every stage of the selection process (Mayr 1988:156). However, determining the probability of the effects of selection is probably more feasible. In this study, a parallel examination of the function of rock mulches and environmental context suggests that the technology would be favored by selection in the particular environmental setting since it serves to compensate for variability in precipitation and low temperatures. Given the high-frequency distribution of these fields, it would appear that they resisted replacement by other forms because natural selection favored their maintenance in the competition with other variant field types.

Acknowledgments

For their valuable insights, comments, and many hours of discussion, I thank Cynthia Herhahn, Bob Leonard, Alysia Abbot, Stephen Post, Ann Ramenofsky, Heidi Reed, Patrice Teltser, and Erin Tyler.

References

Adams, J. E.
1967   Effect of Mulches and Bed Configuration. I. Early-season Soil Temperature and Emergence of Grain Sorghum and Corn. *Agronomy Journal* 59:595–599.

Alderfer, R. B., and F. G. Merkle
1943   The Comparative Effects of Surface Application versus Incorporation of Various Mulching Materials on Structure, Permeability, Runoff, and Other Soil Properties. *Soil Science Society of America Proceedings* 8:79–86.

Anschuetz, K. F.
1992   Saving a Rainy Day: The Integration of Diverse Agricultural Technologies to Harvest and Conserve Water in the Lower Rio Chama Valley, New Mexico. Paper presented at the New Mexico Archaeological Council Symposium on Agriculture, Santa Fe, New Mexico, October 1992.

Anschuetz, K. F., T. D. Maxwell, and J. A. Ware
1986   *Testing Report and Research Design for the Medanales North Project, Rio Arriba County, New Mexico.* Laboratory of Anthropology Notes No. 347, Museum of New Mexico, Santa Fe.

Bandelier, A. F.
1890–   *Final Report of Investigations among the Indians of the Southwestern United States,*
1892   *Carried on Mainly in the Years 1880–1885.* Papers of the Archaeological Institute of America, American Series 3 and 4.

Bugé, D.
1984   Prehistoric Subsistence Strategies in the Ojo Caliente Valley, New Mexico. In *Prehistoric Agricultural Strategies in the Southwest,* edited by S. K. Fish and P. R. Fish, pp. 27–34. Arizona State University, Anthropological Research Papers 33.

Choriki, R. T., J. C. Hide, S. L. Krall, and B. L. Brown
1964   Rock and Gravel Mulch Aid in Moisture Storage. *Crops and Soil* 16(9): 24.

Classen, M. M., and R. H. Shaw
1970   Water Deficit Stress on Corn (Part II: Grain Component). *Agronomy Journal* 62:652–655.

Clutton-Brock, T. H., and P. H. Harvey
1984   Comparative Approaches to Investigating Adaptation. In *Behavioral Ecology: An Evolutionary Approach,* edited by J. R. Krebs and N. B. Davies, pp. 7–29. Sinauer and Associates, Sunderland, Maryland.

Cordell, L. S., A. C. Earls, and M. R. Binford
1984   Subsistence Systems in the Mountainous Settings of the Rio Grande Valley. In *Prehistoric Agricultural Strategies in the Southwest,* edited by S. K. Fish and P. R. Fish, pp. 233–241. Arizona State University, Anthropological Research Papers 33.

Corey, A. T., and W. D. Kemper
1968   *Conservation of Soil Water by Gravel Mulches.* Colorado State University Hydrology Papers 30.

Denmead, O. T., and R. H. Shaw
1960   The Effects of Soil Moisture Stress at Different Stages of Growth on the Development and Yield of Corn. *Agronomy Journal* 52:272–274.

Dunnell, R. C.
1980   Evolutionary Theory and Archaeology. In *Advances in Archaeological Method and Theory,* vol. 3, edited by M. B. Schiffer, pp. 35–99. Academic Press, New York.
1989   Aspects of the Application of Evolutionary Theory in Archaeology. In *Archaeological Thought in America,* edited by C. C. Lamberg-Karlovsky, pp. 35–49. Cambridge University Press, Cambridge.

Endler, J. A.
1986   *Natural Selection in the Wild.* Princeton University Press, Princeton, New Jersey.

Fairbourn, M. L.
1973   Effect of Gravel Mulch on Crop Yields. *Colorado Rancher and Farmer* 24(3): 925–928.

Ferguson, T. J., and E. R. Hart
1985   *A Zuni Atlas.* University of Oklahoma Press, Norman.

Futuyma, D. J.
1986   *Evolutionary Biology.* 2d ed. Sinauer Associates, Sunderland Massachusetts.

Gans, C.
1974   *Biomechanics: An Approach to Vertebrate Biology.* Lippincott, Philadelphia.

Hakimi, A. H., and R. P. Kachru
1978   Silage Corn Responses to Different Mulch Tillage Treatments under Arid and Semiarid Climatic Conditions. *Journal of Agronomy and Crop Science* 147:15–23.

Hibben, F. C.
1937   *Excavation of the Riana Ruin and Chama Valley Survey.* University of New Mexico Bulletin 300, Anthropological Series 2(1).

Ketcheson, J. W.
1970 Effects of Heating and Insulating Soil on Corn Growth. *Canadian Journal of Soil Science* 50:379–384.

Kintigh, K. W.
1984 Late Prehistoric Agricultural Strategies and Settlement Patterns in the Zuni Area. In *Prehistoric Agricultural Strategies in the Southwest,* edited by S. K. Fish and P. R. Fish, pp. 215–232. Arizona State University, Anthropological Research Papers 33.

Kleinendorst, A., and R. Brouwer
1970 The Effect of Temperature of the Root Medium and of the Growing Point of the Shoot on Growth, Water Content, and Sugar Content of Maize Leaves. *Netherlands Journal of Agricultural Science* 18:140–148.
1972 The Effect of Local Cooling on Growth and Water Content of Plants. *Netherlands Journal of Agricultural Science* 20:203–217.

Knoll, H. A., D. J. Lathwell, and N. C. Brady
1964 Effect of Root Zone Temperature on Various Stages of the Growing Period on the Growth of Corn. *Agronomy Journal* 56:143–145.

Lamb, Jr., J., and J. E. Chapman
1943 Effect of Surface Stones on Erosion, Evaporation, Soil Temperature and Soil Moisture. *Journal of the American Society of Agronomy* 35(7): 567–578.

Lang, R. W.
1980 *Archaeological Investigations at a Pueblo Agricultural Site and Archaic and Puebloan Encampments on the Rio Ojo Caliente, Rio Arriba County, New Mexico.* Contract Archeology Division Report 007, School of American Research, Santa Fe.

Lehenbauer, P. A.
1914 Growth of Maize Seedlings in Relation to Temperature. *Physiological Research* 1:247–288.

Leonard, R. D.
1990 Book Review. *Journal of Field Archaeology* 17:348–354.

Leonard, R. D., and A. L. Abbott
1992 Theoretical Aspects of Subsistence Stress and Cultural Evolution. Paper presented at the symposium "Resource Stress, Economic Uncertainty, and Human Response in the Prehistoric Southwest," Santa Fe Institute, Santa Fe, New Mexico, February 1992.

Leonard, R. D., and G. T. Jones
1987 Elements of an Inclusive Evolutionary Model for Archaeology. *Journal of Anthropological Archaeology* 6:199–219.

Leonard, R. D., and H. E. Reed
1993 Population Aggregation in the Prehistoric American Southwest: A Selectionist Model. *American Antiquity* 58(4): 648–661.

Lewontin, R. C.
1978 Adaptation. *Scientific American* 239:156–169.

1979   Sociobiology as an Adaptationist Program. *Behavioral Science* 24:5–14.

Lightfoot, D. R.

1990   The Prehistoric Pebble-Mulched Fields of the Galisteo Anasazi: Agricultural Innovation and Adaptation to Environment. Ph.D. dissertation, Department of Geography, University of Colorado, Boulder.

Maker, H. J., H. E. Bullock, Jr., and J. U. Anderson

1974   *Soil Associations and Land Classification for Irrigation, Valencia County.* New Mexico State University Agricultural Experiment Station Research Report 262, Las Cruces.

Maker, H. J., J. J. Folks, J. U. Anderson, and V. G. Link

1973   *Soil Associations and Land Classification for Irrigation, Rio Arriba County.* New Mexico State University Agricultural Experiment Station Research Report 254, Las Cruces.

Maxwell, T. D., and K. F. Anschuetz

1992   The Southwestern Ethnographic Record and Prehistoric Agricultural Diversity. In *The Gardens of Prehistory: The Archaeology of Settlement Agriculture in Greater Mesoamerica,* edited by T. W. Killion, pp. 35–68. University of Alabama Press, Tuscaloosa.

Mayr, E.

1988   *Toward a New Philosophy of Biology: Observations of an Evolutionist.* Harvard University Press, Cambridge, Massachusetts.

O'Brien, M. J., and T. D. Holland

1989   Variation, Selection, and the Archaeological Record. In *Archaeological Method and Theory,* vol. 2, edited by M. B. Schiffer, pp. 31–79. University of Arizona Press, Tucson.

1992   The Role of Adaptation in Archaeological Explanation. *American Antiquity* 57(1): 36–59.

Othieno, C. O., and P. M. Ahn

1980   Effect of Mulches on Soil Temperature and Growth of Tea Plants in Kenya. *Experimental Agriculture* 16:287–294.

Pittendrigh, C. S.

1958   Adaptation, Natural Selection, and Behavior. In *Behavior and Evolution,* edited by A. Roe and G. G. Simpson, pp. 390–416. Yale University Press, New Haven.

Poesen, J.

1985   Surface Sealing on Loose Sediments: The Role of Texture, Slope and Position of Stones in the Top Layer. In *Assessment of Soil Surface Sealing and Crusting,* edited by F. Callebaut, D. Gabriels, and M. deBoodt, pp. 354–362. Proceedings of the International Symposium on the Assessment of Soil Surface Sealing and Crusting, Ghent, Belgium.

Reed, H. E., and T. D. Maxwell

1990   Darwinian Evolutionary Theory for Archaeology: Some Considerations. Paper presented at the 55th Annual Meeting of the Society for American Archaeology Las Vegas, Nevada, April 1990.

Rindos, D.
1984   *The Origins of Agriculture: An Evolutionary Perspective.* Academic Press, New York.
1989   Undirected Variation and the Darwinian Explanation of Cultural Change. In *Archaeological Method and Theory,* vol. 1, edited by M. B. Schiffer, pp. 1–45. University of Arizona Press, Tucson.

Robbins, J. S., and C. E. Domingo
1953   Some Effects of Severe Soil Moisture Deficits at Specific Growth Stages in Corn. *Agronomy Journal* 45:618–621.

Rouse, I.
1986   *Migrations in Prehistory: Inferring Population Movement from Cultural Remains.* Yale University Press, New Haven.

Sober, E.
1984   *The Nature of Selection: Evolutionary Theory in Philosophical Focus.* MIT Press, Cambridge, Massachusetts.

Tuan, Yi-Fu, C. E. Everard, J. G. Widdison, and I. Bennett
1973   *The Climate of New Mexico.* State Planning Office, Santa Fe.

Wade, M. J., and S. Kalisz
1990   The Causes of Natural Selection. *Evolution* 44(8): 1947–1955.

Walker, J. M.
1969   One-degree Increments in Soil Temperatures Affect Maize Seedling Behavior. *Soil Science Society of America Proceedings* 33(5): 729–736.

Williams, G. C.
1966   *Adaptation and Natural Selection: A Critique of Some Current Evolutionary Thought«.* Princeton University Press, Princeton, New Jersey.

Willis, W. O., W. E. Larson, and D. Kirkham
1957   Corn Growth as Affected by Soil Temperature and Mulch. *Agronomy Journal* 49:323–328.

7

Evolutionary Theory and Native American Artifact Change in the Postcontact Period

Ann F. Ramenofsky

◆◆ My goal in this chapter is to cast the issue of postcontact native artifact change in evolutionary terms and to create a Darwinian framework within which to ask questions about native artifact change during that period. Since the epistemological discussions of the New Archaeology, we have known that explanations do not arise *de novo*. They are embedded in a framework and supported by a set of assumptions and ontologies. Consequently, the construction of explanations begins with a framework. Constructing that framework is the focus of this chapter.

When viewed from a Darwinian perspective, contact between Europeans and Native Americans resulted in an expanded pool of artifactual variation. Such variation had not been present before contact. Because artifacts can be anything altered or produced by humans, the variation brought to the Americas by Europeans occurred at all scales, from microbes to cities. In this context, what new variants native populations tried out and discarded, as well as those which survived, are of evolutionary concern. If new variants persisted, did they outcompete native variants, thereby making them products of selection? Of course, not all variants persist due to selection. Other mechanisms, such as drift (Neiman in press) or sorting (Vrba and Eldredge 1984; Vrba and Gould 1986), could have operated to create the observed patterns of artifact change. Finally, if selection was responsible for frequency changes, then explaining how selection acted is required.

Postcontact artifact change is potentially interesting to both cultural evolutionists and ethnohistorians. While ethnohistorians have always been interested in the contact period, cultural evolutionists should find the topic compelling because it was a time of such dramatic change. Yet, both fields have brought a series of assumptions and ontologies that have precluded the systematic investigation of this topic until the 1990s (e.g., Rogers 1990; Vernon and Cordell 1993).

Traditionally, evolutionary studies in anthropology have been dominated by Cultural Evolution, a framework that places progress as an inherent mechanism of change (e.g., Dunnell 1989a). When viewed from such a goal-oriented or teleological perspective, change during the post-European native record was "in the wrong direction, regressive rather than developmental" (Phillips, Ford and Griffin 1951:419). Thus, even if cultural evolutionists were interested in purported "devolution" (Carneiro 1972) of postcontact Native America (e.g., Service 1962), no theoretical framework existed to accommodate the kind of changes that occurred. The disparity between the direction of the native American record and the developmental assumptions of cultural evolution precluded any serious analysis or discussion of the post-European native record.

Unlike cultural evolution, acculturationists have always been interested in the postcontact native record. Within acculturation, culture, and especially the psychological aspects of culture, were important. Indeed, the first memorandum of acculturation was drafted by a group within the personality and culture section of the Social Science Research Council (Linton 1940). To emphasize the importance of psychology and culture in acculturation, and to separate acculturation from the transformational aspects of cultural evolution, Herskovits (1948) defined the consequences of contact between populations as cultural change, culture contact, or cultural dynamics. The terminological distinction between cultural evolution as mechanistically driven and cultural change as psychologically or culturally driven is still maintained. Because of the psychological emphasis of acculturation, artifacts, if considered at all, were typically viewed symbolically (Hamell 1983; Herskovits 1948:557; Waselkov 1993; White 1975) rather than as a subject of investigation.

Rather than being overlooked or studied as a surrogate of cultural values, an evolutionary framework specifies artifact change as the empirical focus of analysis and has the potential to explain patterns of frequency change. In so doing, evolutionary theory could correct many of the problems imposed by acculturation and anthropological models of cultural evolution, and ultimately contribute to contact period research (Leonard 1993; Ramenofsky 1990, 1991).

Because acculturation was the first scholarly approach to consider seriously postcontact change in native societies, I begin by describing and evaluating acculturation studies of artifacts as developed and used by both ethnologists and archaeologists. I then discuss some aspects of Darwinian theory that suggest why this framework has utility for addressing questions of postcontact artifact change. Finally, I conclude by briefly discussing some of the implications of an evolutionary framework for developing particular explanations of native artifact change.

Ethnological Acculturation

Until the development of American acculturation in the 1930s, no systematic scholarship of post-European, native societies existed. The first generation of Boasian ethnologists were cultural reconstructionists who extracted from native memory, observations, material objects, and documents those traits presumed to obtain to the precontact condition; they created the ethnographic present (Ramenofsky 1987, 1991; Trigger 1981). As a result, descriptions of change that occurred in native societies following European arrival and settlement were viewed as irrelevant because they simply obscured the precontact condition.

Acculturation studies made post-European change of native societies the focus of scholarship (Foster 1960; Herskovits 1948, 1964; Linton 1940; Social Science Research Council 1954). Beyond the commitment to studying and understanding societies undergoing change and to the belief that the changes must be observable or retrievable from documents, there were no common or integrating principles that linked these studies together. Because of political, economic, and social pressure to understand third-world societies undergoing change, however (e.g., Broom and Shevky 1952; Herskovits 1964; Mair 1938), acculturation survived as a field of investigation. As suggested by the scholarly discussions regarding acculturation (e.g., Herskovits 1948, 1958; Linton 1940; Social Science Research Council 1954), the field continually suffered from lack of direction. Even the term "acculturation" had no single referent. It simultaneously defined a temporal period of study, the methods or techniques used to carry out such studies, the descriptions of societies undergoing change, and the changes themselves.

The real strength of acculturation studies resided in the descriptions of societies undergoing change. Although the formats varied, the descriptions were frequently organized into temporal periods that began with contact and continued into the present or recent past. Each period was characterized by a series of traits or changes. The end result was a history of some specific culture undergoing acculturation. Harris (1940), for instance, divided White Knife Shoshoni acculturation into five periods that began in 1825 and terminated in 1877. These descriptions created a vast literature covering all types of contact situations. That such studies were an important contribution to cultural knowledge is demonstrated by the founding and continued success of the journal, *Ethnohistory*.

Acculturationists assumed that culture was uniquely human and that culture explained culture change (Herskovits 1948, 1958; Linton 1940). Linton, for instance, defined culture as an imperfect human structure that changed in response to human discomforts. In essence, culture changed in response to felt needs of the participants of a culture.

Although united in the assumption that culture caused culture change, scholars emphasized different aspects of culture as causal. Herskovits' cultural mechanism was "cultural selectivity" by which he meant cultural values or intentions (1948:537–539). He argued that it was the need to study the nature and processes of cultural selectivity that led anthropology to the study of culture change. Moreover, the principle was so important that it explained not only simple adoptions or rejections but nativistic movements as well.

In contrast Linton (1940), followed by Deagan (1978), Spicer (1961), and others, placed greater weight on the sociopolitical context in which the contact occurred. The relationships between cultures explained subsequent changes. Linton's definitions of directed and undirected contact demonstrate the focus on cultural context. In directed contact, as in Sharp's descriptions of missionaries introducing metal axes to the Yir Yoront of Australia (Sharp 1934a, 1934b, 1952), a dominant society directed the introduction of traits or complexes to subordinate societies and attempted to control subsequent changes. In undirected contact, culture change occurred between equivalent units. No dominant-subordinate distinction existed, and as a result neither society was in a position to introduce or control change in the other.

Invoking cultural values or intentions and cultural setting as causing change is ubiquitous in the acculturation literature, but the particular causal factors varied. Dozier (1961) invoked a special kind of cultural resistance, termed "compartmentalization," to explain the survival of Puebloan religion in the face of directed Spanish contact. Codere (1961), on the other hand, argued that Kwakiutl lost their precontact culture and assimilated into Canadian society quickly because their traditions were so similar to those of the Canadians. Consequently, what appeared as loss was more of a change in style than in fundamental cultural values.

The differences in these causal factors underscore the dilemma of invoking culture to explain cultural change. The belief that culture histories were unique was a legacy of Boasian ethnology. If developmental histories were unique, then so were contact histories. Consequently, the suite of causes operating during the acculturation of Rio Grande pueblos was unique to that setting because Rio Grande pueblos were unique. Another suite of causes pertained to the Kwakiutl or Pomo.

Given these assumptions, it was impossible to move beyond the particulars and create an explanatory framework. Explanations require general principles, and values of resistance, cultural similarity, or directed contact are not general principles. They are culture-specific descriptions. In the absence of an explanatory framework, the best that acculturation studies could produce were empirical generalizations derived from comparing the sequences of change cross-culturally. That such comparison was a common practice is reflected in the inductive structure of edited volumes (Linton 1940; Spicer 1952, 1961). The bulk of the books were devoted to case studies; in the last chapter the editor integrated the studies into a general framework of acculturative change. As Spicer described, these generalizations fell short of the mark:

The same group sometimes changed rapidly its ceremonial interests and practices and under other conditions clung desperately to them; under some circumstances material culture items were replaced or changed rapidly while little else changed, but in other situations social structure and religion changed rapidly while material culture underwent small change. In some circumstances there was rapid change in all aspects of culture at the same time; under other circumstances there were marked differentials. In short *the comparative analysis carried out by the seminar led to an abandonment of a search for generalizations framed in terms of a universal differential susceptibility to change of aspects of culture.* (Spicer 1961:542, emphasis added)

Ethnological acculturationists brought the subject of postcontact change to the attention of anthropologists; through participant observation and historical research they constructed histories of culture change of numerous societies. These stand as lasting contributions. Although ethnological acculturationists sought universal principles that could account for acculturation, they never reached that goal. Their assumptions about the uniqueness and causal role of culture in acculturation resulted in elaborate descriptions of change but no general principles that could explain why change occurred.

Archaeological Acculturation

American archaeologists have always been consumers of ethnological ideas and approaches; it is not surprising that in research of the postcontact period, archaeologists adopted the framework of acculturation. Significant differences exist, however, between archaeology and ethnology, and these differences made archaeological studies of acculturation considerably less robust than ethnological studies.

Ethnological studies of acculturation began with behavior, whether observed or documented. Even though there was no framework for explaining why cultures changed, ethnologists proceeded on a case-by-case basis to describe how cultures changed. Archaeological studies of acculturation began with artifacts (e.g., Bamforth 1993; Brain 1979; Brown 1979; Charlton and Fournier 1993; Ceci 1982; Deagan 1990; Quimby and Spoehr 1951; Rogers 1990, 1993; Vernon 1988; and White 1975), and artifacts are not behavior. To invoke cultural behavior as causal required a bevy of assumptions: (1) that artifacts reflect cultural traditions; (2) that native artifact change of the postcontact period is a product of and reflects culture contact; and (3) that cultural causes can be inferred from the description and analysis of artifacts. The number of assumptions coupled with the lack of an explanatory framework created inherently weak products.

In the simplest archaeological studies, archaeologists asserted that European contact caused artifact change. Kidder (1936:273), for instance, suggested that Spanish influence was responsible for a change in the shape of bowl rims at Pecos.

Behind the statement were observations and assumptions: the rim shape was new, appeared quickly, occurred in strata that postdated 1600, and resembled Spanish rims. It followed, therefore, that Spanish contact was causal.

As ethnological acculturation developed, archaeologists used a combination of cultural and functional causes to account for artifact change. Quimby and Spoehr (1951) created a classification of pre- and post-European artifacts that examined change across technology, form, material, and use. Some post-European changes, such as the replacement of stone by metal, were explained by the functional superiority of metal over stone. Causes of other changes were not readily apparent; Quimby and Spoehr suggested a series of causes including "utility, convenience, and prestige" (1951:146).

The tendency to use a suite of cultural factors to explain postcontact artifact change continues into the present. Bamforth (1993) used efficiency, changing cultural values, and the introduction of European forms to explain the pattern of postcontact artifact frequencies at the Chumash site of Helo. Stone persisted in fishing-related activities because the activity became less important historically and because the Chumash were resisting infiltration by missionaries. Metal, however, replaced stone in shell-bead production; this activity was labor intensive, and metal drills were more efficient than stone for this task.

Rogers (1990) defined five cultural processes to account for eighteenth-century artifact change among the Arikara. Addition and replacement explained the steady increase in diversity and abundance of European items in Arikara assemblages between 1681 and 1775. Between 1776 and 1805, Euro-American items decreased in frequency after which they again increased. Rogers invoked rejection of Europeans to account for the decrease in European-American artifacts; cultural transformation in which the Arikara lost their autonomy and became incorporated into a European system accounted for the subsequent and final increase of Euro-American products.

Because archaeologists have wanted to explain postcontact artifact change in cultural terms, they have sought guidance in ethnological studies. Yet, unlike ethnologists, archaeologists do not have behavior, memory, or documents to guide their endeavors. Assumptions about the relationship between artifacts and cultural behavior replaced observed behavior. Had there been an explanatory framework in ethnological acculturation comparable to that in cultural evolution, archaeological assumptions of the relationship between artifacts and behavior could have worked better than they have. Archaeologists might have created studies of artifact change similar in structure to the typological studies of chiefdoms (e.g., Peebles and Kus 1977). Without either a theoretical framework or the behavior, archaeological studies of acculturation became tautological, and tautologies are not explanatory in science. Culture behavior caused the changes in artifacts, and artifacts reflected the behavior.

In the end then, there exist some descriptions of post-European native arti-facts, and there are some notions that cultural resistance or prestige account for the changes. Unfortunately, no systematic body of knowledge explains the form and pattern of native artifact change.

Darwinism and Archaeological Evolution

Artifacts, not culture, are the focus of my enquiry, which makes artifact change an archaeological problem rather than an ethnological one. Explaining artifact change requires a theoretical framework in which causation is external to the subject of explanation. Darwinian evolution is such a theory. Besides separat-ing causes of change from change itself, Darwinian evolution offers a deeper insight into why cultural factors do not explain artifact change.

Darwinian evolution is a historical process defined as changes in the frequen-cies of variants from one generation to the next. The theory has three compo-nents: individuals vary morphologically, physiologically, and behaviorally; some part of that variation is heritable with the result that individuals more closely resemble their relatives than nonrelatives; individuals differ in the number of off-spring they produce (Lewontin 1984; Mayr 1988). Adaptation, not initially part of Darwin's theory, was added later to link the components (Brandon 1984; Burian 1983; Lewontin 1984:245–247; Mayr 1988).

According to Darwin, adaptation is the consequence of "the struggle for exis-tence." In a finite world, there is competition between individuals for resources; because of that competition, differences between individuals matter. Fitness, or adaptedness (Brandon 1984; Burian 1983; Mayr 1988; O'Brien and Holland 1992), is the difference among individuals that could contribute to reproductive success. Realized fitness, by contrast, describes actual reproductive success. In other words, individuals who leave more offspring relative to other individuals are, by definition, more fit.

Two aspects of Darwinian adaptation are particularly important for creating explanations of biological change. First, fitness differentials are relative; no opti-mal set of variants results in a perfect adaptation. Rather, individuals vary only slightly in their ability to "get by," and getting by is context specific (Braun 1990; O'Brien and Holland 1992). Second, because successful adaptations are the prod-uct of past differences in fitness, Darwinian adaptation is a consequence of evolu-tionary change. It is not a cause. Explaining why can only be done by analyzing what has already happened. Thus, explanations of evolutionary change are his-torical explanations.

Variation, heredity, and reproductive fitness constitute the necessary compo-nents of selection, but they do not describe the evolutionary process. Evolution is a two-step process. In the first step, phenotypic variation is produced. The production of this variation is nondirected, or random, with respect to natural selection, but the variation provides the "raw material" on which selection operates. In the second step, selection operates on the pool of phenotypic variation resulting in differential persistence of variants. Selection requires understanding all those environmental factors that affect the reproductive success of individuals. Because the evolutionary steps are independent of one another, evolutionary change is opportunistic. Evolutionary change is not driven by intention nor is it teleological.

Although important, natural selection is not the only mechanism that perpetuates some variants at the expense of others. For example, sampling error, or drift, has long been recognized as an important mechanism of evolutionary change (Wright 1931). More recently, and as a consequence of the discovery of neutral features (Kimura 1983; King and Jukes 1969), evolutionary theorists have suggested that hierarchical sorting may play a substantial role in patterning variation through time (Mayr 1988; Vrba and Eldredge 1984; Vrba and Gould 1986).

Sorting is actually a kind of hierarchical sweeping that occurs when selection operates. Because selection operates at different scales of inclusion, variants at all scales lower than the target of selection will be sorted, or "swept," with those that are under selection. The sorted traits then become part of the package of variation that persists. Traits at scales below the target of selection are neutral with respect to fitness. When, for instance, the individual organism is the target of selection, variants at the scale of organs or genes experience the same evolutionary fate as that of the individual.

In sum, Darwinian evolution is a two-step process with the generation of variation independent of the fate of that variation. Evolutionary mechanisms operate resulting in patterned variation through time. Although Darwin argued that natural selection was the principal mechanism of evolutionary change, modern evolutionary theory accords explanatory significance to both drift and sorting.

The extension of evolutionary theory to cultural behavior involves only a few additional definitions. It requires, however, major changes in the way we conceptualize the archaeological record and cultural behavior.

First, the evolution of human cultural behavior, or the products of that behavior, does not require unique principles to explain its form and pattern (Dunnell 1980; 1989b; Neiman 1990, in press; O'Brien and Holland 1990; and Rindos 1984). Second, artifacts are part of the human phenotype (Leonard and Jones 1987). Because selection operates on the phenotype, it also applies to behavior and the products of behavior resulting in changing frequencies of variants through time.

Third, Dunnell's definitions of style and function are crucial within archaeological evolution because they specify that not all frequency changes in phenotypic variants are a product of selection (Dunnell 1978, 1980). The definitions are, in effect, models that describe different types of variants (Neiman 1990:177–181 and Teltser 1988:28–32 for discussion). Dunnell defines stylistic variants as neutral in that they do not affect fitness. They behave stochastically through time and are primarily a product of drift (see Neiman 1990:169–177 for an extended discussion of this point). Functional variants, on the other hand, affect Darwinian fitness of the population. Changes in the frequencies of functional variants can be explained by deterministic processes. Consequently, they are predictable in principle (Neiman, in press).

Finally, not all variants that have nonrandom distributions are the product of selection. As I discussed in reference to biological evolution, sorting may be a cause of the patterning of variation. Sorting has received some attention in the archaeological literature (Abbott et al. 1992; Neff 1992; Neiman 1990; and Teltser, chapter 1), but, as I will argue, it is particularly important in the postcontact period. Although the package in which sorted traits occur is functional, the sorted traits are initially neutral with respect to fitness. At some later time they may become the target of selection or other evolutionary mechanisms.

In summary, then, the evolutionary process begins with the production of variation. Through sexual reproduction and cultural transmission humans are constantly producing new genotypic and phenotypic variants. Because artifacts are part of the human phenotype, they are part of the pool of variation. In the second step, evolutionary processes—including selection, sorting, and drift—operate on the pool of variation. If variants contribute to fitness, then they are defined as functional and subject to selection. Through time these variants behave deterministically, yet not all deterministic changes in trait frequencies are a product of selection. Variants that are tied to selected variants will be sorted and will appear as if they are the product of the selection. Still other variants, defined as stylistic, have no affect on fitness and are Markovian in nature.

The Evolutionary Process and Native Artifact Change

Viewing postcontact native artifact change as a two-step evolutionary process creates a fundamentally different explanatory framework than previous efforts in acculturation. First, cultural values and traditions are not causally relevant to explaining artifact change. Humans are cultural animals, which means that some parts of artifacts are cultural products. If cultural values, learning, and tradition are inherent parts of artifacts, these values and traditions are part of what must be explained; they cannot explain artifacts.

These statements do not imply that cultural motives or values are unimportant to evolutionary explanations. Within an evolutionary framework, these factors fit comfortably within the first step of the process. Cultural intent, such as the desire to increase one's prestige or the dislike of Europeans, may motivate human action.

As a result, European artifacts—raw materials, technologies, or forms—may be adopted or rejected. These behaviors and their consequences change the pool of variants on which evolutionary processes act.

Evaluated from an evolutionary perspective, acculturationists have confused the production of variation with causes of differential persistence of variants. As a result, they have made a two-step process into a one-step, Lamarckian process. As Rindos (1984:69–74) has pointed out, Lamarck understood the importance of environment in evolutionary change, but the intentional, or teleological, aspect of his evolutionary theory cannot explain human cultural change. The postcontact record repeatedly demonstrates that human intent does not explain cultural change. Indeed, change in human societies occurred independently of intentions. I will describe one example.

Earlier in my discussion of ethnological acculturation, I mentioned the introduction of metal axes to the Yir Yoront as an example of Linton's directed contact or, in Lamarckian terms, directed variation. In that experiment, the missionaries at Mitchell River wanted to "raise the living standards" (Sharp 1952:70) of the Yir Yoront. Accordingly, they restricted introduction of many European variants, such as alcohol, but freely distributed metal axes to individuals because axes were considered to be a genuine improvement. Although metal axes replaced stone axes, the "unintended" outcome was that the position of adult males changed dramatically. Males no longer "owned" a key artifact in the Yir Yoront assemblage; in addition, their trading relationships changed. As a result, Yir Yoront men lost much of their status. If cultural change is a one-step process, then we must argue that missionaries intended to change status relationships among the Yir Yoront. Alternatively, when cultural evolution is conceived as a two-step process, then evolutionary mechanisms are causal in the changes of Yir Yoront, and these mechanisms are independent of the production of variation. Indeed, the missionaries could not predict the outcome of their well-intended actions.

Incorporating cultural intentions within the first step of evolution means that other mechanisms, namely selection, sorting, and drift, occur in the second step and account for the frequency changes of variants. Even though selection may be of primary interest in understanding artifact change among populations of the postcontact period, sorting undoubtedly is operative and plays as significant a role as selection in sculpting the pattern of postcontact artifact change. Moreover, unlike the prehistoric record where differentiating between sorting and selection may be difficult, if not impossible, the temporal accessibility, coupled with the documentary record of the historical period, creates the possibility of differentiating between these mechanisms. A brief description of selection and sorting will highlight the importance of sorting.

Within 100 years of its introduction, the horse had diffused as far east as Texas, north into Canada, and south into Mexico (Ewers 1955). This rapidity suggests that the horse was a functional trait that greatly increased the fitness of individuals within populations. The strength of the horse out-competed humans and dogs as a means of transport; the speed of the horse gave it a unique advantage in hunting. Consequently, individuals who owned horses reproduced in greater numbers than others. This evolutionary advantage is expressed as the florescence of eighteenth-century Plains societies so well documented historically.

On the other hand, artifacts are an extension of the individual phenotype, and selection operates on individuals. When selection operates on individuals, artifacts will necessarily be sorted deterministically. During the postcontact period, the severity of selection operating on individuals was great because of the introduction of infectious diseases (e.g., Ramenofsky 1987, 1990, among others). As a consequence of the attrition of peoples, artifact frequencies necessarily decreased. Indeed, it is this sorting of artifacts that has allowed archaeologists to track the presence and action of infectious diseases as a selective agent.

The case of Ishi (Kroeber 1967) is a simple and dramatic example of both selection and sorting. Because Ishi was the last surviving Yahi, he could demonstrate how to reduce stone, make fire, and numerous other variants. When Ishi died of pneumonia, however, his knowledge also died. (See Dunnell 1991 for a similar point.)

Simply stated, because selection and sorting result in the same kind of frequency patterns, and because Native Americans were under heavy selective pressures during the postcontact period, both mechanisms were operating, sometimes separately, sometimes simultaneously. Differentiating between these mechanisms on historical time scales is possible and important for explaining the pattern and form of postcontact artifact change. For instance, as cultural knowledge of artifact technology was lost because people died, European artifacts may have affected fitness with the result that these forms increased and replaced native artifacts. In other contexts, such as the diffusion of the horse onto the Plains, selection operated on the European form, and that form increased the fitness of the individuals.

To summarize briefly, if evolutionary theory is the framework for explaining postcontact artifact change, then changes must be explained as a two-step process. Intention is one source of variation that operates during the first step, but it does not explain why variants are differentially represented in subsequent generations. Selection, sorting, and drift account for differential representation over time. Because of the new disease loads, much of the archaeological record of change may be due to sorting.

Implications and Conclusion

I have shown why acculturation failed to explain native artifact change during the postcontact period. I have also described evolutionary theory and discussed why it is a potentially useful theoretical framework for constructing explanations of postcontact, native artifact change. A number of implications derive from establishing evolutionary theory as a framework for constructing particular explanations of postcontact artifact change.

First, at the scale of continent, contact between Europeans and Native Americans resulted in artifact flow. Prior to the Columbian voyages, artifact histories of Europeans and Native Americans had evolved in isolation. Consequently, while artifacts were an extension of phenotype among both peoples, the forms, technologies, and products of all kinds were different. After 1492, Europeans and Native Americans transmitted knowledge and products, and the result was a greatly expanded pool of variation.

Second, because of the flow, artifactual diversity increased. Besides new variants in both Europe and the Americas, individuals combined variants that were products of different evolutionary histories to create new evolutionary combinations. Remodeling European files into chisels or fleshers, inlaying lead in tobacco pipes, and Southeastern colono-ware are examples. Furthermore, even though I focus on changes in artifacts among Native Americans, flow, by definition, is bidirectional. Not only did European products change the pool of variation in the Americas, but Native artifacts changed the pool of artifact variation of European colonists in the Americas and those who remained in Europe. The introduction of the potato or tobacco to Europeans are obvious examples.

Third, the expansion of the pool of variation increased the rate of evolutionary change. Fisher (1930) and Haldane (1932) demonstrated mathematically that as the number of variants increases, the rate of evolutionary change also increases. Even though the postcontact period is brief in evolutionary time, that brevity is further compressed by the rate of evolutionary change. Thus, changes that, in other settings, might have occurred over several generations may have occurred within a single generation. This difference in rate has obvious consequences for the transmission of variants within generations and the perpetuation of variants between generations.

Finally, given the increased diversity and increased rates of change, no simple generalizations can account for the perpetuations and change of artifacts across the last 500 years. Acculturationists have naively assumed that all European products or technologies were superior to native products and this superiority resulted in change in native artifacts and societies. Brain, for instance, stressed:

> The initial cultural advantage, of course, was technological. Whatever the motivations of the Europeans may have been, and whatever the auspices under which those motivations were translated into action, it was their technology that enabled the Europeans to implement their grand schemes, and also first attracted the Indians. This initial infatuation with European hardware and trinkets was the key to economic dependency,

which then led to political, social, and religious domination of the Indian. . . . (Brain 1979:270–271)

Within evolutionary theory, no European product is, a priori, superior to a native product. Superiority varies by historical context, and context changes over time. European guns, for instance, were initially a liability. They were slow, cumbersome, noisy, and they rusted (e.g., Ewers 1972; Linton 1940; Ray 1974). Consequently, guns did not replace bows and arrows everywhere. Among the bison hunters of the Plains, bows and arrows persisted until the eighteenth century when the technology of guns changed.

I am suggesting, then, that evolutionary explanations must be tied in time and space, and to particular artifact histories. Constructing these explanations at the scale of continent will involve different mechanisms than constructing explanations of change in native ceramics or house construction among the Rio Grande puebloans. Despite the differences in particular selective agents in particular contexts, the same processes operated, namely the continual production of undirected variation and the operation of evolutionary mechanisms on those variants. Some variants, perhaps a substantial number, were neutral with respect to fitness. Consequently, they either declined to zero or varied stochastically through time. Other variants, however, affected fitness. Changes in these variants were the consequence of selection operating on them directly. However, selection operating at higher scales sorted or swept traits at lower scales.

In the end, using an evolutionary framework will create not only a fundamentally different understanding of the form and pattern of native artifact change but, in the long run, will yield a body of knowledge regarding the causes and consequences of those changes that are fundamentally different from our current understanding.

Acknowledgments

I would like to thank Ana Steffen, Patrice Teltser, Bob Leonard, and Robert Dunnell, as well as Heidi Reed, and especially Fraser Neiman, for their helpful criticisms on earlier versions of the ideas presented here. I would also like to thank Kristen Hawkes, Jim O'Connell, and the graduate students at the University of Utah who listened to a slightly different version of the ideas discussed here. My stimulating discussions with both faculty and students helped clarify my view of evolutionary theory.

References

Abbott, A. L., R. D. Leonard, and G. T. Jones
1992   Explaining the Change From Biface to Flake Technology: A Selectionist Applica-
        tion. Paper Presented at the 57th Annual Meeting of the Society for American
        Archaeology, Pittsburgh, Pennsylvania.

Bamforth, D. B.
1993   Stone Tools, Steel Tools: Contact Period Household Technology at Helo. In *Eth-
        nohistory and Archaeology: Approaches to Postcontact Change in the Americas,* edited
        by J. D. Rogers and S. M. Wilson, pp. 51–72. Plenum Press, New York.

Brain, J. P.
1979   *Tunica Treasure.* The Peabody Museum of Archaeology and Ethnology Paper 71.
        Cambridge, Massachusetts.

Brandon, R.
1984   Adaptation and Evolutionary Theory. In *The Conceptual Issues in Evolutionary
        Theory,* edited by E. Sober, pp. 58–82. The MIT Press, Cambridge, Massa-
        chusetts.

Braun, D. P.
1990   Selection and Evolution in Nonhierarchical Organization. In *The Evolution of Po-
        litical Systems,* edited by S. Upham, pp. 62–86. Cambridge University Press,
        Cambridge, Massachusetts.

Broom, L., and E. Shevky
1952   Mexican in the United States: A Problem in Social Differences. *Sociology and
        Social Research* 36 (3).

Brown, I. W.
1979   Functional Group Changes and Acculturation: A Case Study of the French and
        the Indian in the Lower Mississippi Valley. *Mid-Continental Journal of Archaeology*
        4:147–165.

Burian, R. M.
1983   "Adaptation." In *Dimensions of Darwinism,* edited by M. Grene, pp. 287–314.
        Cambridge University Press, Cambridge, Massachusetts.

Carneiro, R. L.
1972   The Devolution of Evolution. *Social Biology* 19:247–258.

Charlton, T. H., and P. G. Fournier
1993   Urban and Rural Dimensions of the Contact Period: Central Mexico, 1521–
        1620. In *Ethnohistory and Archaeology: Approaches to Postcontact Change in the
        Americas,* edited by J. D. Rogers and S. M. Wilson, pp. 201–214. Plenum Press,
        New York.

Ceci, L.
1977   *The Effects of European Contact and Trade on the Settlement Pattern of Indians in
        Coastal New York, 1524–1665.* Ph.D. dissertation, The City University of New
        York, New York.

1982   The Value of Wampum among the New York Iroquois: A Case Study in Artifact Analysis. *Journal of Anthropological Research* 38:97–107.

Codere, H.

1961   Kwakuitl. In *Perspectives on American Indian Culture Change,* edited by E. Spicer, pp. 431–516. University of Chicago Press, Chicago.

Deagan, K. A.

1978   Cultures in Transition: Fusion and Assimilation Among the Eastern Timucua. In *Tacachale: Essays on the Indians of Florida and Southeastern Georgia During the Historic Period,* edited by J. T. Milanich and S. Proctor, pp. 89–119. Florida State Museum, Gainesville.

1990   Accommodation and Resistance: The Process and Impact of Spanish Colonization in the Southeast. *In Columbian Consequences: Archaeological and Historical Perspectives on the Spanish Borderlands East,* vol. 2, edited by D. H. Thomas, pp. 297–314. Smithsonian Institution Press, Washington, D.C.

Dozier, E. P.

1961   Rio Grande Pueblos. In *Perspectives on American Indian Culture Change,* edited by E. H. Spicer, pp. 94–186. University of Chicago Press, Chicago.

Dunnell, R. C.

1978   Style and Function: A Fundamental Dichotomy. *American Antiquity* 43:192–202.

1980   Evolutionary Theory in Archaeology. In *Advances in Archaeological Method and Theory,* vol. 3, edited by M. B. Schiffer, pp. 35–99. Academic Press, New York.

1989a   The Concept of Progress in Cultural Evolution. In *Evolutionary Progress,* edited by M. H. Nitecki, pp. 169–194. University of Chicago Press, Chicago.

1989b   Aspects of the Application of Evolutionary Theory in Archaeology. In *Archaeological Thought in America,* edited by C. C. Lamberg-Karlovsky, pp. 35–49. Cambridge University Press, Cambridge, Massachusetts.

1991   Methodological Impacts of Catastrophic Depopulation on American Archaeology and Ethnology. In *Columbian Consequences: The Spanish Borderlands in Pan-American Perspective,* vol. 3, edited by D. H. Thomas, 561–580. Smithsonian Institution Press, Washington, D.C.

Ewers, J. C.

1955   *The Horse in Blackfoot Culture.* Bureau of American Ethnology Bulletin 159, Washington, D.C.

1972   Influence of the Fur Trade on Indians of the Northern Plains. In *People and Pelts: Selected Papers of the Second North American Fur Trade Conference,* edited by Malvina Bolus, pp. 1–26. Peguis Publishers, Winnipeg.

Fisher, R. A.

1930   *The Genetical Theory of Natural Selection.* Clarendon Press, Oxford.

Foster, G. M.

1960   *Culture and Conquest.* Viking Fund Publication in Anthropology 27. New York.

Haldane, J.B.S.

1932   *The Causes of Evolution.* Longmans, Green, New York.

Hamell, G. R.
1983   Trading in Metaphors: The Magic of Beads. In *Proceedings of the 1982 Glass Trade Bead Conference,* edited by C. F. Hayes, pp. 5–28. Museum and Science Center Research Records 16, Rochester.

Harris, J. S.
1940   The White Knife Shoshoni of Nevada. In *Acculturation of Seven North American Indian Tribes,* edited by R. Linton, pp. 39–118. Appleton-Century-Crofts, New York.

Herskovits, M. J.
1948   *Man and His Works.* Alfred Knopf, New York.

1958   *Acculturation: The Study of Culture Contact,* 2d edition. Peter Smith, Gloucester, Massachusetts.

1964   *Cultural Dynamics.* Alfred Knopf, New York.

Kidder, A. V.
1936   *The Glaze Paint, Culinary, and Other Wares. The Pottery of Pecos,* vol. 2, by A. V. Kidder and Anna O. Shepard, 388 pp. Yale University Press. New Haven, Connecticut.

Kimura, M.
1983   *The Neutral Theory of Molecular Evolution.* Cambridge University Press, Cambridge, Massachusetts.

King, J. L., and T. H. Jukes
1969   Non-Darwinian Evolution. *Science* 164:788–798.

Kroeber, T.
1967   *Ishi in Two Worlds: A Biography of the Last Wild Indian in North America.* University of California Press, Berkeley.

Leonard, R. D.
1993   The Persistence of the Explanatory Dilemma in Contact Period Studies. In *Ethnohistory and Archaeology: Approaches to Postcontact Change in the Americas,* edited by J. D. Rogers and S. M. Wilson, pp. 31–48. Plenum Press, New York.

Leonard, R. D., and G. T. Jones
1987   Elements of an Inclusive Evolutionary Model for Archaeology. *Journal of Anthropological Archaeology* 6:199–219.

Lewontin, R. C.
1984   Adaptation. In *Conceptual Issues in Evolutionary Biology,* edited by E. Sober, pp. 235–251. MIT Press, Cambridge, Massachusetts.

Linton, R. (editor)
1940   *Acculturation of Seven American Indians Tribes.* Appleton-Century-Crofts, New York.

Mair, L. P. (editor)
1938   *Method of Culture Contact in Africa.* International Institute of African Languages and Cultures, Memorandum XV. Oxford University Press, Oxford, England.

Mayr, E.
1988   *Toward a New Philosophy of Biology: Observations of an Evolutionist.* Harvard University Press, Cambridge, Massachusetts.

Neff, H.
1992   Ceramics and Evolution. *Archaeological Method and Theory,* vol. 4, edited by M. B. Schiffer, pp. 141–193. University of Arizona Press, Tucson.

Neiman, F. D.
1990   *An Evolutionary Approach to Archaeological Inference: Aspects of Architectural Variation in the 17th-Century Chesapeake.* Ph.D. dissertation, Department of Anthropology, Yale University, New Haven, Connecticut.
1995   Stylistic Variation in Evolutionary Perspective: Implications for Decorative Diversity and Inter-Assemblage Distance in Illinois Woodland Ceramic Assemblages. *American Antiquity* in press.

O'Brien, M. J., and T. D. Holland
1990   Variation, Selection, and the Archaeological Record. In *Archaeological Method and Theory,* vol. 2, edited by M. B. Schiffer, pp. 31–80. University of Arizona Press, Tucson.
1992   The Role of Adaptation in Archaeological Explanation. *American Antiquity* 57: 36–59.

Peebles, C. S., and S. M. Kus
1977   Some Archaeological Correlates of Ranked Societies. *American Antiquity* 42:421–448.

Phillips, P., J. A. Ford, and J. B. Griffin
1951   *Archaeological Survey in the Lower Mississippi Alluvial Valley, 1940–1947.* Peabody Museum of Archaeology and Ethnology Papers 25. Cambridge, Massachusetts.

Quimby, G. I., and A. Spoehr
1951   Acculturation and Material Culture—I. *Fieldiana Anthropology* 36 (3). Chicago Natural History Museum, Chicago.

Ray, A. J.
1974   *Indians in the Fur Trade: Their Role as Trappers, Hunters, and Middlemen in the Lands Southwest of Hudson Bay 1660–1870.* University of Toronto Press, Toronto.

Ramenofsky, A. F.
1987   *Vectors of Death: The Archaeology of European Contact.* University of New Mexico Press, Albuquerque.
1990   Loss of Innocence: Assessing Archaeological Explanations of Aboriginal Change in the Sixteenth-Century Southeast. In *Columbian Consequences: Archaeological and Historical Perspectives on the Spanish Borderlands East,* vol. 2, edited by D. H. Thomas, pp. 31–48. Smithsonian Institution Press, Washington, D.C.
1991   Historical Science and Contact Period Studies. In *Columbian Consequences: Archaeological and Historical Perspectives in Pan-American Perspective,* vol. 3, edited by D. H. Thomas, 437–452. Smithsonian Institution Press, Washington, D.C.

Reed, H. E., and T. Maxwell

1990   Darwinian Evolutionary Theory for Archaeology: Some Considerations. Paper Presented at the 55th Annual Meeting of the Society for American Archaeology. Las Vegas, Nevada.

Rindos, D.

1984   *The Origins of Agriculture: An Evolutionary Perspective.* Academic Press, New York.

Rogers, J. D.

1990   *Objects of Change: The Archaeology and History of Arikara Contact with Europeans.* Smithsonian Institution Press, Washington, D.C.

1993   The Social and Material Implications of Culture Contact on the Northern Plains. In *Ethnohistory and Archaeology: Approaches to Postcontact Change in the Americas,* edited by J. D. Rogers and S. M. Wilson, pp. 73–88. Plenum Press, New York.

Service, E. R.

1962   *Primitive Social Organization: An Evolutionary Perspective.* Random House, New York.

Sharp, L.

1934a   The Social Organization of the Yir Yoront Tribe, Cape York Peninsula. *Oceania* 4:404–431.

1934b   Ritual Life and Economics of the Yir Yoront. *Oceania* 5:19–42.

1952   Steel Axes for Stone Age Australians. In *Human Problems in Technological Change: A Casebook,* edited by E. H. Spicer, pp. 69–90. Russell Sage Foundation, New York.

Social Science Research Council

1954   Acculturation: An Exploratory Formulation. *American Anthropologist* 56:973–1002.

Spicer, E.

1961   Types of Contact and Processes of Change. In *Perspectives on American Indian Culture Change,* edited by E. Spicer, pp. 517–544. University of Chicago Press, Chicago.

Spicer, E. (editor)

1952   *Human Problems in Technological Change, a Casebook.* Russell Sage Foundation, New York.

Teltser, P. A.

1988   *The Mississippian Archaeological Record on the Malden Plain, Southeast Missouri: Local Variability in Evolutionary Perspective.* Ph.D. dissertation, Department of Anthropology, University of Washington, Seattle.

Trigger, B. G.

1981   Archaeology and the Ethnographic Present. *Anthropologica* 23:3–17.

Vernon, R.

1988   Seventeenth-Century Apalachee Colono-Ware as a Reflection of Demography, Economics, and Acculturation. *Historical Archaeology* 22:76–82.

Vernon, R., and A. S. Cordell
1993   A Distributional and Technological Study of Apalachee Colono-Ware from San Luis de Talimali. In *The Spanish Missions of La Florida,* edited by B. G. McEwan, pp. 418–442. University Press of Florida, Gainesville.

Vrba, E. S., and N. Eldredge
1984   Individuals, Hierarchies and Processes toward a more Complete Evolutionary Theory. *Paleobiology* 10:146–171.

Vrba, E. S., and S. J. Gould
1986   The Hierarchical Expansion of Selection: Selection and Sorting Cannot Be Equated. *Paleobiology* 12:217–228.

Waselkov, G. A.
1993   Historic Creek Indian Responses to European Trade and the Rise of Political Factions. In *Ethnohistory and Archaeology: Approaches to Postcontact Change in the Americas,* edited by J. D. Rogers and S. M. Wilson, pp. 123–131. Plenum Press, New York.

White, J. R.
1975   Historic Contact Sites as Laboratories for the Study of Culture Change. *The Conference on Historic Site Archaeology Papers* 9:153–163.

Wright, S.
1931   Evolution in Mendelian Populations. *Genetics* 16:97–159.

8

The Evolutionary Significance of Ceremonial Architecture in Polynesia

Michael W. Graves and Thegn N. Ladefoged

◆◆ With the recognition that the prehistory of Polynesia has substantially more time-depth than first assumed (Emory and Sinoto 1961; Suggs 1961), archaeologists have begun to examine the twin problems of change through time and spatial variability in the archaeological record of the region (Fig. 8.1). Initially, these problems were addressed by employing methods from culture history (Green 1963; Sinoto 1966) and culture reconstruction (Green et al. 1967; Suggs 1961). More recently, archaeologists have drawn theoretical inspiration from processual approaches that emphasize evolutionary perspectives (Kirch 1984; Kirch and Green 1987). The rationale offered by Clark and Terrell (1978) and Suggs (1961) for an evolutionary or ecological approach to the region's prehistory is warranted by the concept of "islands as laboratories" in which the archaeological record can be investigated under relatively controlled conditions. Despite some exaggeration of its potential, this notion of islands as laboratories is useful since islands have clearly demarked physical boundaries, and Polynesian islands are relatively diverse in natural environmental structure (e.g., distance from continents and other archipelagoes, size and elevation, rainfall, temperature, seasonality, and resource abundance and distribution). Because they are naturally set apart, it is possible to compare prehistoric development on islands characterized by different environmental attributes.

Additionally, archaeologists working in Polynesia—regardless of the perspective adopted—have tended to record the same kinds of archaeological phenomena and to utilize similar variables in their research. Architecture used for ceremonial purposes is one part of the archaeological record of Polynesia that has

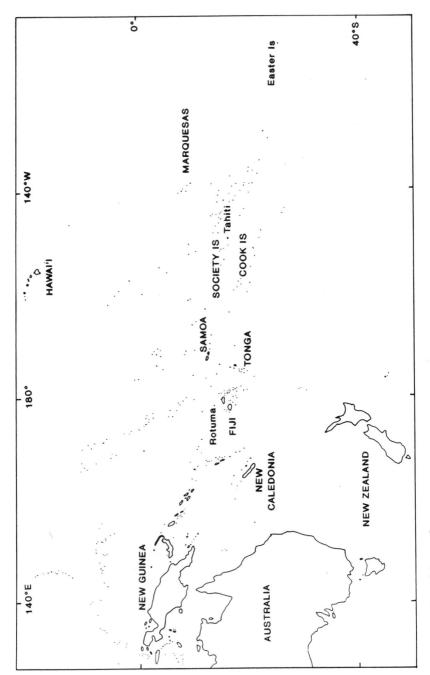

Figure 8.1. Map of the Pacific

Figure 8.2. Representation of re-erected statues at Ahu Akivi, Easter Island, adapted from Bellwood (1987: Fig. 70).

received considerable attention by both researchers and the public. The architectural remains are relatively abundant, sometimes occur as large structures, and are often known to or are identifiable by archaeologists. For example, on Easter Island the large carved stone image heads (*moai*) are found atop stone foundations (*ahu*) (Fig. 8.2). Hawai'i and the Society Islands (including Tahiti) are well known for their temples (*heiau* and *marae*) associated with stone foundations (Figs. 8.3 to 8.5). In the Marquesas, ceremonial dancing grounds (*tohua*) were constructed (Fig. 8.6). Similar kinds of structures exist throughout Polynesia, and all have been linked through archaeological, historical, and oral historical research to the performance of ritual and ceremonial activities. The homologous relationships among the human populations and the ceremonial architecture of Polynesia have been made previously (Bellwood 1970, 1979; Emory 1943, 1970; Green 1993) and form a core assumption of the research presented here. Therefore, it is potentially possible to employ a common framework for the interpretation of the distribution of prehistoric ceremonial architecture through time and space in Polynesia.

The first objective of this paper is to describe how ceremonial architecture in the region has been identified in archaeological terms. Such identification is necessary both to highlight the potential for systematic study of this portion of the archaeological record and to suggest some of the problems that archaeologists must eventually confront in such studies. Next, we illustrate how ceremonial architecture can be interpreted from the perspectives of cultural evolution and biological, or scientific, evolution. Thus, we shall be concerned with the theoretical principles represented by these two evolutionary perspectives. Each suggests a different kind of explanation for the development of ceremonial architecture, and each is linked to a different hypothesis in which the relationship between ceremonial

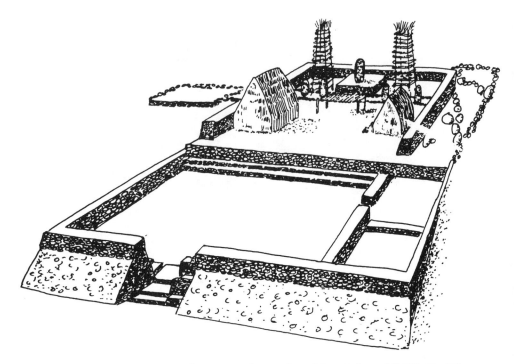

Figure 8.3. Representation of a Hawaiian *heiau,* adapted from Bellwood (1987: Fig. 58).

architecture and environmental structure is specified. Finally, we offer a prelimi-nary evaluation of the empirical sufficiency of both cultural and scientific evolu-tion with respect to explanations for the development of ceremonial architecture in Polynesia.

The Identification of Ceremonial Architecture

Archaeologists have at least three, not necessarily exclusive, options for the identification of ceremonial architecture. First, we can proceed theoretically to define a concept of ceremony or ritual whose application to a set of archaeologi-cal remains or inferred behaviors is relatively straightforward and whose variabil-ity we expect to explain within the originating theoretical framework. Such a linkage is necessary, since the phenomena accounted for by a particular theoreti-cal perspective should be congruent with what we have observed and recorded from the archaeological record. Although not explicitly enunciated by archae-ologists, the dominant perspective on ceremonial architecture shares much in common with that of style, that is, "lacking detectable selective values" (Dunnell

1978:199). This view considers ceremonial architecture as a form of cultural expression, in most cases being the stylized manifestation of social complexity. As an alternative, we present a conceptualization anticipating our later attempt to sketch a model explaining why such architecture may be said to have selective value. From this perspective, ceremonial architecture refers to a portion of the archaeological record with selective value, but value that does not directly contribute to subsistence acquisition, production, maintenance, or storage, or to human reproduction. Archaeologically, ceremonial architecture would then consist of a subset of all the physical manifestations of structures or buildings that cannot be established as portions of residential or resource areas.

While the definition provided above is sufficiently general to include all potential ceremonial architecture, it may also be unsatisfying for those who would hope to see ceremonial architecture defined in its own terms, not as a residual category of culture. A second approach, then, is to develop a contextual and behavioral definition for ceremonial architecture. At minimum, ceremonial architecture would then represent the location at which ritual behaviors are performed. Rappaport (1979) lists a number of characteristics associated with ritual which may help archaeologists develop expectations for its archaeological manifestations, including formality (i.e., stylized and repetitive behaviors), information transmission, and the establishment of sacredness. In Polynesia, Goldman (1970) argues

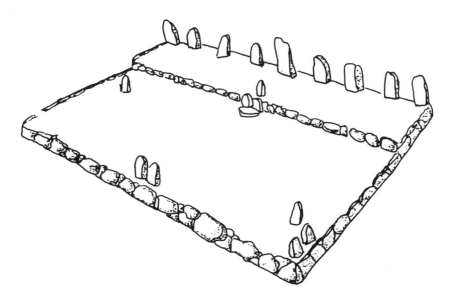

Figure 8.4. Representation of Hawaiian Necker Island *heiau*, adapted from Bellwood (1987: Fig. 55).

that ritual involves the transposition of human qualities with those associated with the divine. This transposition is accomplished through sacrifice and worship, and utilizes concepts and deities drawn from Polynesian cosmology. For both Goldman (1970) and Valeri (1985), ritual transposition in Polynesia is founded on differentiation, in terms of hierarchy and separation. Sacrifice and worship thus produce and affirm both cosmological and social distinctions.

The combination of information transmission and sacredness in ritual helps to further our previous definition of ceremonial architecture as that part of the archaeological record distinguished from direct resource production and human reproduction. In general, Polynesian ceremonial architecture includes a partially or completely paved or outlined court segmented into front and back areas by an *ahu* (altar), uprights, or other smaller features or structures such as pits, houses, and scaffolding. Within the court are few contemporaneous features indicative of food production or preparation, or other domestic activities. Ceremonial architecture is usually spatially discrete from residential features and structures. The separation is accomplished, at varying scales, by the orientation and arrangement of ceremonial architecture, physical separation, and the architectural elements used to complete the structure. Additionally, ceremonial architecture incorporates spatial relationships with other ceremonial structures, topographic features, and

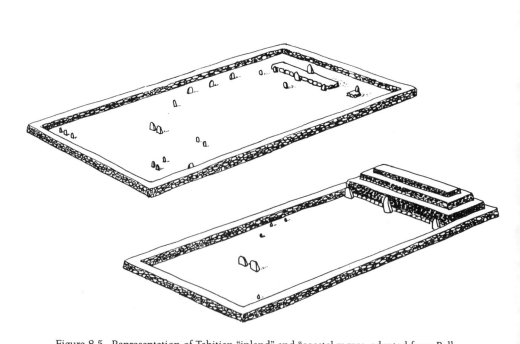

Figure 8.5. Representation of Tahitian "inland" and "coastal *marae*, adapted from Bellwood (1987: Fig. 39).

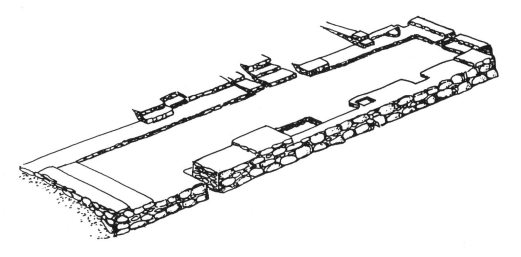

Figure 8.6. Representation of Marquesan *tohua*, adapted from Bellwood (1987: Fig. 51).

visible features of the ocean and sky. Separation appears to be the underlying canonical theme of Polynesian ceremonial architecture which ties that architecture to the enduring quality of sacredness.

Other characteristics of Polynesian architecture are more variable and include the shape and form of structures and foundations, the size and height of built areas, volume of rock or earthen foundations, the number of features in the court, construction materials, and the specific architectural elements employed. These vary for a variety of reasons related to differentiation and hierarchy, including functional and social organizational differences, the deity (or deities) represented, placement on the landscape, and raw materials available. Because of this variability, we suggest that the attributes that represent the canonical qualities of separateness may be the most useful for identifying the archaeological manifestations of such architecture.

Finally, a third way in which ceremonial architecture can be identified is through historical and contemporary records. From the time of the arrival of Europeans and Americans in Polynesia during the seventeenth to nineteenth centuries, documentary records identify locations where rituals and ceremonies were performed. Additionally, oral traditions as well as contemporary Polynesians, identify sites, including those with indications of ceremonial architecture, throughout the region.

Altogether, these three sources of information provide archaeologists with the means to deploy a systematic, comprehensive, and theoretically informed basis for identifying and investigating ceremonial architecture in the archaeological record of Polynesia. Each source would be associated with a somewhat different, yet overlapping, assemblage of ceremonial architecture; and although each source would emphasize some sets of ceremonial architecture over others, the combination of all three would likely maximize our ability to identify all the varieties of ceremonial architecture that exist in the archaeological record of Polynesia. Thus, the combined sources make it possible to employ ceremonial architecture in the evaluation of different interpretations for its development throughout Polynesia.

Evolutionary Perspectives and Ceremonial Architecture

Cultural Evolution

Two main approaches for studying change in the archaeological record via processes or principles of evolution can be distinguished: cultural evolution and biologically based evolution (Dunnell 1980). Cultural evolution is best known to most archaeologists through the writings of our contemporaries (Adams 1966; Flannery 1972; Hill 1977; Price 1982; Sanders and Webster 1978) but has enjoyed earlier periods of popularity as a mode of anthropological interpretation (Hawthorne and Belshaw 1957; Wolf 1964). In Polynesia, cultural evolution has been, and continues to be, the dominant interpretive approach following the seminal works of two cultural anthropologists, Marshall Sahlins (1955, 1957, 1958; Sahlins and Service 1960) and Irving Goldman (1955, 1957, 1960, 1970). The main adherents today, however, are archaeologists (e.g., Cordy 1981; Green et al. 1967; Kirch 1984, 1990a; Kirch and Green 1987; Suggs 1961). Typically, cultural evolutionists have emphasized the adaptation of groups (at the scale of islands or archipelagoes) to their natural and social environments. As we shall subsequently show, the development of and variation in Polynesian social complexity—often monitored by observations of ceremonial architecture—have been the common themes which have linked virtually all cultural evolutionary research, both archaeological and anthropological.

The history and nature of cultural evolution have been explored by others (e.g., Dunnell 1980; Durham 1992; Sahlins and Service 1960; Service 1962; Wolf 1964) and the results of that work need not be repeated here. Instead, we briefly describe the history of cultural evolutionary research in Polynesia. This review is necessary since the development of modern cultural evolution was closely tied to this region and the adoption of a cultural evolutionary perspective by archaeologists in Polynesia occurred somewhat independently of that by the New Archaeology in the United States (see Dunnell 1980:75–83).

The publication of M. Sahlins's *Social Stratification in Polynesia* in the late 1950s was a milestone in Americanist cultural evolutionary studies. Sahlins's book

(1958) was the first comparative ethnohistorical investigation of social complexity in which environmental variation was identified as a factor promoting particular patterns of social configurations in Polynesian culture. That Sahlins has since distanced himself from this work and this perspective has not affected its singular significance, especially for archaeologists. First, Sahlins's work (1957; 1958:248) established Polynesian societies as cases of adaptive radiation or differentiation from a "single cultural genus." This model has continued to structure most cultural evolutionary accounts of Polynesian prehistoric change (cf., Kirch 1984; Kirch and Green 1987), even those at odds with his original environmental emphasis (Goldman 1955, 1970). Second, the view of cultures as "cohesive wholes" (Sahlins 1958:247) established the functional linkage between separate components of social systems, such as status rankings, political integration, and deference.[1] Again, such an integrated view of Polynesian cultures was commonplace among cultural evolutionists, even those who held antithetical views about the causal forces in cultural evolution (e.g., Goldman 1955:680; 1957:156–157). Goldman (1955:690), for instance, linked religion and political authority, and a change in one implied a change in the other. Thus, the differentiation of historic Polynesian societies into three types—Traditional, Open, and Stratified—was the outcome of evolutionary change from relatively less to relatively more social complexity (Goldman 1970:20). This involved the increasing role and impact of both religion and government in evolutionary change, the result of status rivalry.

For Sahlins, different levels of sociopolitical organization in Polynesia reflected the particular adaptation resulting from the interplay of environment and technology. The mechanism by which change and differentiation occurred was (after White 1949) a greater harnessing of energy or productivity (Sahlins 1958:247), which was largely dependent on the environmental diversity of an island since traditional Polynesian technology was similar from one place to another. Environmental diversity, in turn, was linked to greater resource productivity. Therefore, those Polynesian societies associated with high volcanic islands such as Tahiti and Hawai'i were able to develop more means to produce energy (i.e., food) and were consequently the locations of greatest social stratification and political development.

Clearly, what separates the cultural evolutionary models of Goldman and Sahlins are the functional linkages and adaptive transformations emphasized by each. For Sahlins, environmental diversity and productivity correlate with Polynesian variation in social stratification. The environment thus establishes the parameters for possible levels of cultural development. Goldman, on the other hand, privileges the role of status rivalry in the development of varying levels of social stratification among Polynesian societies. Here, the motivational force of status rivalry was thought to establish the "push" toward the level of social complexity achieved in different parts of Polynesia. The role of environment was clearly secondary but instrumental since it effectively set the upper limits on the level of complexity achieved.

Goldman's work, focused as it was on identifying the link between status rivalry and the development of Polynesian societies, was clearly the most influential in the earliest archaeological attempts to identify cultural evolutionary trends in eastern Polynesia. Suggs (1961) discussed how the initial construction of *tohua* (ceremonial platforms or places) in the Marquesas might indicate the elaboration of status rivalry. The temporal variation he identified for these structures as well as for *ma'ae* (temples), from simple to more complex, was suggested to indicate increasing prestige of the priesthood.

Both Sahlins (1958) and Goldman (grudgingly, in a 1960 publication) found agreement in the proposition that increases in cultural elaboration in Polynesian societies were partly a function of greater environmental diversity or high resource productivity. This notion is structured on a Malthusian-like assumption that human potential will rise to match the productivity of the environment in which societies are found. It also highlights one of the progressive features of cultural evolution in Polynesia, whereby change occurs from simple to complex as populations colonize, settle, and increase on new islands in the area. Not surprisingly, this idea has been the foundation for a number of subsequent archaeological studies in Polynesia. Peebles and Kus (1977:426) generalized for Hawai'i that "the greater the productivity of an *ahupua'a* [a territorially based community], the greater the number of royal *heiau* [temples]." They imply that such a correlation might be used to examine the development of chiefly control in Hawaiian society.

Kirch has remarked on the great potential of ceremonial architecture for archaeological discussions of political changes in precontact Polynesian societies. Such structures, he suggests, should serve as markers reflecting the various stages of sociopolitical adaptation among Polynesian chiefdoms (Kirch 1984:286). Subsequently, in a paper discussing the variation in monumental architecture in Hawai'i and Tonga, Kirch (1990b:206) argues that these structures "played a key role as visual markers of chiefly dominance and hegemony." Although these two island societies are homologously related, Kirch suggests that the appearance of large-scale ritual architecture in each was a result of cultural convergence. He draws upon the distribution of *luakini heiau* (temples where human sacrifices are thought to have occurred) on the island of Moloka'i to propose that greater labor investment in ceremonial architecture occurred in the Kona district of the island; the Kona district had high productivity due to a dense concentration of fishponds that were constructed along its coastline. More recently, Kirch (1992:16) plots the distribution of major temples and primary zones of irrigation on the island of O'ahu and suggests that the temples and zones of irrigation are spatially associated and that the appearance of temples is a function of the surplus produced by irrigated agriculture.

The view that the construction and elaboration of ceremonial architecture are a result of changes in food productivity is also found in Kolb's (1991) research on the island of Maui. Kolb (1991:380–383) concludes his study with the observations that *heiau* construction in different districts of Maui approximates the productivity, either naturally determined or humanly induced, of those districts. Thus, these ceremonial structures are viewed as indicators of the relative amount of power exercised by the chiefs of those districts through time, and power is generally a function of the surplus produced through economic or subsistence development.

Both anthropologists and archaeologists who have adopted a cultural evolutionary perspective in Polynesia employ the archipelago, the island, or the society as their scale for analysis. These then become their units of evolutionary change. Within this perspective, ceremonial architecture is generally treated as a functional reflection of the political constituents (authority, rivalry, and power) of the social system. Even when the hegemonic role of authority and its expression through ceremonial architecture is explicitly set within the framework of political economy (Earle 1991; Kolb 1991), concomitant changes in population size or density, social complexity, and ceremonial architecture take on an adaptationist character when placed within the possibilism of environmental productivity (Brumfiel and Earle 1987:2–3). Dunnell (1980:44–46) notes that these changes occur because of the typological concepts and generalizations about progress which underlie most archaeological views about cultural evolution or change. In this context, causality is lodged in the sequence of changing variables, and archaeological investigation is devoted to identifying the onset of change in order to discover one or more prime movers.

Despite these drawbacks, the comparative hypothesis first forwarded by Sahlins, and subsequently elaborated by archaeologists on a smaller scale, remains provocative. Is there an effect of environmental structure on the development of social complexity and ceremonial architecture in Polynesia? The association that some cultural evolutionists have noted between large ceremonial sites and the productive potential of certain environments suggests that they may have identified a pattern of general interest but have yet to frame the question in evolutionary terms which are not at the same time typological and progressive.

Scientific Evolution

Evolutionary theory based on biological principles has rarely been used to interpret the prehistory of Polynesia or Oceania and thus is poorly known to most archaeologists working in the region (but see Allen 1992; Graves et al. 1990;

Hunt 1987, 1989; Ladefoged 1993). Nonetheless, we believe the perspective of scientific evolution has exceptional potential because it can help to identify new ways of thinking about the explanation of change and variability in the archaeological record. Scientific evolution does so by emphasizing the selective mechanisms for the persistence or loss of cultural variability through time. Following Dunnell (1980:84–85) we believe that scientific evolution differs from cultural evolution with respect to ontology and, consequently, that the two perspectives differ in the kind of explanation they seek from the archaeological record.

As an alternative to cultural evolution, selectionist models should describe the operation of dynamic principles and from these posit particular configurations of variables and concomitant patterns of material-behavioral variation. The cause for change within these models would then be lodged in theory rather than being the outcome of empirical generalizations. Evolutionary ecologists and, more recently, archaeologists have sought to use models consistent with or derived from biological evolutionary theory to explain the differential persistence or occurrence of human traits. We develop a model that may explain certain aspects of the evolution of ceremonial architecture in the late prehistory of Polynesia. The model focuses on the underlying environmental context that can provide the selective basis for the construction and elaboration of ceremonial structures.

Dunnell (1989) initiated this process by sketching a model which suggests that not all human energy is directly devoted to individual reproduction, or to food and material production or maintenance—what we might think of as the major domains over which selection would be likely to operate. Some of this other energy is devoted to storage, either biologically or culturally, a trait under some selective control. Yet for Dunnell (1989:47) there is another domain of energy expenditure, which from a strictly reproductive point of view he infelicitously labels as "waste." We prefer the term superfluous, which we think better captures the intent of Dunnell and which might be less offensive. Superfluous activity is human energy expended on acts that do not immediately and directly contribute to one's food supply or storage, or reproduction. All animals, including humans, engage in some superfluous activity. The construction, maintenance, and use of ceremonial architecture represent examples of superfluous activities as defined by Dunnell. Note that this definition is also congruent with our earlier description of how ceremonial architecture might be identified in the archaeological record.

The fact that such behaviors are superfluous, however, does not mean that they are either culturally or selectively unimportant. Dunnell (1989:47–48) argues that the selective value of such activities is twofold: (1) superfluous activities help to stabilize population levels below "carrying capacity" by diverting energy away from activities that would be necessary to maintain populations at a higher level; and (2) during periods of resource scarcity, superfluous activities can be temporarily abandoned and thus create an interval of time in which individuals can contribute relatively more energy to subsistence, reproduction, or storage. An important implication of this proposition is that superfluous behavior may indirectly and significantly contribute to the increased survivorship of offspring through lower population numbers or lower rates of population increase than that which might be otherwise experienced.

Finally, Dunnell (1989:47) suggests that superfluous behaviors are fixed by selection (i.e., have a regular occurrence) when "environmental perturbations are severe and/or unpredictable." The importance of this approach, as observed by Dunnell (1989:48), is that it makes it unnecessary to interpret the appearance and elaboration of superfluous behaviors from the progressive ontology of cultural evolution. Dunnell does not develop the model further, but rather leaves it incomplete in several respects. Because of the intriguing possibilities, we provide additional formulation to the model by first describing the measurement of environmental perturbations. We also consider the various dimensions along which superfluous traits might be measured. Next we show how superfluous behavior might have at least one other selective advantage besides those advantages proposed by Dunnell. Finally, we describe the expectations of this model in relationship to the initial occurrence, persistence, change in scale, and loss of superfluous behavior.

What is meant by severe or unpredictable perturbations and how may these two qualities of perturbations co-occur to fix superfluous traits? For us, severe perturbations refer to extreme variations in climatic or environmental conditions, such as hurricanes, droughts, flooding, or environmental degradation. When such extreme conditions occur, additional labor must be diverted to resource production even as output diminishes, and resources may become scarce, especially if the conditions persist. Unpredictable perturbations are those variations whose occurrences are relatively unpatterned through time or those difficult to estimate. Care must be exercised to consider the interaction of these two dimensions of perturbations, since environments which experience severe perturbations (i.e., exhibit high variation from the mean) also tend to be the locations that experience them most often, thus rendering the perturbations and their associated effects relatively predictable through time and space. The use of the word "predictability" here refers to the likelihood or relative certainty of perturbations and thus is different from the way that evolutionary ecologists often use the term to connote production or resource reliability. Environmental contexts differ in the severity and predictability of perturbations, and in the spatial and temporal predictability of distributions of resources. Additionally, the geographic positioning of human populations relative to one another and in relation to the spatial and temporal variability of resources available to them represents a final dimension to our consideration of perturbations. The effects of environmental perturbations can be lessened when human populations are located near one another. Proximity, of course, increases the likelihood that they will both experience the same perturbations. These dimensions have implications for the selective value of superfluous behavior.

Superfluous behavior can be measured or monitored in several different ways.It may also be related to different aspects of environmental perturbations and selective advantage. For our purposes here, we differentiate the origin, or the earliest occurrence, of superfluous behavior from its persistence or continued occurrence through time. We also distinguish the scale of superfluous behavior as a categorical variable (although we recognize that it might ultimately be treated as a continuous one), which has two attribute states: small and large. Thus, there is both small- and large-scale (i.e., monumental) ceremonial architecture. Finally, the geographic location in which ceremonial architecture occurs, or its density within an area, represents a final measure of superfluous behavior.

Dunnell identified population dampening and the option for switching to alternative productive behaviors as the primary advantages that might accrue to individuals engaged in superfluous behaviors. Yet, one other advantage which this behavior may confer on individuals is that it may establish a social context for resource and labor pooling, especially when it involves large-scale increments of such behaviors (e.g., as in the building of monumental ceremonial architecture).

Conceived in this way, a selectionist model of superfluous behavior can be linked to evolutionary ecology. Such behavior can be an alternative behavioral pattern which persists because it results in the reduction of risk under conditions of resource uncertainty. It may share the outcome of risk reduction, along with behavioral strategies such as population movement, subsistence change or intensification, and food storage (Smith 1988:233). Moreover, the circumstances that would favor superfluous behaviors over these strategies can be generally estimated.

If resource alternatives are limited or if intensification of resource production or storage would tend to increase human populations within environments subject to unpredictable and severe perturbations, then changes to food production or storage will eventually fail. Similarly, population movement out of such areas would result in loss of property or resource rights, especially if such relocations became long-term or permanently established elsewhere.

Resource sharing within a population is ineffective when all members experience relativity the same conditions at the same time, thus rendering no advantage of such behaviors. Pooling resources over large areas (across populations) may be effective (as we discuss below) but is affected by the spatial and temporal scale of resource variability. Only when the timing of resource disparities are complementary across geographic localities would pooling through exchange be advantageous (Rautman 1993).

Dunnell (1989:48) suggests that superfluous traits should originate at the geographic margins of a regionally distributed archaeological complex. Although he does not explicitly state why this should be, we conclude that this is where environmental perturbations are likely to be more severe and thus where superfluous behaviors are most likely to be first established at detectable levels. However, the long-term predictability of resource perturbations in such locations makes it unlikely that superfluous behaviors will necessarily persist for very long. Instead, we propose that the persistence of superfluous traits should be linked to a combination of moderately severe perturbations and irregular occurrence of this variability through time and across space. These conditions would maximally combine severity and unpredictability, thus fixing superfluous traits in a population. At the same time, such conditions would render other behavioral responses, such as direct exchange across locations, less effective. We also anticipate that the loss of, or marked reduction in the frequency of, superfluous traits would occur when moderate and irregular environmental perturbations diminish in their temporal and geographic effects, either through changing environmental conditions, alterations to resource availability, or by dramatic reductions in population.

Thus far we have emphasized the origins and persistence of superfluous traits in terms of the advantages first suggested by Dunnell. Yet, we propose that where there are marked scalar changes in superfluous behavior (i.e., the construction of monuments), these changes can often be explained as the result of interpopulation integration. Under conditions of marked (and sometimes complementary) spatio-temporal variation in resource availability, the pooling of resources (including labor for constructing ceremonial architecture) among separate populations in near proximity is advantageous.

As evolutionary ecologists and archaeologists Boone (1983, 1992), Dyson-Hudson and Smith (1978), and Ladefoged (1993) have noted, such integration is often preceded by intergroup aggression and the subsequent dominance of one group over another. These researchers suggest that such aggression occurs when there are relatively stable and predictable food resources for which other groups might vie through warfare or tribute, and which could be obtained at a lower cost than local food resources. The stimulus for intergroup aggression is likely to be most intensely felt where diverse environments occur in sufficiently close proximity, and where those living in less productive areas are at greater risk and would be faced earlier, or more regularly, with the problems of provisioning themselves with sufficient quantity or quality of food. Such environments would include areas where the year-to-year reliability of food is lowered because of unpredictable perturbations in climatic patterns, as well as areas where the costs of applying additional labor to increase food production are high relative to potential returns. These environments and the resources they support are uncertain in relation to the reliability of production adequate to feed people.

Individuals living in these environments are more likely to employ aggression in order to obtain additional supplies of food or other resources, given the benefits of aggression in relation to its costs. Political integration may occur under these conditions when the disparity of resource distribution is not immense and where the populations of different groups are relatively equivalent in size. Thus, integration may substitute for continued intergroup aggression, especially where those who instigate and participate most often in aggression are also likely to benefit from suprapolity integration.

To summarize, we have described the environmental conditions under which first intergroup aggression and then suprapolity integration may occur. It is with integration that we anticipate the elaboration of superfluous traits, perhaps by increasing the scale of ceremonial architecture. Integration contributes to such superfluous elaboration by providing mechanisms for pooling labor and resources. Such pooling across environmental boundaries buffers individuals from perturbations, the environmental constraints that may be experienced within certain locations, and the effects of endemic aggression.

Obviously, integration may preferentially benefit some individuals or groups more than others. We anticipate a tendency to locate elaborated superfluous traits in a limited number of places in territories associated with those most often sponsoring intergroup aggression and providing much of the leadership for suprapolity integration. These territories will be characterized by comparative resource limitations, and thus political integration will provide long-term benefits through labor and resource pooling. The construction of monumental architecture in the leaders' political districts may also symbolize (and to some anthropologists, serve to create and maintain) the underlying structure of social relations.

The superfluous behavior of constructing monumental architecture offers selective advantages in several different ways. On one hand, superfluous behavior serves to divert energy away from population expansion where maintaining the expansion would be impractical. On the other hand, the pooling of labor and resources across territories as a consequence of political integration can confer selective advantages to individuals who will have access to resources during periodic climatic or environmental disturbances.

Implications of the Selectionist Model for Explaining Polynesian Ceremonial Architecture

The value of the selectionist evolutionary model lies in its explication of temporal, spatial, and scalar variability in ceremonial architecture which is not well accounted for by other evolutionist hypotheses. The model does not assume a typological progression of change from one stage to another, nor does it assume that monumental architecture is a simple reflection or correlate of social complexity. At the same time, the model directs our attention to a different set of relationships among the environment, behavioral patterns, and material outcomes.

In the remainder of this paper, we will explore some of the expectations of the model.

Under the selectionist model, we would expect some of the earliest occurrences of religious features in regions or localities in Polynesia, which after the establishment of human populations experienced the greatest perturbations. Some evidence suggests that early prehistoric religious sites are located in the environmental contexts predicted by the superfluous behavior model. The rapid proliferation of ceremonial architecture on Easter Island (Bahn and Flenley 1992) and on the two most leeward inhabited Hawaiian islands of Necker and Nihoa (Emory 1928; Cleghorn 1988) conforms to these expectations. These islands are small and isolated, thus rendering them vulnerable to environmental perturbations, in particular drought compounded by distance to the nearest permanently inhabited island. The well-documented abundance of religious architecture on Necker and Nihoa islands is explained as an example of selection for superfluous behavior during the colonization and early establishment of Hawaiian settlers on islands whose environment is marginal for agricultural production. Neither Nicker nor Nihoa was apparently occupied at the time of European contact, and each may represent the limiting case for the relationship between severe environmental perturbations and superfluous traits.

The widespread and nearly contemporaneous distribution of ceremonial architecture throughout Easter Island is evidence for the selective advantage of superfluous traits within a somewhat less severe environment. Additionally, some evidence of agricultural expansion and intensification exists. Most anthropologists agree, however, that the ratio of effort devoted to superfluous behaviors and terrestrial food production was weighted toward the superfluous behaviors, especially in comparison to virtually all other populations of East Polynesia. This "esoteric efflorescence," as it was termed by Sahlins (1955), is made less anomalous under the selectionist model of superfluous behavior. The construction of stone platforms and the use of stone to carve large images were "intensified" not because of some inherent need as implied by Sahlins. Rather, such behaviors proliferated relatively early in the settlement history of the island because their effect was to stabilize the population of Easter Island at lower levels.

In Polynesia, we may expect the construction of religious architecture to persist in areas that experience moderate variation from the mean for food production or procurement, and where variation is difficult to predict. On both Tahiti and Mo'orea in the Society Islands, the two largest valleys—Papeno'o and 'Opunohu, respectively—have disclosed the densest concentration of *marae* (C. Cristino personal communication 1990; Descantes 1990). In both cases, distance from the coastline appears to structure variability in number and density of *marae*. In the case of Papeno'o Valley some of these religious features are located in excess of 15 km inland. None of the religious features in these interior valleys is thought to date to an early stage of occupation of either island. Rather the features appear to date from the initial stage of permanent colonization of these interior localities, which occurred during the late prehistoric era through the early historic period. Thus, these inland valleys satisfy the prediction of the selectionist model that superfluous behavior should flourish in unpredictable environments. We suggest that distance from the coast makes these localities particularly subject to unpredictable environmental perturbations. These perturbations have less to do with limited rainfall, since the valleys are extremely wet locations, and are more likely a function of transport costs associated with maintaining interaction with coastal groups on which the inland populations would have been somewhat dependent for fish and certain food staples. This case highlights that not all environmental perturbations are entirely natural in origin; human populations and their intergroup relations are part of the environmental structure promoting the proliferation of superfluous traits. In comparison to other parts of Tahiti and Mo'orea, such traits spread more quickly within these valleys through this late interval of time than elsewhere on these islands.

The superfluous model was devised to account for the appearance and proliferation of superfluous artifacts or features in the archaeological record. As Dunnell (1989:48–49) notes, however, the model may also enable us to explain the disappearance of such complexes or climaxes. He suggests that the disappearance may occur when the productive potential of a region or locality changes, and aspects of superfluous behavior may disappear since they no longer enjoy a selective advantage. In Hawai'i, during the late prehistoric period, agriculture expanded rapidly along the leeward coasts of the larger islands as Hawaiians discovered and then pursued the possibilities of extensive dryland farming in upper elevations. Large field systems proliferated on the drier slopes of Hawai'i, Maui, Moloka'i, and possibly Kaua'i. These agricultural systems increased the productivity of their districts substantially, and such opportunities would have diminished the selective advantage of population dampening that construction of superfluous ceremonial architecture formerly enjoyed. Interestingly, these changes in agricultural productivity occurred at approximately the same time that Kolb (1991) documented a decrease in the labor investment in *heiau* construction and remodeling on the island of Maui.

On Easter Island archaeologists have documented the collapse of *moai* quarrying and carving and *ahu* construction in the late prehistoric or early proto-historic periods (Bahn and Flenley 1992). The collapse has been treated as either enigmatic or as the consequence of decreased agricultural production. Stevenson's (1986:77) research on the south coast of the island indicates a marked decline in the human population of the island at this time. Although this decrease has been attributed to precontact, human-induced environmental change, it is equally possible that the decrease may reflect the onset of proto-historic population collapse associated with the introduction of European diseases. Whatever the precise timing for and origin of the massive depopulation, the effect would have been the same, that is, an increase in the ratio of persons to potential food supply. Again, the model predicts and the archaeological record indicates the loss of superfluous architectural construction after this time.

The selectionist model involving labor and resource pooling suggests that large-scale superfluous traits should appear with interpolity integration. Further, if integration is achieved through intergroup aggression in contexts of moderate differences in regional productive capacity, then monumental architecture should tend to occur in the more marginal areas of an island. Several studies now suggest that the largest *luakini heiau* in Hawai'i are located in districts with relatively low potential for productivity, districts which do not have significant areas of land for pondfield agriculture. These include Kirch's (1990b) review of Moloka'i, where most of the largest *heiau* are located along the south coast. Whereas Kirch (1990b) implies that this coast is productive and rich because it contains a number of fishponds, we would argue differently. The general aridity and the limited opportunity for agricultural intensification along this coast would have motivated groups to use aggression more often to increase access to agricultural products from the north and east coast of the island. The abundance of *heiau* are a signal of this process, not a sign of the inherent productivity of the south Moloka'i coast. While the fishponds along the Kona coast of Moloka'i did improve productivity, their construction was sponsored by the elite of the district, and the resulting output of fish was largely reserved for elite consumption or use.

Additional survey data from both Maui and Hawai'i islands suggest that the densest array of large *heiau* is located along the leeward coasts of these islands. Fewer large religious structures are found on the wetter and presumably more productive coasts of either island. The same is true on Maui, despite the likely destruction of numerous *heiau* in drier areas under sugarcane or pineapple cultivation today. Further, despite Kirch's (1992) claim that large *heiau* on O'ahu are associated with areas containing pondfield agriculture (i.e., high productivity), we suspect closer examination of the record will prove otherwise. The evidence from Hawai'i thus appears to support resource pooling and integration across territories of differential productive potential as the likely mechanisms for the predominance of large ceremonial architecture in the less productive portions of the islands.

Based on a selectionist model, Ladefoged (1993) predicted that monumental religious or mortuary architecture on the island of Rotuma in west Polynesia should occur more often in districts where intergroup aggression was more often employed and whose elite were the main beneficiaries of interdistrict integration. The construction of monumental architecture in conjunction with intergroup aggression would have contributed to the integration of the island into a single polity. Thus, the largest structures—those requiring the greatest labor invest-ment—should be unevenly distributed through space with their densest occur-rence in, or adjacent to, the less productive areas of Rotuma. The integration of the island into a single polity would have had important long-term selective ad-vantages in buffering against environmental perturbations that differentially af-fected the island, such as droughts or hurricanes. Archaeological, environmental, and ethnohistorical data from Rotuma confirm the spatial association between monumental ceremonial architecture and natal districts of paramount chiefs (sau). These variables are inversely related to terrestrial productivity measures and sug-gest that resource buffering in times of stress was achieved through the elabora-tion of superfluous traits (Ladefoged 1993).

Conclusion

These cases from both East and West Polynesia suggest that the hypothesis derived from cultural evolutionary empirical generalization is incorrect. The dis-tribution of large or monumental ceremonial architecture in either Hawai'i or Rotuma does not occur as a positive function of environmental productivity. We have outlined an alternative selectionist model based on the advantages accruing to resource pooling and population dampening where moderate and irregular en-vironmental perturbations occur across islands with moderate regional resource disparities. Superfluous traits (i.e., construction of ceremonial architecture) can lead to population dampening that could have selective advantages for popula-tions. In addition, the two linked processes of intergroup aggression and supra-polity integration combine to favor greater investments in large-scale superfluous traits in the less productive territories. This model provides a direct functional role for ceremonial architecture in the adaptation of individuals and groups to particular environmental circumstances. As such, it stands in contrast with mod-els of architecture as ideological style or those which employ architecture as an indicator of other behavioral patterns or processes (e.g., chiefly power).

We make no claim that evolutionary theory, or any particular selectionist model for that matter, will necessarily account for all material variability. As noted above, the interpretation offered here for superfluous traits does not, and is not intended to, account for stylistic variation in ceremonial architecture. This model is general, however, in the sense that it is derived from evolutionary theory, and we establish a set of conditions for the application of the model and specify the measures of superfluous traits to which the model should accord. Thus, the ap-proach developed here is comprehensive. It accounts for a greater number of the instances of ceremonial architecture in Polynesia than any other alternative. We may also extend its application to new cases in Polynesia where the appropriate environmental conditions prevail (e.g., the Marquesas Islands or New Zealand). Finally, this model should also apply to other regions of the world, again where comparable environments are found.

Our model is also comprehensive in that it can account for several dimensions of ceremonial architecture, including its initial occurrence, its persistence (or failure), locational patterning, and change in scale. The identification of selective advantages (e.g., population dampening and resource pooling) accruing to superfluous traits provides a functional context in which the place of reconstructionist inference is clearly specified and delimited. In other words, this model is coherent in ways that other cultural evolutionary explanations are not.

Nonetheless, the superfluous model continues to be underdetermined with respect to empirical sufficiency. The spatial patterning of ceremonial architecture provided here in support of the model is broadly congruent with expectations but can hardly be considered a rigorous test. Temporal patterning—historical change—is still lacking in most cases. Additionally, we must eventually confront the important methodological issue, that measures of superfluous traits alone will not constitute a sufficient test of the model. Traits linked to alternative behavioral patterns (e.g., agricultural intensification, storage, and population movement) must also be systematically monitored. This was implicit in Dunnell's original formulation of waste and its application to Woodland archaeological phases in the midwestern United States. Only by detailing the historical and spatial distribution of those alternative traits can we evaluate the relative contribution of superfluous traits to evolutionary change, and thus to the selectionist model. In making these evaluations we can begin to identify the geographically and temporally variable processes of change, persistence, and loss in ceremonial architecture. Doing so would complete the ontological shift in explanation that Dunnell (1982) has suggested is necessary for evolution to come of age in archaeology.

Acknowledgments

A portion of this paper originated as a presentation by Graves at the XVII Pacific Science Congress, held in Honolulu, Hawai'i, in May and June of 1991 and subsequently published (Graves and Sweeney 1993). This paper and our research have benefited from extensive discussions with and comments from our colleague Terry Hunt. We thank Joan Lawrence who drew the illustrations. Others who have helped improve this paper include Patrice Teltser, Sarina Pearson, Ann Ramenofsky, Roger Green, JoAnne Van Tilburg, Helen Leach, Maria Sweeney, C. Kēhaunani Cachola-Abad, Doug Sutton, Alex Brewis, and Peter Sheppard. And although he may be alarmed with what we have done with his original proposition, we dedicate this paper to Robert C. Dunnell.

Note

1. Occasionally, Sahlins (1955, 1958:138) argued that ritual and ceremonial sites might be nonadaptive elements. This had to be the case, because Sahlins found that variation in ritual architecture and behavior did not always correctly correlate with the expectations generated from the model linking environmental diversity with sociopolitical organization. For example, overelaborated ceremonial activities persisted as "nonadaptive survivals" (Sahlins 1958:138) when a Polynesian group on an atoll or small island had diverged from a Polynesian society of a higher level in a more productive environment. And in the case of Easter Island, Sahlins (1955) had earlier argued that the evolutionary pathway toward greater agricultural productivity was blocked on this island by environmental and geographic conditions peculiar to it. Hence, the "esoteric efflorescence" as represented by the considerable investment in labor for religious architecture and sculpture was a substitute for limited agricultural opportunities. In other words, the religious domain, rather than subsistence, was expanded and intensified.

References

Adams, R. McC.
1966   *The Evolution of Urban Society*. Chicago: Aldine Publishing Company.

Allen, M. S.
1992   Temporal Variation in Polynesian Fishing Strategies: The Southern Cook Islands in Regional Perspective. *Asian Perspectives* 31:183–204.

Bahn, P., and J. Flenley
1992   *Easter Island, Earth Island*. Thames and Hudson, London.

Bellwood, P.
1970   Dispersal Centers in East Polynesia, with Special Reference to the Society and Marquesas Islands. In *Studies in Oceanic Culture History*, vol. 1, edited by R.C. Green and M. Kelly, pp. 93–104. Pacific Anthropological Records No. 11. Bernice P. Bishop Museum, Honolulu.

1979   *Man's Conquest of the Pacific: The Prehistory of Southeast Asia and Oceania*. Oxford University Press, New York.

1987   *The Polynesians: Prehistory of an Island People*, 2d ed. Thames and Hudson, Ltd., London.

Boone, J. L.
1983   Noble Family Structure and Expansionist Warfare in the Late Middle Ages: A Socioecological Approach. In *Rethinking Human Adaptation: Biological and Cultural Models*, edited by R. Dyson-Hudson and M. A. Little, pp. 79–96. Westview Press, Boulder, Colorado.

1992   Competition, Conflict, and the Development of Social Hierarchies. In *Evolutionary Ecology and Human Behavior*, edited by E. A. Smith and B. Winterhalder, pp. 301–337. Aldine de Gruyter, New York.

Brumfiel, E. M., and T. K. Earle

1987   Specialization, Exchange, and Complex Societies: An Introduction. In *Specialization, Exchange, and Complex Societies*, edited by E. M. Brumfiel and T. K. Earle, pp. 1–9. Cambridge University Press, Cambridge.

Burrows, E. G.

1939   Breed and Border in Polynesia. *American Anthropologist* 41:1–21.

Clark, J., and J. Terrell

1978   Archaeology in Oceania. *Annual Review of Anthropology* 7:293–319.

Cleghorn, P. L.

1988   The Settlement and Abandonment of Two Hawaiian Outposts: Nihoa and Necker Islands. *Bishop Museum Occasional Papers* 28:35–49.

Cordy, R.

1981   *A Study of Prehistoric Social Change: The Development of Complex Societies in the Hawaiian Islands*. Academic Press, New York.

Descantes, C.

1990   Symbolic Stone Structures: Protohistoric and Early Historic Spatial Patterns of the 'Opunohu Valley, Mo'orea, French Polynesia. Master's thesis, Department of Anthropology, University of Auckland, Auckland, New Zealand.

Dunnell, R. C.

1978   Style and Function: A Fundamental Dichotomy. *American Antiquity* 43:192–202.

1980   Evolutionary Theory and Archaeology. *Advances in Archaeological Method and Theory*, vol. 3, edited by M. B. Schiffer, pp. 35–99. Academic Press, New York.

1982   Science, Social Science, and Common Sense: The Agonizing Dilemma of Modern Archaeology. *Journal of Anthropological Research* 38:1–25.

1989   Aspects of the Application of Evolutionary Theory in Archaeology. In *Archaeological Thought in America*, edited by C. Lamberg-Karlovsky, pp. 35–49. Cambridge University Press, Cambridge.

Durham, W. H.

1992   Applications of Evolutionary Culture Theory. *Annual Review of Anthropology* 21: 331–355.

Dyson-Hudson, R. and E. A. Smith

1978   Human Territoriality: An Ecological Reassessment. *American Anthropologist* 80: 21–41.

Earle, T.

1991   The Evolution of Chiefdoms. In *Chiefdoms: Power, Economy, and Ideology*, edited by T. Earle, pp. 1–15. Cambridge University Press, New York.

Emory, K. P.

1928   *Archaeology of Nihoa and Necker Islands*. Bernice P. Bishop Museum Bulletin No. 53. Honolulu.

1943   Polynesian Stone Remains. In *Studies in the Anthropology of Oceania and Asia Presented in Memory of Roland Burrange Dixon*. Papers of the Peabody Museum of

American Archaeology and Ethnology, Harvard University, vol. 20, pp. 9–21. Harvard University Press, Cambridge, Massachusetts.

1970 A Re-examination of East-Polynesian Marae: Many Marae Later. In *Studies in Oceanic Culture History*, vol. 1., edited by R. C. Green and M. Kelly, pp. 73–92. Pacific Anthropological Records 11. Bernice P. Bishop Museum, Honolulu.

Emory, K. P., and Y. H. Sinoto

1961 *Hawaiian Archaeology: Oahu Excavations.* Bishop Museum Special Publication, 49. Honolulu.

Flannery, K. V.

1972 The Cultural Evolution of Civilizations. *Annual Review of Ecology and Systematics* 3:399–426.

Goldman, I.

1955 Status Rivalry and Cultural Evolution in Polynesia. *American Anthropologist* 57: 680–697.

1957 Cultural Evolution in Polynesia: A Reply to Criticism. *Journal of the Polynesian Society* 66:158–164.

1960 The Evolution of Status Systems in Polynesia. In *Selected Papers of the Fifth International Congress of Anthropological and Ethnological Sciences,* edited by Wallace, pp. 255–260. University of Pennsylvania Press, Philadelphia.

1970 *Ancient Polynesian Society.* University of Chicago Press, Chicago.

Graves, M. W., and C. Erkelens

1991 Who's in Control? Method and Theory in Hawaiian Archaeology. *Asian Perspectives* 30:1–18.

Graves, M. W., and M. Sweeney

1993 Ritual Behaviour and Ceremonial Structures in Eastern Polynesia: Changing Perspectives on Archaeological Variability. In *The Evolution and Organisation of Prehistoric Society in Polynesia,* edited by M. W. Graves and R. C. Green, pp. 102–121. New Zealand Archaeological Association, Monograph No. 19, Auckland.

Graves, M. W., T. L. Hunt, and D. Moore

1990 Ceramic Production in the Mariana Islands: Explaining Change and Diversity in Prehistoric Interaction and Exchange. *Asian Perspectives* 29:211–234.

Green, R. C.

1963 *A Review of the Prehistoric Sequence of the Auckland Province.* New Zealand Archaeological Association Monograph, 2. Auckland.

1993 Community-Level Organisation, Power and Elites in Polynesian Settlement Pattern Studies. In *The Evolution and Organisation of Prehistoric Society in Polynesia,* edited by M. W. Graves and R. C. Green, pp. 9–12. New Zealand Archaeological Association Monograph, no. 19. Auckland.

Green, R. C., K. Green, R. A. Rappaport, A. Rappaport, and J. Davidson

1967 *Archeology on the Island of Mo'orea, French Polynesia.* Anthropological Papers of the American Museum of Natural History, vol. 51, pt. 2. New York.

Hawthorne, H. B., and C. S. Belshaw
1957   Cultural Evolution or Cultural Change?—The Case for Polynesia. *The Journal of the Polynesian Society* 66:18–35.

Hill, J. N.
1977   Introduction. In *Explanation of Prehistoric Change,* edited by J. N. Hill, pp. 1–16. University of New Mexico Press, Albuquerque.

Hunt, T. L.
1987   Patterns of Human Interaction and Evolutionary Divergence in the Fiji Islands. *The Journal of the Polynesian Society* 96:299–334.

1989   *Lapita Ceramic Exchange in the Mussau Islands, Papua New Guinea.* Ph.D. dissertation, Department of Anthropology, University of Washington, Seattle.

Kirch, P. V.
1982   The Impact of the Prehistoric Polynesians on the Hawaiian Ecosystems. *Pacific Science* 36:1–14.

1984   *The Evolution of the Polynesian Chiefdoms.* Cambridge University Press, Cambridge.

1990a   The Evolution of Sociopolitical Complexity in Prehistoric Hawaii: An Assessment of the Archaeological Evidence. *Journal of World Prehistory* 4:311–345.

1990b   Monumental Architecture and Power in Polynesian Chiefdoms: A Comparison of Tonga and Hawaii. World Archaeology 22:206–222.

1992   The Archaeology of History, vol. 2. In *Anahulu: The Anthropology of History in the Kingdom of Hawaii,* edited by P. V. Kirch and M. Sahlins. University of Chicago Press, Chicago.

Kirch, P. V. and R. Green
1987   History, Phylogeny, and Evolution in Polynesia. *Current Anthropology* 28:431–456.

Kolb, M. J.
1991   *Social Power, Chiefly Authority, and Ceremonial Architecture in an Island Polity, Maui, Hawaii.* Ph.D. dissertation, Department of Anthropology, University of California, Los Angeles.

Ladefoged, T. N.
1993   *Evolutionary Process in an Oceanic Chiefdom: Intergroup Aggression and Political Integration in Traditional Rotuman Society.* Ph.D. dissertation, Department of Anthropology, University of Hawai'i, Honolulu.

Peebles, C. S., and S. Kus
1977   Some Archaeological Correlates of Ranked Societies. *American Antiquity* 28:431–448.

Price, B. J.
1982   Cultural Materialism: A Theoretical Review. *American Antiquity* 47:709–741.

Rappaport, R. A.
1979   *Ecology, Meaning, and Religion.* North Atlantic Books, Richmond, California.

Rautman, A. E.
1993   Resource Variability, Risk, and the Structure of Social Networks: An Example from the Prehistoric Southwest. *American Antiquity* 58:403–424.

Sahlins, M.

1955   Esoteric Efflorescence in Easter Island. *American Anthropologist* 57:1045–1052.

1957   Differentiation by Adaptation in Polynesian Societies. *Journal of the Polynesian Society* 66:291–300.

1958   *Social Stratification in Polynesia.* University of Washington Press, Seattle.

Sahlins, M., and E. Service (editors)

1960   *Evolution and Culture.* The University of Michigan Press, Ann Arbor.

Sanders, W. T., and D. Webster

1978   Unilinealism, Multilinealism, and the Evolution of Complex Societies. In *Social Archeology: Beyond Subsistence and Dating,* edited by C. L. Redman, et al. pp. 249–302. Academic Press, New York.

Service, E.

1962   *Primitive Social Organization.* Random House, New York.

Sinoto, Y. H.

1966   A Tentative Prehistoric Cultural Sequence in the Northern Marquesas Islands, French Polynesia. *The Journal of the Polynesian Society* 75:287–303.

Smith, E. A.

1988   Risk and Uncertainty in the 'Original Affluent Society': Evolutionary Ecology of Resource-Sharing and Land Tenure. In *Hunters and Gatherers 1: History, Evolution, and Social Change,* edited by T. Ingold, D. Riches, and J. Woodburn, pp. 222–251. Berg Publishers, Oxford.

Stevenson, C. M.

1986   The Socio-Political Structure of the Southern Coastal Area of Easter Island: AD 1300–1864. In *Island Societies: Archaeological Approaches to Evolution and Transformation,* edited by P. V. Kirch, pp. 69–77. Cambridge University Press, Cambridge.

Suggs, R. C.

1961   *The Archaeology of Nuku Hiva, Marquesas Islands, French Polynesia.* Anthropological Papers of the American Museum of Natural History, vol. 49, pt. 1. New York.

Valeri, V.

1985   *Kingship and Sacrifice.* University of Chicago Press, Chicago.

White, L. A.

1949   *The Science of Culture: A Study of Man and Civilization.* Farrar Straus, New York.

Wolf, E. R.

1964   The Study of Evolution. In *Horizons of Anthropology,* edited by S. Tax, pp. 108–119. Aldine Publishing Company, Chicago.

9

The Nature and Premise of a Selection-Based Archaeology

Michael J. O'Brien and Thomas D. Holland

◆◆ In recent years there has been a growing acceptance in archaeology that an emerging paradigm offers a powerful means of explaining variation in the material record. That paradigm, often referred to as evolutionary, or selectionist, archaeology, is new and largely undeveloped, but positive signs point toward future growth and development. We have been among the proponents of integrating a Darwinian-evolutionary paradigm into Americanist archaeology, with our earliest effort (O'Brien and Holland 1990) building on the work of Dunnell (e.g., 1978a, 1980, 1982, 1988, 1989) and others (e.g., Leonard and Jones 1987). We also admit that many of the early efforts—ours included—were perhaps not as self-critical as they should have been. Evolutionary archaeology has reached the point that it is appropriate to assemble a book such as this one that examines how the selectionist approach developed, where it is likely to head in the next several years, and what the limits of its explanatory power are.

For several reasons, we believe that this is the appropriate time to take stock. First, in reviewing the history of scientific paradigms, it is clear that for anything other than the most profound of paradigms to take hold requires a considerable amount of time and reiteration. So it has been with evolutionary archaeology, which we view as being neither a novel concept nor a particularly profound one. It might have been profound back in 1859, but after Darwin published *On the Origin of Species*, it theoretically should have been a relatively uncomplicated matter to extrapolate "descent with modification" to humans and, by extension, to features that affect their fitness. For reasons we will discuss later, however, this extrapolation was slow to be made. Not even Darwin wanted to admit that humans were necessarily a product of natural selection and other evolutionary processes (many of which were unknown or misunderstood), a view that is still pervasive in anthropology and which inhibits the acceptance of an internally consistent approach to the study of humans and the materials they manufacture, use, and discard. Evolutionary archaeology, however, has made the claim that humans, like any other organisms, are directly affected by selection and that the material record reflects the effects of selection. In our view Darwinian-evolutionary theory provides the most powerful means of integrating our knowledge of human history and of explaining the variation evident in the vast archaeological record that is testament to that history.

The second reason for our belief that this is an appropriate time to take stock of the developmental history and future course of evolutionary archaeology is that unless other archaeologists understand the basic tenets of the approach and are convinced of its powerfulness relative to explaining variation in the archaeological record, there is no reason to suspect that it will be accepted. The field of archaeology is a graveyard of paradigms that have come and gone over the years, and while in our introductory paragraph we stated that there are signs of a healthy future for evolutionary archaeology, we are not so naive as to believe that it can flourish without constant attention. The failure of the approach to engage the discipline as a whole will result, if not in death, then, at the very least, in severe retardation. Unlike many other approaches that have been proposed in the discipline, evolutionary archaeology, because it is driven by data, needs full participation by researchers. Stated more directly, no other approach requires such a massive amount of data. Our goal as more-than-casual proponents is to help ensure that the basic tenets of evolutionary archaeology are clearly stated and, importantly, are not overstated.

We elsewhere (O'Brien et al. 1994) drew a parallel between the infant state of evolutionary archaeology and Lewontin's metaphor in which he compared the beginning stages of population genetics to an ore-processing machine: "Occasionally some unusually clever or lucky prospector would come upon a natural outcrop of high-grade ore, and part of the machinery would be started up to prove to its backers that it really would work. But for the most part, however, the machine was left to engineers, forever tinkering, forever making improvements, in anticipation of the day when it would be called upon to carry out full production" (1974:189). Happily, chapters in this book and other books, and articles (e.g., Dunnell and Feathers 1991; Feathers 1990a, 1990b; O'Brien et al. 1994) have begun to stamp out marketable products. We focus attention on some of those products in the next few pages. Despite these much needed additions, however, it is important that those weighing the merits of the approach—as well as those who have embraced it wholeheartedly—understand precisely what the basic tenets of the approach are. Even among those archaeologists committed to an evolutionary approach, there is disagreement over some of its aspects. This, of course, is to be expected, but we believe those differences should be emphasized more than they have been. We begin by examining some of the common ground, then discuss several basic premises that, while integral to applying selectionist theory to archaeological remains, have not been addressed fully in previous position statements. Many of those oversights are redressed in this book, and we reference the chapters throughout. We also point out two critical issues that students of evolutionary archaeology must be aware of—quantified essentialism and untestable adaptationist arguments—lest our efforts be questioned on methodological grounds.

Darwinian-Evolutionary Theory and the Study of Humans

A growing list of authors (e.g., Dunnell 1978a, 1980, 1982, 1989; Leonard 1989; Leonard and Jones 1987; O'Brien and Holland 1990, 1992; Rindos 1984) have begun to flesh out the basic tenets of a Darwinian-evolutionary paradigm for archaeology. Whether called evolutionary or selectionist, or even Darwinian, the tenets and models operate on the same general premise, that is, that humans are subject to the process of selection just as is anything else organic. It is abundantly evident that all the authors whose works are included here believe strongly that humans not only are *not* immune from the selection process by virtue of their being "culture-bearing animals," but to the contrary, are even more subject to the process on account of their capacity for culture, however defined (see Rindos 1985, 1986). It is human culture that has created the vast pool of variation that selection subsequently has sculpted into organisms so complex that they appear to be immune from the evolutionary process.

Therein lies the difficulty that many archaeologists appear to have with incorporating an evolutionary paradigm into their work. It seems as if humans have escaped selection because they, through an "extrasomatic . . . temporal continuum of things and events dependent upon signaling" (White 1959:3) can make enough adjustments in the face of changing physical and social environments to stay ahead of the game. This incorrect view, unfortunately, is taught in every anthropology course from introductory classes to graduate seminars and has set the human phenotype apart from the rest of the organismic world. We would argue, however, that culture has not set humans apart. To be sure, the fact that we have culture—and this is not the forum in which to debate what culture is and is not—makes us different, but this difference is simply a part of the variation expressed by all organisms. We see neither a need nor a rational basis for separating humans from the purview of selection. Neither do we see a need to apply the modifier *cultural* to the term *selection* when dealing with humans (O'Brien and Holland 1990). We do not deny that there are different mechanisms by which variation can be transmitted, but we do not see the term selection used by itself as obscuring this fact.

Archaeology, of course, has always had an intense interest in evolution in one guise or another (see Teltser, chapter 1), though the perspectives that have been offered are most decidedly non-Darwinian. Rather, emphasis for the most part has been placed on the vague notion of progress toward more complex social, economic, and political organization. Donald Campbell (1956, 1965, 1975) and other social scientists have noted that Darwinian evolution is quite capable of accounting for human behavior, but this is certainly a minority opinion and, to our knowledge, was not introduced into archaeology until the late 1970s (Dunnell 1978a, 1978b), except in an oblique fashion (e.g., Meggers et al. 1965). The so-called "new archaeology" of the 1960s celebrated the reemergence of evolution as a topic of interest (Marks and Staski 1988:151), but it borrowed its brand of evolution from anthropologists such as White (e.g., 1949, 1959), together with a particular emphasis on "culture" and how it changed through time (see Dunnell 1980, 1982). As opposed to the neo-Darwinian perspective of change being a process of replacement of one form by another, the anthropological and archaeological perspective rendered change as a series of transformational steps from one cultural stage to another. Cultural groups were placed along a continuum based on certain criteria, and, within certain limits, they were grouped into types. In other words, analytical emphasis was placed on commonalities in form as opposed to differences in function, with the end result being the creation of modal types (see Teltser, chapter 4). The focus that was placed on formulating and describing these types immediately removed archaeology from the purview of a Darwinian perspective, which focuses instead on differences between and among organisms (Dunnell 1988).

One paradigm, behavioral archaeology—more specifically that branch of behavioral archaeology proposed and later expanded by Schiffer (e.g., 1975, 1976, 1978)—broke rank with other approaches and actually comes close to evolutionary archaeology in terms of some of its underlying premises. At its core, behavioral archaeology has as its scope of interest "the study of material objects regardless of time or space in order to describe and explain human behavior" (Reid et al. 1975:864)—a logical extension of the view that archaeology itself is "the study of relationships between human behavior and material culture" (Reid et al. 1975:864). As we have pointed out elsewhere (O'Brien and Holland n.d.), the type of work conducted under the rubric of behavioral archaeology has varied considerably over the years, and certainly not all of it is even remotely compatible with evolutionary archaeology. For example, any search for universal laws (or "general principles," to use Richard Gould's [1980:140] term) that govern behavior is not only incompatible with an evolutionary approach but is doomed to fail. We point this out because we want to make it clear that our focus on behavior—especially on the outputs of behaviors (or "activities," to use Schiffer's [1976] term)—has little or nothing in common with ethnographic analogy, which in the 1970s and 1980s became the centerpiece of many behavioral-archaeology studies. As Teltser points out in chapter 1, under an evolutionary perspective analytical emphasis shifts from cultural systems to specific classes of *behaviors*.

The Basic Premise of Evolutionary Archaeology

The basic position adopted in this book is that the objects observed in the archaeological record are, in fact, fossilized remnants of successful human phenotypes (see Dunnell 1988; O'Brien and Holland 1990, 1992). Furthermore, these fossilized remnants potentially can contribute as much information about human fitness and adaptation as can any purely biological feature (Neff 1992; O'Brien and Holland 1990, 1992; O'Brien et al. 1994). This view is a radical departure from the mainstream anthropological perspective. For whatever reason or reasons, the view that most anthropologists have of the human phenotype is limited to those things that are biologically based (e.g., cranial capacity and blood type).

Virtually all general anthropology texts pay a great deal of attention to the concept of evolution for the first two or three chapters—up to the point when neanderthals are encountered and somehow disposed of—after which time the concept virtually is ignored with the exception of a few small digressions such as sickle-cell anemia or lactose intolerance. It somehow is assumed, at least tacitly, that human evolution stopped (or at least significantly slowed down) some time after the appearance of the opposable thumb and the first artifact that it touched. This view results from three conditions that anthropologists and archaeologists must contend with that biologists generally do not have to. First, the time frame that forms the arena in which we ask our questions is but an evolutionary blink of an eye. For example, archaeologists interested in the selective advantages offered by ceramic cooking vessels, or in the advantages of one type of temper over another, must, by definition, limit their scope to no more than a few thousand years. Sufficient depth of resolution for our eyes to easily focus on the subtle changes that selection might have wrought over that period is not available.

Second, the archaeological record is biased. More importantly, the record also must be recognized as a catalog of relative successes. We sometimes fail to grasp the immense range of unsuccessful variation that may, or may not, have existed in the past. Just as we often viewed dinosaurs in the past as evolutionary failures, the same "dinosaur premise" often leads us to view archaeological forms in the black-and-white arena of winner and loser. But in fact, when we examine shell-tempered pottery in relation to sand-tempered wares (and by extension the humans that manufactured and used them, as Neff points out in chapter 5), we are not looking at a simple winner-loser situation. Both types of ceramic wares are highly evolved, as well as highly successful, technologies at particular times and in particular places. It is difficult to place the two wares on the sliding scale of relative fitness until we have first examined them relative to the myriad unsuccessful (or at least less successful) competing variants, and it is precisely these variants that are most commonly lost to (or at least not recognized in) the archaeological record.

The third condition, and in our view the most insidious, is self-imposed. For whatever reason, anthropologists are incapable of shrugging free of intention as the ultimate explanatory device (see Ramenofsky, chapter 7). Intention, however, explains nothing but how variation might be generated. Many early aviators must have leapt from cliffs, propelled by hopeful inventions and the intent of flying. Ultimately, it was the ability to overcome gravity—not intent—that determined which aviators survived to pass their genes and inspiration on to others. The ingrained notion that behavior is conditioned by intent renders our research as really nothing more than a cataloging of automatic adjustments made by humans in the face of physical or social environmental change, or both. Under this view, as both Jones et al. (chapter 2) and Ramenofsky (chapter 7) note, change is rendered as a directional process, with the direction in large part being preordained. If we buy in to such a view, no wonder we start to believe that humans are exempt from selection.

Humans, however, are not products of their intentions. Intent certainly plays a proximal role in shaping variation, but that variation is the very thing on which selection operates, just as it operates on heritable genetic variation. Any adaptation—defined as a trait (feature) that increases fitness and that has been shaped by selection (see Dunnell 1978a; O'Brien and Holland 1990, 1992)—begins life as a variant, regardless of whether the trait is a strictly biological one or a cultural one. Selection, in fact, is blind to the source of variation and thus could not care less whether the trait is inherited genetically or culturally. It certainly does not pay attention to whether or not the proximal cause of the variant was human intent (see Jones et al., chapter 2).

This is not to say that intentions explain the generation of variation, only that, like a host of other agents, they can spawn variation. Neither does this imply that intent controls the amount of variation created. At a given time only limited intentionally created variants may be available, but this says nothing about *unintentional* variants that are constantly being generated. In this regard, Rindos (1984:4) notes that "man may indeed select, but he cannot direct the variation from which he must select." Neither can he control the amount of variation in a population.

The human phenotype actually is a plethora of genetically, as well as culturally, transmitted features, making it at once both a truly remarkable as well as a complicated entity. We do not need to complicate the issue further by establishing two theories to guide research—one based in biology to cover the genetic aspects and the other in anthropology to cover everything else. Dunnell (chapter 3) makes this point forcefully in his discussion of Durham's (1991) formulation of a cultural evolution that is parallel to genetic evolution. There is no need for such a dual construction; one theory—Darwinian evolution—will do nicely. What is needed are methods and techniques that enable us to understand the evolutionary histories of the organisms and the features they exhibit. Those histories are reflected in the material remains—the products of human behavior—left behind by the makers and users of the items that ended up in the archaeological record. Archaeologists, like paleontologists, have access to an incredible record of when and where certain phenotypic variation took place. The key to using the material remains in an evolutionary perspective lies in changing our perspective to include those remains as parts of past phenotypes.

If behavior can be subsumed under phenotype, why should the notion of phenotype not be logically extended to include the products of behavior? Biologists (e.g., Bonner 1980, 1988; Dawkins 1990), for the most part, routinely include such things as spiderwebs and bird nests in their concept of phenotype, and we see no reason not to extend in similar fashion the notion of the human phenotype to include such things as projectile points and pottery, or as Graves and Ladefoged (chapter 8) amply demonstrate, such artifacts as ceremonial architecture in Polynesia. Since selection works on the phenotype—the vehicle that carries and protects the germ-line replicators (the genes)—then, with regard to humans, those things they manufacture and use to modify their environment are subject to selection in the same way any somatic feature is.

An important point to keep in mind—and one that sometimes has been obscured—is that selection does not work on the features themselves, though even biologists routinely refer, in shorthand notation, to selection "for" certain features. In fact, selection does not select "for" anything, whether it be features or phenotypes. It selects *against* certain phenotypes as opposed to others. Sober (1984) makes the distinction between selection "for" certain features and selection "of" certain individuals that carry adaptive features, but again, it should be borne in mind that what really happens is that selection as a process (not as a force [see Sober 1984]) operates against certain organisms. And just as importantly, selection operates against those individuals *at a particular time and in a particular place.* As Stephen Gould (1986) notes, "History matters." In other words, possession of a particular feature may be advantageous in one selective regime—which is space- and time-bound—but not in another. It makes little sense to concoct evolutionary scenarios that are spaceless and timeless, and to expect those scenarios to have any explanatory power.

A Case of Misplaced Emphasis

In archaeology, like in any field of inquiry, theory has to have explanatory power, a point made over and over throughout this book. As Dunnell notes (chapter 3), "Using evolutionary terms and concepts as just another set of interpretive algorithms misses the whole point to evolutionary theory in the first place—it is a scientific theory." The measured success of evolutionary theory is in *explaining* why certain organisms that exhibit certain phenotypic traits do better than their conspecifics that do not exhibit those traits. The success of evolutionary theory has to turn on this point, but there is considerable debate even in biology over what is meant by an organism's "doing better." Do we restrict "better" to include only reproductive success? Is the only meaningful measure of an organism's adaptiveness whether or not it actually outreproduces its conspecifics? If so, then evolutionary archaeology has an immediate problem. To demonstrate that possession of a feature or features has increased the fitness of an individual or group of individuals, we would have to show that over time the individual or group left more offspring than did an individual or group of individuals that did not possess the feature or features. Without an enormous skeletal sample and the ability to differentiate between possessors and nonpossessors, our efforts would fail.

The success of any evolutionary study, however, whether it be in archaeology or biology, in fact, does not hinge on the concept of actual reproductive success (O'Brien and Holland 1992, 1995). On the other hand, we see the potential failure of evolutionary archaeology to engage the discipline as being connected intricately to this misconception. Most evolutionary archaeologists have shrugged off the problem as being unimportant, but we believe this is shortsighted. Why should we expect widespread acceptance of a paradigm that, at first glance, fails to account for what is perceived as the cornerstone of Darwinian evolution, that is, increased reproductive success (the normal measure of fitness)? Biologists and philosophers (e.g., Brandon 1990; Burian 1983) have long wrestled with this point, often in terms of the so-called "tautology problem" implied by the term later used by Darwin, "survival of the fittest." The issue is simply this: Does fitness apply to the actual (realized) reproductive success of organisms, or does it apply to the potential for success—what Mills and Beatty (1979) term the *propensity* for organisms to be successful? In other words, when is fitness measured, before or after (perhaps long after) an organism reproduces?

As we state elsewhere (O'Brien and Holland 1992:40), "Realized fitness simply refers to the fact that organism *a* is more fit (better adapted) than organism *b*, if in fact organism *a* outreproduced organism *b* in a specific environment." Thus, "Degree of adaptation, in this sense, is an empirical property of the organism (or of the class) in question, but one which can only be known post hoc" (Burian 1983: 299). But surely what Darwin meant by "survival of the fittest" was the "*tendency* of organisms that are better engineered to be [more] reproductively successful [than those that are not]" (Burian 1983:299, emphasis added). Thus Brandon (1990:11) views the underlying tenet of Darwin's natural selection as simply, "If *a* is better adapted than *b* in environment *E*, then (probably) *a* will have greater reproductive success than *b* in *E*." This definition can be termed expected fitness. Note Brandon's use of the term "probably." This is neither an attempt to waffle nor a clever disguise of an internal contradiction of evolutionary theory. It simply draws attention to the important and interesting aspects of evolution, as Williams (1966:159) notes: "Measuring reproductive success focuses attention on the rather trivial problem of the degree to which an organism actually achieves reproductive success. The central biological problem is not survival as such, but *design* for survival" (emphasis added).

Anthropology, we suspect (O'Brien and Holland 1995), has avoided an emphasis on Darwinian-evolutionary theory because of a misinterpretation of what is implied by the notion of fitness and the fact that sociobiology is so closely linked to the concept. The backlash to the application of evolutionary theory to the study of humans was and still is a reaction to sociobiology, which might best be characterized as a venue for studies that supposedly demonstrate a genetic basis for specific behaviors. As Rambo (1991) and others have demonstrated, however, biological mechanisms do not provide explanations for the development of cultural differences. Why should we ever have thought that they do? The answer to this question rests on confusion of evolutionary principles with biological mechanisms such as genetic inheritance. Genetic inheritance, however, is not what is important to evolutionary theory. Of central concern is that variation present and that it is heritable by whatever means. And this is the *only* thing that is important.

Sociobiology, unfortunately, at least in many of its early formulations, has emphasized fitness maximization, as if all organisms always perform all their functions so as to increase the number of viable offspring they leave behind. In other words, they act to maximize their genetic contribution to posterity. We say "unfortunately" because (1) we do not believe that fitness maximization is a universal phenomenon (see below) and (2) this misplaced emphasis has been transferred to humans. This has, in turn, led to patently silly—or at best "shoehorned"—conclusions about human behavior as well as to a backlash by anthropologists such as Sahlins (1976), who gleefully pointed out the failure of inclusive fitness (Hamilton 1964) to account for human institutions such as kinship systems.

Such exposés usually wind up by totally discounting Darwinian-evolutionary theory in general as an applicable paradigm under which to examine human behavior. The problem, however, is not with evolutionary theory but with beanbag approaches to using it to try to answer potentially interesting questions. We do not need to throw out the theory; we need to throw out inappropriate applications of it. In the example cited above, for example, Hamilton (1964) never argued that organisms maximize their inclusive fitness. Rather, he modeled mathematically what would happen if an organism, or group of organisms, maximized its fitness. The distinction is critical. Nothing in evolutionary theory says that organisms must act according to some maximizing principle (O'Brien and Holland 1995). As Dawkins (1990:188–189) insightfully notes, "Individuals do not consciously strive to maximize anything; they behave as if maximizing something. . . . [They] may strive for something, but it will be a morsel of food, an attractive female, or a desirable territory, not inclusive fitness."

Evolutionary archaeology, at least to our knowledge, has not bitten on the bait. No one has claimed that the manufacture of ceramic containers came about as an attempt on the part of prehistoric peoples to maximize their reproductive success or even that better engineered vessels necessarily led to an increase in realized fitness. What has been claimed (e.g., Dunnell and Feathers 1991; Feathers 1990b; O'Brien and Holland 1990, 1992, 1995; O'Brien et al. 1994) is that it can be demonstrated that users of superior pot-making technologies were potentially more fit than those using other technologies. "Superior" is derived empirically by engineering-design analysis and experimentation. But, as we have always maintained (O'Brien and Holland 1990, 1992; O'Brien et al. 1994), this type of engineering-design analysis is only the first step in a long analytical process. Importantly, it remains to be demonstrated if the technologies under investigation were indeed superior and how they might have affected the fitness of the users.

In other words, detailed engineering studies of technologies allow us to document change and, under proper conditions, to determine whether certain technological products came under selective control, that is, became adaptations (see O'Brien and Holland 1992), but this process tells us little or nothing about why the products changed, or if the changes actually could have caused humans to reproduce differentially. The next step, once adaptations have been identified (and sorted out from those features that are not adaptations), is to link engineering data to other aspects of the archaeological record (O'Brien and Holland 1992; O'Brien et al. 1994). For example, data from Woodland-period sites in the central Mississippi River valley indicate that changes in ceramic technologies, together with other technological and social changes, had significant impact on the reproductive success of human groups residing in the area (O'Brien and Holland 1992;

see Buikstra et al. 1986; Holland 1989; O'Brien 1987). No one has argued that the analytical process is simple or straightforward (see below), but in no sense is it linked to an endless search for deliberate fitness maximization.

Potential Pitfalls of an Evolutionary Approach

Darwin's salient contribution to science was the recognition that the process of evolution was composed of two independent components: (1) the generation of a pool of variants, and (2) the subsequent selection of a subset of those variants. Likewise, the selectionist approach, as applied to the archaeological record, can be viewed as consisting of two independent steps: (1) the identification and quantification of variation and (2) the subsequent inference of the history of selection of those variants. Archaeology, whether in a selectionist vein or not, has always had an intrinsic interest in variation and change. But all too often this interest is played out as an attempt to document similarities and differences in the material record for the express purpose of creating artifact types and cultural-temporal units. Unfortunately, the resulting types—bound tightly as they are within an essentialist straitjacket (see below)—are at odds with the goals of a selectionist approach. The true subject of evolution is change, not merely similarities and differences.

To study change, variation available to the selection process must be identified and quantified. Therein lies the stumbling block. How do we construct meaningful units to measure variation (see papers by Dunnell and Teltser, chapters 3 and 4 respectively)? And, more importantly, how do we interpret the data within an evolutionary framework? It is one thing to say that the units of measurement must be derived directly from the theory—a point covered by all of the authors in this book—and another actually to get down to the business of choosing the units. Likewise, it is one thing to produce a pile of data and another to construct a logical argument in which selection is seen as operating on phenotypic features. Several risks are involved, all of which hinge on an incomplete understanding of the evolutionary process. Two such risks—quantified essentialism and adaptationist "just-so" stories—are discussed below. Failure to recognize these pitfalls will render evolutionary archaeology as a sterile exercise in measurement and will cause doubt to be cast on its explanatory ability as well.

Quantified Essentialism

More than a few authors have presented their attempts to operationalize selectionist theory, but all too often these attempts have been little more than "quantified essentialism." Though professing to break with the essentialist view, much of the so-called "selectionist research" continues to produce and use types, though these "types" are statistical phenomena bounded by a set of breakpoints rather than the usual, named, gestalt constructs with which archaeologists are so familiar. Seldom is variation conceived of as existing on a continuous spectrum, but rather, variation is viewed as, and subsequently lumped into, a small number of manageable, albeit quantified, classes. For example, after elaborate X-ray analysis to determine temper-particle size, undecorated shell-tempered ceramics from the middle Mississippi River valley may be rendered into some set of analytical classes (e.g., very fine, fine, medium, coarse, very coarse) that in practice differ very little from the paste-based types (e.g., Mississippi plain, Bell plain, and associated varieties) defined by Phillips (1970) and that have been used by a generation of archaeologists. The difference is that the new "types" are predicated on measurable, though arbitrary, differences.

This is not to argue that the lumping associated with quantified essentialism is inherently wrong. Quite the contrary, lumping is necessary. It is possible to treat 100 sherds from a site (or 100 projectile points) as 100 independent variations, but it probably is unproductive. When lumping is required, it should be done in a straightforward manner, with few preconceptions. The resulting classes that we create are simply units by which to measure variation; they are not "things" that have a profound essence (see below). More importantly, it does us little good to document variation in the archaeological record if we are unable to relate that variation to selective processes that operated in the past.

What we term quantified essentialism is the end result of a failure to appreciate that evolution is not a transformational process. Evolution is a replacement-based process that produces new kinds; it does not gradually transform one thing into another.[1] Archaeology is rife with the notion of transformation, nowhere more noticeably than in the concept of type, one of the stalwarts of archaeological analysis. As we have said, there is nothing inherently wrong with the concept of the modal type as long as we realize its place in analysis. Two things should be borne in mind. First, there are "types" of types, some of which are ill-suited for measuring the effects of selection. For example, stylistically based types can be excellent temporal markers, but no matter how they are formulated, they most assuredly are ill-suited for understanding the effects of selection, a point Teltser makes in chapter 4. However, as she also points out, the tried-and-true types that have formed the backbone of Americanist chronological studies can be used in evolutionary studies to monitor such things as rates of trait transmission. Without a proper understanding, however, of (1) the differences between stylistic and functional features (see Dunnell 1978a, 1978b; O'Brien and Holland 1990) and (2) why, from an evolutionary point of view, the distinction has to be made between the two, we run the definite risk of blindly taking measurements and professing to practice evolutionary archaeology.

Second, theoretical units and empirical units differ significantly, as Dunnell and Teltser point out in chapters 3 and 4, respectively. Ideational units such as inches allow us to treat dimensions such as size in a quantitative fashion, but the mere fact that we document a change in size over time—through the use of ideational units—in and of itself "explains" nothing. It is the theoretical units that are used to describe and explain change. In essence, until we specify the scale of analysis (e.g., attribute, artifact, assemblage), partition the archaeological record into appropriate analytical units (see Dunnell, chapter 3), and determine whether a trait is stylistic or neutral, our efforts to construct a reasonable evolutionary archaeology will be nothing more than trivial exercises.

Functional features are those that affect the Darwinian fitness of populations in which they occur; stylistic features exhibit no detectable selective values. Thus, functional features (more precisely, certain expressions of features) offer organisms solutions to problems. The problem is in identifying functional features, which are not always easy to distinguish from stylistic features. The solution to the problem lies in monitoring the behavior of features over time (Dunnell 1978a; O'Brien and Holland 1990, 1992). Traits under selection should begin at some point during their life histories to increase in frequency at a steadily decelerating rate toward some optimal value. Eventual selection against the trait, resulting from changes in the selective environment, reverses the trend and sends the curve downward: "As selection favors new characteristics that arise, the fall-off in frequency of variants being replaced should be rapid. Given the rapidity with which variation can be generated among groups of humans, successive sigmoid curves with abrupt truncations should be the rule rather than the exception" (O'Brien and Holland 1992:49). This type of curve is decidedly different from that exhibited by stylistic (neutral) features, whose "behavior should be more adequately accommodated by stochastic processes" (Dunnell 1978a:199). Teltser (chapter 4) points out that "in the absence of selective pressures, the frequency of a given variant has equal probability of increasing or decreasing at any given point in time." More specifically, it is the Markovian nature of stylistic features that sets them apart from functional features, that is, those under selection (Dunnell 1978b; O'Brien and Holland 1990, 1992).

The bottom line is that the features being measured must be functional, and the units used to measure the features must be capable of handling minute variation. The tracking of what happens to a feature through time is a tedious process (see Braun 1985, 1987 for an example) requiring numerous data points that extend across the life of the trait. The more data points, the more precise the curve. It should be obvious that for this type of analysis actual measurements are needed, as opposed to nominal units built around modes. Without such detail, we will be hard-pressed to identify functional features accurately and to track their life histories, and it is these life histories upon which our evolutionary explanations depend.

Adaptationist "Just-So" Stories

The identification of functional features—adaptations—and the measurement of variation constitute only the first phase of a two-step process. Variation can be measured, but unless the variation is explained, why should we bother quantifying it in the first place? This next step can be treacherous, though the end products seduce us by their elegance and seeming accommodation of data. These "just-so" stories are neat little explanations tethered loosely to evolutionary principles by the unguarded use of the word "selection." Measurable variation too often becomes prima facie evidence for a groundless cause-and-effect relation between an artifact and some nebulous concept of fitness and adaptation. The terms "selection," "selective forces," and "selective agents" become a ready means of understanding patterns that emerge from our analysis of data for which we have no other ready explanation. We are reminded of Bertrand Russell's comment on Hindu cosmology. The world, according to Hindus, is held aloft by a large elephant, which in turn stands on the back of a tortoise. When Russell (1957:7) asked what the tortoise stood upon, his informant replied, "Suppose we change the subject." Likewise, when the question is asked, Why should there be selection for some variant over another? many of the archaeological papers we see rely on an unwritten "suppose we change the subject" clause.

In their often-cited paper, "The Spandrels of San Marco and the Panglossian Paradigm: A Critique of the Adaptationist Programme," S. Gould and Lewontin (1979) heap extensive criticism and ridicule on biologists who identify adaptations as solutions to problems and who then set about the business of trying to determine how the traits functioned. Their criticism centers around the notion that organisms are integrated wholes and that phylogenetic development, pathway development, and engineering constraints should be considered equally in identifying adaptations and their functions. In reality, contrary to the criticisms of Gould and Lewontin, most biologically based adaptationist programs are based on the type of holistic approach they advocate. Surely, adaptations are solutions to problems posed by the environment, though not in any directed (and, with regard to humans, necessarily in any intentional) way. When biologists colloquially speak of, say, fur as being a "solution" to loss of body heat in squirrels, we doubt seriously that they believe squirrels actually set out to evolve fur to keep warm. Although Gould and Lewontin's criticism is a caricature of most modern biological research into adaptations, it most assuredly is applicable to most anthropological research, in which adaptations are viewed as almost die-cut solutions to environmental perturbations.

The result of this mind-set in anthropology, as Gould and Lewontin note for some biological analyses, is the construction of seemingly plausible explanations of objects' functions in forms that ultimately are not testable. This criticism against the construction of "just-so" stories applies to a wide range of archaeological analysis, regardless of whether the analysis is purportedly evolutionary or not. We raise the point because we do not want to see the same criticism leveled against archaeological studies carried out under the banner of Darwinian evolution. How do we escape this dilemma? Mayr (1988:154) is correct that "the student of adaptation has to sail a perilous course between a pseudoexplanatory reductionist atomism and stultifying nonexplanatory holism." It might appear at first glance that the only way to escape Gould and Lewontin's criticism is to sort out adaptations from nonadaptations correctly and then to identify the proper function of every adaptation (O'Brien and Holland 1992:44). In essence this is correct, but no one (except Gould and Lewontin) ever said we had to get it right on the first try. In other words, there is nothing inherently wrong with the "try-until-you-get-it-right" approach to understanding the proper function of adaptive features. The only crime is in being satisfied with the conclusion simply because the data appear to fit the argument. We view this as perhaps the biggest pitfall of evolutionary archaeology but certainly one over which it does not have sole claim.

Evolution and Engineering

The potential of evolutionary theory to explain variation in the archaeological record must begin with the realization that the process of evolution can be summarized essentially as one of overcoming limitations. All organisms, and by extension all populations, are inherently bounded; they are constrained by some manner of limitation—environmental, technological, reproductive, even psychological—and evolutionary change simply is the surmounting of some obstacle. The adaptive radiation seen when a species breaks loose from the confinement of an old niche is testament to this view. (So, too, may be the punctuated equilibria seen in the fossil record.) Seen closer to home, the oftentimes rapid and widespread adoption of a new technological innovation (e.g., ceramic vessels) within and among populations illustrates the same point.

The most intuitive means of judging success at overcoming limitations is to look at raw numbers, with population growth of both individuals and individual traits being the best (though by no means the only) index of evolutionary success. As we stressed earlier, however, what we are interested in is the potential fitness of an individual or group as opposed to the actual fitness. This does not imply that we are not interested in those adaptive features that by inference we believe to be important to reproductive fitness. In fact, why would we focus on anything else? Those are the very features that contribute to an organism's success in overcoming limitations. This is not vulgar sociobiology but rather simple pragmatism. The more closely tied some aspect of human culture is to reproduction, the more closely the existing biological models can apply. It is not an accident that Rindos's

(1984; see also O'Brien and Wilson 1988) coevolutionary model for the origin of agriculture is perhaps the most successful example to date of the application of Darwinian thought to an archaeological problem. On a smaller scale, the suggestion by Buikstra et al. (1986; see also O'Brien 1987) that the increase in starchy-seed use seen in the midwestern archaeological record for the Middle Woodland period (ca. 200 B.C. to A.D. 400) is concomitant with an increase in fertility, is best explained, we believe, within an evolutionary framework (Holland 1989).

Unfortunately, most archaeological remains cannot be tied directly to human reproduction. For example, few archaeologists would buy the argument that subtle variation in projectile-point notching has anything to do with human fitness. This is not to say that projectile-point notching necessarily is unrelated to reproduction, just that the ties are sufficiently stretched to be unpalatable to most archaeologists. The same is true for variation in ceramic tempering agents. Yet, projectile-point notches and tempering agents are part of an adaptive system, and notched projectile points and ceramic vessels are part of a human phenotypic response, just as mulched fields (Maxwell, chapter 6) and ceremonial architecture (Graves and Ladefoged, chapter 8) are phenotypic responses. As we noted earlier, our attempts to show that notching and temper are functional dimensions—and therefore contributors to fitness—are destined for ridicule unless we can show how certain notching patterns or temper types allowed humans to overcome an environmental problem (Dunnell 1978a, 1978b).

We have argued extensively (O'Brien and Holland 1990, 1992, 1995; O'Brien et al. 1994) that engineering-design analysis offers an appropriate basis from which to construct plausible (and we emphasize the word plausible) arguments relative to fitness, and thus overcome the "just-so" hurdle. As Sober (1984:81) notes, "A careful engineering analysis can in principle permit us to make reasonable judgments about fitness differences in advance of finding out who lives and dies." It is apparent from even a casual examination of On the Origin of Species that Darwin had an extreme fascination with engineering design, referring to some features such as the eye as "organs of extreme perfection and complication." To Darwin, the better engineered a feature was, the more potentially fit the organisms bearing that feature were. We see no reason, given our basic belief in the notion of an extended phenotype, to exclude the engineering design of such things as pots from our purview. But again, it must be kept squarely in mind that the link between determining certain features to be adaptations and deciding what the features are adaptations for rests on inference. For example, engineering studies can demonstrate how certain features confer on an organism the ability to run quickly, but we make the inference that that ability gives certain organisms a decided selective advantage over those that do not possess the feature.

In opposition to the stark presence or absence of features is the more typical case of two or more populations or individuals possessing alternate states of a feature. In the above example one organism, or group of organisms, contained a feature that allowed it to run faster than those organisms without the feature. However, we would more likely find a situation where the organisms all contained the feature, but it would be engineered differently in some organisms than in others. In other words, the situation is not that one group has legs and the other does not but rather that one group has longer legs than the other, or a different type of knee joint, or an almost infinite number of other possibilities. The really interesting question that arises is, Do (did) measurable engineering differences affect the relative fitness of the organisms differentially? Likewise, did measurable differences in pottery have any affect on the relative fitness of prehistoric humans? For example, was there a selective advantage in the central Mississippi River valley around A.D. 900 of using crushed mussel shell as a tempering agent as opposed to another material such as sand? Feathers (1990a, 1990b) and Dunnell and Feathers (1991) present logical arguments that there were. Likewise, was there a selective advantage after A.D. 100 in producing thin-wall cooking vessels? Again, logical arguments have been constructed for why there was such an advantage (Braun 1985, 1987; O'Brien 1987; O'Brien et al. 1994). Importantly, the arguments are derived directly from Darwinian-evolutionary theory, complete with conditions and expectations, and are amenable to engineering analysis.

Neff's work (chapter 5) begins to shed light on the manner and degree that a common substance—pottery clay—can vary within a relatively small area, though how that variation plays into the hands of selection still is unknown. His central tenet is that an evolutionary archaeology must pay equal attention to what Eldredge (1985) calls genealogy (history) and ecology (the selective environment). Neff's paper is important because it is one of the few examples where the selectionist paradigm has been translated into practice, using real data sets to examine the effects of selection on potters and their pot-making behaviors. All of Neff's recent work (Neff 1992, 1993, and chapter 5, this volume) revolves around the persistence of different types of vessels and what that tells us about the differential success of certain pottery-making phenotypes.

Maxwell (chapter 6) takes a similar engineering approach in his analysis of a systemic artifact, that is, agricultural-field architecture in the Rio Chama region of northwestern New Mexico. In one of the more convincing case studies presented so far, he provides compelling evidence that variation in mulching practices can be linked to the potential fitness of differing groups, even though, and this is important, the dates of use of the mulched fields are unknown. Thus, one does not have to date the fields immediately to suggest, in light of experimentation, that rock-mulch technology would be favored by selection in that particular physical environment. While Maxwell's observations still are preliminary, they nevertheless represent the type of approach and analysis that is sorely needed if selectionism is to be considered a viable paradigm.

A common roadblock to incorporating an evolutionary approach into archae-ology is a failure on the part of archaeologists to ask themselves whether they are more interested in problems or solutions. We suspect that most researchers would probably argue that the solutions are of greatest interest, and yet if this were the case, we would need to go no further than the artifacts that we recover. Artifacts represent solutions to roadblocks that our ancestors encountered. Rock-mulched fields are a solution, as are shell-tempered ceramics, Clovis points, and wall-trench houses. They are, at various points in time, solutions that in turn are bounded by a new set of limitations that, at some later date, also might be over-come. As counterintuitive as it may seem, solutions as a focus of interest should take a back seat to a focus on problems and limitations.

For example, at site 23BU239, a multicomponent site in southeastern Mis-souri, the lithic assemblage from Late Archaic levels (3000 to 1000 B.C.) is pre-dominantly of quartzite (75 to 100 percent), while the overlying Woodland levels (1000 B.C. to A.D. 900) produced assemblages that were composed almost exclu-sively of chert artifacts (O'Brien et al. 1989). Similar quartzite and chert distribu-tions have been noted from other portions of the Western Lowland and the Ozark Escarpment. Quartzite and chert artifacts clearly are responses to problems; that is, they represent viable solutions to some problem within the confines of an ex-isting technology. What we as archaeologists are (or at least should be) interested in is not the fact that quartzite was used so extensively by Late Archaic peoples but rather why it was used, and what changed so that chert became a more viable solution during the Woodland period. Was it simply a technological hurdle that was cleared, or was the shift a result of some other limiting factor, such as a change in resource availability? For instance, it has been suggested (Holland 1984; Perttula 1984) that the use of quartzite and rhyolite tools during the Late Archaic in southeastern Missouri may have represented selection for a durable edge at the expense of sharpness. But why was durability valued over sharpness, if indeed it was? Perhaps the answer is functional, that is, the materials being processed did not require sharp tools as much as they required durable-edged tools, or the answer may relate to some broader aspect of the cultural system, such as the settlement-subsistence pattern (e.g., hunters may have been required to travel greater distances to lithic sources).

What is important is that simply measuring variation with no idea as to why that particular measurement might relate to the problem at hand, while it will quantify variation within the assemblage, probably will not supply the informa-tion that is needed. In this particular example, use-wear or blood-residue analyses that identify activities for which the artifacts were used; engineering studies that quantify edge durability; or even trace-element analysis that helps to pinpoint sources of materials will generate more usable data. These same types of analysis have been at the forefront of some behavioral archaeology studies (e.g., Schiffer and Skibo 1987; Skibo et al. 1989; Vaz Pinto et al. 1987), leading to our earlier statement that significant similarities exist between that approach and evolutionary archaeology.

We believe that while variation in the archaeological record can be identified and measured in a thousand different ways, variation that relates back to technological limitations will prove the most illuminating. For example, Ramenofsky (chapter 7) examines the post-contact-period use of European items in terms of the properties afforded by the introduced materials—properties that affected function, durability, and energy costs. She points out that we need not rely on age-old explanations such as acculturation to explain why one group would immediately use the material goods of another group. In fact, "explanations" grounded in concepts such as diffusion and acculturation explain nothing. On the other hand, explanations tied to how contact-period groups solved technological problems by switching to guns and iron knives have considerable merit.

Ceramic archaeometrists, working on replicas of midwestern pottery, have begun assembling a wealth of information on how variation in temper size and composition affects such properties as resistance to crack propagation, resistance to abrasion, resistance to thermal shock, and resistance to impact (Bronitsky and Hamer 1986; Feathers 1989, 1990a, 1990b; Feathers and Scott 1989; Dunnell and Feathers 1991; Hoard 1992; Hoard et al. n.d.; Schiffer and Skibo 1987; see O'Brien et al. 1994 for review). The extent to which these properties enter into the selection process, and by inference affect the adaptiveness and fitness of the prehistoric potters who made and used the vessels, is, of course, an inferential process. Importantly, however, it is a process separate from the act of measuring variation. What is significant is that the variation is measured, not in some willy-nilly manner, but with an eye to identifying key attributes and limitations in the process of selection. By focusing on variation bounded by mechanical constraints, we at least are examining variation that was physically available to selection's agents, both environmental and cultural.

Conclusion

As with works subscribing to other schools, much of what has been published under a selectionist title has only a tenuous grasp of the basic tenets of the underlying paradigm. As two of selectionism's strongest proponents, we feel that we are in a position to say this without triggering a self-defense reflex on the part of our colleagues. Our position is that those who espouse a selectionist approach are in a struggle for the attention of the profession. It is our goal to effect a complete paradigm shift within archaeology, not simply to amuse ourselves with academic debates. As it is with any emerging paradigm, progress has been made in laying the groundwork, but the future of evolutionary archaeology lies in demonstrating, through examples, how variation in the archaeological record can be explained in terms of potential fitness, that is, how prehistoric peoples, through changes in functional phenotypic features, overcame environmental limitations. Progress is being made in this direction, albeit slowly, and publication of this book represents a strong push forward.

Several of the chapters herein represent excellent case studies of how a selectionist perspective can be applied to the archaeological record. We need to take steps to insure that gains in attracting the attention of archaeologists to this perspective are not lost amid a cloud of "all-talk, no-product" rhetoric. As all the authors whose works are included here state unequivocally, we cannot continue to dress up old arguments in new terminology and expect them to fly. Neither can we supply vacuous explanations, or simply believe that measuring variation, in and of itself, constitutes a selectionist approach. To be sure, quantifying variation is essential to evolutionary archaeology, but it has never been more than a means to an end. It is insufficient to state that variation exists, or even that change occurred. We ultimately must get back to the "why?" and to do so, we must identify variation that has empirical meaning within the realm of the selective process.

We have advocated the use of engineering studies as a means of winnowing the spectrum of variation to a manageable level. Certainly, the range of human endeavors will never be fully accounted for by recourse to stress tests and X-ray diffraction, but we believe engineering-design analysis represents a good point from which to start. We believe that aspects of the archaeological record that impinge most directly on technological, reproductive, and replicative limitations will prove the most useful in the long run. Technological considerations, especially, are applicable to the archaeological record. We do not discount the applicability of an evolutionary approach to more intangible arenas such as art, kinship, or political organization; we simply believe that selectionist models dealing with these topics will always prove more tenuous. However, as Graves and Ladefoged (chapter 8) point out, even things such as the evolution of ceremonial architecture can be subsumed under a selectionist perspective, with promising results.

The solution to understanding the past is not simply to measure everything within reach and hope that some pattern emerges from the bowels of a computer. Although we still agree with our earlier observation, that if we can measure variation so can the process of selection (O'Brien and Holland 1990), we also appreciate that the selective process, while capable of measuring variation, is not *required* to do so. From an infinite pool of variability, there is but a finite amount of variation that will ever come under selective control, and to identify that finite amount of variation, our research must have a purpose and a goal. We are left with the realization that the biases inherent in the archaeological record will preclude any anthropological paradigm, no matter how inclusive, from explaining everything. Large patches of our understanding of the past must forever remain a mystery. Ultimately, it is not necessarily the role of science to explain phenomena—archaeological or otherwise—as much as it is to order observable phenomena into a system consistent with our perception of reality.

Acknowledgments

We thank Patrice Teltser and two reviewers for many extremely helpful comments on an earlier version of our chapter.

Note

1. The important differences between essentialism and materialism within an archaeological framework have been addressed elsewhere (e.g., Dunnell 1980, 1982, 1989; O'Brien and Holland 1990), and the reader is urged to consult those references.

References

Bonner, J. T.
1980   *The Evolution of Culture in Animals.* Princeton University Press, Princeton, New Jersey.
1988   *The Evolution of Complexity.* Princeton University Press, Princeton, New Jersey.

Brandon, R. N.
1990   *Adaptation and Environment.* Princeton University Press, Princeton, New Jersey.

Braun, D. P.
1985   Absolute Seriation: A Time-Series Approach. In *For Concordance in Archaeological Analysis: Bridging Data Structure, Quantitative Technique, and Theory,* edited by C. Carr, pp. 509–39. Westport, Kansas City, Missouri.
1987   Coevolution of Sedentism, Pottery Technology, and Horticulture in the Central Midwest, 200 B.C.–A.D. 600. In *Emergent Horticultural Economies of the Eastern Woodlands,* edited by W. F. Keegan, pp. 153–181. Occasional Paper No. 7. Center for Archaeological Investigations, Southern Illinois University at Carbondale.

Bronitsky, G., and R. Hamer
1986   Experiments in Ceramic Technology: The Effects of Various Tempering Materials on Impact and Thermal-Shock Resistance. *American Antiquity* 51:89–101.

Buikstra, J. E., L. Konigsberg, and J. Bullington
1986   Fertility and the Development of Agriculture in the Prehistoric Midwest. *American Antiquity* 51:528–546.

Burian, R.
1983   Adaptation. In *Dimensions of Darwinism,* edited by M. Grene, pp. 287–314. Cambridge University Press, New York.

Campbell, D. T.
1956   Adaptive Behavior from Random Response. *Behavioral Science* 1:105–110.
1965   Variation and Selective Retention in Sociocultural Evolution. In *Social Change in Developing Areas: A Reinterpretation of Evolutionary Theory,* edited by H. R. Barringer, G. I. Blanksten, and R. W. Mack, pp. 19–48. Schenkman, Cambridge, Massachusetts.
1975   On the Conflicts between Biological and Social Evolution and between Psychology and Moral Tradition. *American Psychology* 30:1103–1126.

Dawkins, R.
1990   *The Extended Phenotype: The Long Reach of the Gene.* New edition. Oxford University Press, Oxford, England.

Dunnell, R. C.
1978a   Style and Function: A Fundamental Dichotomy. *American Antiquity* 43:192–202.
1978b   Archaeological Potential of Anthropological and Scientific Models of Function. In *Archaeological Essays in Honor of Irving B. Rouse,* edited by R. C. Dunnell and E. S. Hall, Jr., pp. 41–73. Mouton, The Hague.
1980   Evolutionary Theory and Archaeology. In *Advances in Archaeological Method and Theory,* vol. 3, edited by M. B. Schiffer, pp. 35–99. Academic Press, New York.
1982   Science, Social Science, and Common Sense: The Agonizing Dilemma of Modern Archaeology. *Journal of Anthropological Research* 38:1–25.
1985   Methodological Issues in Contemporary Americanist Archaeology. In *Proceedings of the 1984 Biennial Meeting of the Philosophy of Science Association,* vol. 2, edited by P. D. Asquith and P. Kitcher, pp. 717–744. Philosophy of Science Association, East Lansing, Michigan.
1988   Archaeology and Evolutionary Theory. Unpublished paper delivered at the University of Missouri–Columbia.
1989   Aspects of the Application of Evolutionary Theory in Archaeology. In *Archaeological Thought in America,* edited by C. C. Lamberg-Karlovsky, pp. 35–49. Cambridge University Press, New York.

Dunnell, R. C., and J. K. Feathers
1991   Late Woodland Manifestations of the Malden Plain, Southeast Missouri. In *Stability, Transformation, and Variation: The Late Woodland Southeast,* edited by M. S. Nassaney and C. R. Cobb, pp. 21–45. Plenum Press, New York.

Durham, W. H.
1991   *Coevolution: Genes, Culture and Human Diversity.* Stanford University Press, Stanford, California.

Eldredge, N.
1985   *Unfinished Synthesis.* Oxford University Press, Oxford.

Feathers, J. K.

1989   Effects of Temper on Strength of Ceramics: Response to Bronitsky and Hamer. *American Antiquity* 54:579–588.

1990a   An Evolutionary Interpretation for the Predominance of Shell Tempering in Late Prehistoric Southeastern Missouri Ceramics. Paper presented at the 55th Annual Meeting of the Society for American Archaeology, Las Vegas.

1990b   *An Evolutionary Explanation for Prehistoric Ceramic Change in Southeast Missouri.* Ph.D. dissertation, University of Washington. University Microfilms, Ann Arbor, Michigan.

Feathers, J. K., and W. D. Scott

1989   Prehistoric Ceramic Composite from the Mississippi Valley. *Ceramic Bulletin* 68: 554–557.

Gould R. A.

1980   *Living Archaeology.* Cambridge University Press, New York.

Gould, S. J.

1986   Evolution and the Triumph of Homology, Or Why History Matters. *American Scientist* 74:60–69.

Gould, S. J., and R. Lewontin

1979   The Spandrels of San Marco and the Panglossian Paradigm: A Critique of the Adaptationist Programme. *Proceedings of the Royal Society of London* B205:581–598.

Hamilton, W. D.

1964   The Genetical Theory of Social Behaviour I, II. *Journal of Theoretical Biology* 7:1–52.

Hoard, R.

1992   *Technological Dimensions of Woodland-Period Cooking Vessels from Missouri.* Ph.D. dissertation, University of Missouri–Columbia. University Microfilms, Ann Arbor, Michigan.

Hoard, R. J., M. J. O'Brien, M. G. Khorasgany, and V. S. Gopalaratnam

n.d.   A Materials-Science Approach to Understanding Limestone-Tempered Pottery from the Midwest. Unpublished manuscript.

Holland, T. D.

1984   Archaeological Testing of the Route 60, Butler County Project. Report on file, American Archaeology Division, University of Missouri–Columbia.

1989   Fertility in the Prehistoric Midwest: A Critique of Unifactoral Models. *American Antiquity* 54:389–426.

Leonard, R. D.

1989   Resource Specialization, Population Growth, and Agricultural Production in the American Southwest. *American Antiquity* 54: 491–503.

Leonard, R. D., and G. T. Jones

1987   Elements of an Inclusive Evolutionary Model for Archaeology. *Journal of Anthropological Archaeology* 6:199–219.

Lewontin, R. C.
1974   *The Genetic Basis of Evolutionary Change.* Columbia University Press, New York.

Marks, J., and E. Staski
1988   Individuals and the Evolution of Biological and Cultural Systems. *Human Evolution* 3:147–161.

Mayr, E.
1988   *Toward a New Philosophy of Biology: Observations of an Evolutionist.* Harvard University Press, Cambridge, Massachusetts.

Meggers, B. J., C. Evans, and E. Estrada
1965   *Early Formative Period of Coastal Ecuador: The Valdivia and Machalilla Phases.* Smithsonian Contributions to Anthropology 1, Smithsonian Institution.

Mills, S., and J. Beatty
1979   The Propensity Interpretation of Fitness. *Philosophy of Science* 46:263–286.

Neff, H.
1992   Ceramics and Evolution. In *Archaeological Method and Theory,* vol. 4, edited by M. B. Schiffer, pp. 141–193. University of Arizona Press, Tucson.
1993   Theory, Sampling, and Technical Studies in Archaeological Ceramic Analysis. *American Antiquity* 58:23–44.

O'Brien, M. J.
1987   Sedentism, Population Growth, and Resource Selection in the Woodland Midwest: A Review of Coevolutionary Developments. *Current Anthropology* 28: 177–197.

O'Brien, M. J., and H. C. Wilson
1988   A Paradigmatic Shift in the Search for the Origin of Agriculture. *American Anthropologist* 90:958–965.

O'Brien, M. J., and T. D. Holland
1990   Variation, Selection, and the Archaeological Record. In *Archaeological Method and Theory,* vol. 2, edited by M. B. Schiffer, pp. 31–79. University of Arizona Press, Tucson.
1992   The Role of Adaptation in Archaeological Explanation. *American Antiquity* 57: 36–59.
1995   Behavioral Archaeology and the Extended Phenotype. In *Reconstruction Theory: A Behavioral Approach to the Archaeological Record,* edited by A. E. Nielsen, J. M. Skibo, and W. H. Walker. Salt Lake City: University of Utah Press.

O'Brien, M. J., R. L. Lyman, and T. D. Holland
1989   Geoarchaeological Evidence for Prairie-Mound Formation in the Mississippi Alluvial Valley, Southeastern Missouri. *Quaternary Research* 31:83–93.

O'Brien, M. J., T. D. Holland, R. J. Hoard, and G. L. Fox
1994   Evolutionary Implications of Design and Performance Characteristics of Prehistoric Pottery. *Journal of Archaeological Method and Theory* 1.

Perttula, T. K.
1984   Prehistoric Use of Rhyolite in the Current River Valley, Eastern Ozark Highland, Southeast Missouri. *Missouri Archaeological Society Quarterly* 1:3, 11, 15.

Phillips, P.
1970   *Archaeological Survey in the Yazoo Basin, Mississippi, 1949–1955.* Papers of the Peabody Museum of American Archaeology and Ethnology, no. 60. Harvard University, Cambridge Massachusetts.

Rambo, A. T.
1991   The Study of Cultural Evolution. In *Profiles in Cultural Evolution,* edited by A. T. Rambo and K. Gillogly, pp. 23–109. Anthropological Papers No. 85, Museum of Anthropology, University of Michigan, Ann Arbor.

Reid, J. J., M. B. Schiffer, and W. L. Rathje
1975   Behavioral Archaeology: Four Strategies. *American Anthropologist* 77:864–869.

Rindos, D.
1984   *The Origins of Agriculture: An Evolutionary Perspective.* Academic Press, New York.
1985   Darwinian Selection, Symbolic Variation, and the Evolution of Culture. *Current Anthropology* 26:65–88.
1986   The Evolution of the Capacity for Culture: Sociobiology, Structuralism, and Cultural Selection. *Current Anthropology* 27:315–332.

Russell, B.
1957   *Why I Am Not a Christian and Other Essays on Religion and Related Subjects.* New York, Simon and Schuster.

Sahlins, M.
1976   *The Use and Abuse of Biology: An Anthropological Critique of Sociobiology.* The University of Michigan Press, Ann Arbor.

Schiffer, M. B.
1975   Archaeology as Behavioral Science. *American Anthropologist* 77:836–848.
1976   *Behavioral Archeology.* Academic Press, New York.
1978   Methodological Issues in Ethnoarchaeology. In *Explorations in Ethnoarchaeology,* edited by R. A. Gould, pp. 229–247. University of New Mexico Press, Albuquerque.

Schiffer, M.B., and J. M. Skibo
1987   Theory and Experiment in the Study of Technological Change. *Current Anthropology* 28:595–622.

Skibo, J. M., M. B. Schiffer, and K. C. Reid
1989   Organic-Tempered Pottery: An Experimental Study. *American Antiquity* 54:122–146.

Sober, E.
1984   *The Nature of Selection: Evolutionary Theory in Philosophical Focus.* MIT Press, Cambridge, Massachusetts.

Vaz Pinto, I., M. B. Schiffer, S. Smith, and J. M. Skibo
1987   Effects of Temper on Ceramic Abrasion Resistance: A Preliminary Investigation. *Archeomaterials* 1:119–134.

White, L. A.
1949   *The Science of Culture: A Study of Man and Civilization*. Farrar, Straus and Giroux, New York.
1959   *The Evolution of Culture: The Development of Civilization to the Fall of Rome*. McGraw Hill, New York.

Williams, G. C.
1966   *Adaptation and Natural Selection: A Critique of Some Current Evolutionary Thought*. Princeton University Press, Princeton, New Jersey.

◆◆ Index